CW01649506

Read *ary*

2 CORINTHIANS

2 CORINTHIANS

Jerry W. McCant

Sheffield Academic Press

Copyright © 1999 Sheffield Academic Press

Published by Sheffield Academic Press Ltd
Mansion House
19 Kingfield Road
Sheffield S11 9AS
England

Printed on acid-free paper in Great Britain
by Bookcraft Ltd
Midsomer Norton, Bath

British Library Cataloguing in Publication Data

A catalogue record for this book is available
from the British Library

ISBN 1-84127-031-8
1-84127-032-6 pbk

With abiding love
and great admiration
I dedicate this volume to
my son, Jonathan
who inspired and gave me the strength
to complete this task

Contents

Abbreviations

AB	Anchor Bible
ABC-ClioLC	ABC-Clio Literary Companion
ABD	David Noel Freedman (ed.), *The Anchor Bible Dictionary* (New York: Doubleday, 1992)
ACNT	Augsburg Commentary on the New Testament
AusBR	*Australian Biblical Review*
BAGD	Walter Bauer, William F. Arndt, F. William Gingrich and Frederick W. Danker, *A Greek-English Lexicon of the New Testament and Other Early Christian Literature* (Chicago: University of Chicago Press, 2nd edn, 1958)
BBB	Bonner biblische Beiträge
BDF	Friedrich Blass, A. Debrunner and Robert W. Funk, *A Greek Grammar of the New Testament and Other Early Christian Literature* (Cambridge: Cambridge University Press, 1961)
BFCT	Beiträge zur Förderung christlicher Theologie
BHT	Beiträge zur historischen Theologie
CBQ	*Catholic Biblical Quarterly*
CC	Calvin's Commentaries
CIBPI	Current Issues in Biblical Patristic Interpretation
ConNT	Coniectanea neotestamentica
DGRA	Dictionary of Greek and Roman Antiquities
EB	Expositors Bible
EBib	Etudes bibliques
EGNT	Expositors Greek New Testament
EvT	*Evangelische Theologie*
FRLANT	Forschungen zur Religion und Literatur des Alten und Neuen Testaments
GNTG	Grammar of the New Testament Greek
HCNT	Harper's Commentary of the New Testament
Hesp	*Hesperia*
HNT	Handbuch zum Neuen Testament
HTKNT	Herders theologischer Kommentar zum Neuen Testament
HTR	*Harvard Theological Review*
IB	*Interpreter's Bible*
ICC	International Critical Commentary
Int	*Interchange*
JBL	*Journal of Biblical Literature*
JCE	*Journal of Christian Education*
JSNTSup	*Journal for the Study of the New Testament*, Supplement Series
JTS	*Journal of Theological Studies*

KJV	King James Version
LAE	*Life of Adam and Eve*
LCL	Loeb Classical Library
LEC	Library of Early Christianity
LSJ	H.G. Liddell, Robert Scott and H. Stuart Jones, *Greek-English Lexicon* (Oxford: Clarendon Press, 9th edn, 1968)
MeyerK	H.A.W. Meyer (ed.), Kritisch-Exegetischer Kommentar über des Neue Testament
MNTC	Moffatt NT Commentary
MSA	Metaphor and Symbolic Activity
NAB	*New American Bible*
NASB	*New American Standard Bible*
NAWG	Nachrichten von der Akademie der Wissenschaften in Göttingen
NCB	New Century Bible
NEB	*New English Bible*
NICNT	New International Commentary on the New Testament
NIV	New International Version
NovT	*Novum Testamentum*
NRSV	New Revised Standard Version
NTD	Das Neue Testament Deutsch
NTS	*New Testament Studies*
PB	Postmodern Bible
PC	Proclamation Commentaries
Ph	Phoenix
RAC	*Reallexikon für Antike und Christentum*
RB	*Revue biblique*
REB	Religious Book Club
REG	Revue Etude arecques
RSV	Revised Standard Version
SBL	Society of Biblical Literature
SBLDS	SBL Dissertation Series
SBT	Studies in Biblical Theology
SC	Sources chétiennes
SCHNT	Studia ad corpus hellenisticum Novi Testamenti
Scrip.	Scriptura
SE	*Studia Evangelica I, II, III* (= TU 73 [1959], 87 [1964], 88 [1964], etc.)
SJT	Southwestern Journal of Theology
SMA	Studies in Mediterranean Archaeology (Goteborg: Astroms)
SNTSMS	Society for New Testament Studies Monograph Series
SUNT	Studien zur Umwelt des Neuen Testaments
TDNT	Gerhard Kittel and Gerhard Friedrich (eds.), *Theological Dictionary of the New Testament* (trans. Geoffrey W. Bromiley; 10 vols.; Grand Rapids: Eerdmans, 1964–)

TEV	Today's English Version
TNTC	Tyndale New Testament Commentaries
UNT	Untersuchungen zum Neuen Testament
WBC	Word Biblical Commentary
ZNW	*Zeitschrift für die neutestamentliche Wissenschaft*
ZTK	*Zeitschrift für Theologie und Kirche*

Introduction

1. A Defense that Does not Defend

Formally, 2 Corinthians, except for chs. 8–9, conforms to the species of judicial rhetoric. As in most rhetorical literature, we have mixed genres. The thesis of this study is that Paul's goal is not self-defense. He needs no defense because he is an 'apostle of Jesus Christ by the will of God' (1.1). The Corinthian appraisal poses no threat to his apostolic office. Rhetorical goals subvert the judicial functions to promote Paul's pastoral and epideictic goals. This strategy seeks a reorientation of Corinthian criteria for apostleship and the gospel. Paul desires to 'build up' and not to 'tear down' the church.

A disavowal of 'defense' at 12.19, after presenting a sustained defense suggests that irony and parody are frolicking on every page. Indeed, 2 Corinthians reads almost like a commentary on 1 Cor. 4.2-4:

> Morever, it is required of stewards that they be found trustworthy. But with me it is a very small thing that I should be judged by you or by any human court. I do not even judge myself, but I am not thereby acquitted. It is the Lord who judges me.

If it is 'a very small thing' that Corinth indicts him, one might expect that if he offers a defense, it will be parodic.

Most scholarship concerned with 'defense' in 2 Corinthians has focused on chs. 10–13. G.A. Kennedy (*NT Interpretation*, pp. 86-96) argues that chs. 1–7 are also a 'defense speech'. Witherington argues that chs. 1–7, 10–13 are judicial, and deliberative rhetoric in chs. 8–9 supports the judicial goals in the remainder of the letter. Hans Dieter Betz ('Paul's Apology', pp. 15-16) thinks Paul consciously imitates the Socratic apology and thinks this humanistic, Socratic-Cynic tradition has antecedents in the Delphic religion. In a strong riposte, Judge alleges that Betz's 'whole thesis rests in the end upon a single word in St Paul, the word apology, when Paul says 'Don't think that this has been an apology that I have been making' (2 Cor. 12.19). Judge ('Paul and Socrates', pp. 106-107, 109) contends that Paul is 'parodying whatever it was that they were imposing upon him'. Rigaux thinks of 2 Corinthians 10–13 as 'apologetic or polemic autobiography' (p. 123) and Stowers (1986, p. 173) labels it 'ironic apology'. Wüllner (p. 152) identifies 1 Corinthians 4, 9 and 2 Corinthians 10–13 as 'parody' and Danker (p. 280) entertains the possibility of 'a parody of the Greco-Roman epideictic pattern'.

Although Betz appears to take 2 Corinthians 10–13 as a serious apologia, even he can think of it as 'self-parody'. He notes that the 'Foolish Discourse' relies on parody and ascertains that 12.2-4 and 12.7-10 are parodies but stops short of identifying the entire speech as parodic. Like the Platonic Socrates, Betz says Paul employs 'self-parody' ('Paul's Apology', p. 9ff.). This study argues that it is not self-parody but a parody of defense. Surely a 'Foolish Discourse' (11.1–12.18) already suggests parody. This fact alone does not verify that all of 2 Corinthians is parodic, but it is suggestive and invites investigation into that possibility.

Parody is 'a department of pure criticism' (C. Stone, p. 18). An art of imitation, parody imitates serious writing or speech but with slight changes makes the serious appear ridiculous. Genres related to parody include satire, burlesque, irony, sarcasm and invective as a distortion of satire.

> A keen, creative form of mimicry or indirect commentary, parody, which is similar to political cartoons and caricature, derives from the Greek for 'false song' and parallels the tone, diction, style or themes of a serious work to create incongruity, disparagement or dissonance (Snodgrass, p. 351).

One of the earliest parodies, the anonymous and undated *Batrachomyomachia* (*The Battle of Frogs and Mice*, sixth century BCE), carries to epic proportions Athena's war on vermin in a comic spoof of Homer's *Iliad*. Parody derides words, situations, sentimentality, posturing and overblown rhetoric through exaggeration or misapplication.

Few parodies imitate every phrase of the original but they must catch the ring of the original and appear spontaneous. A parody may accomplish its purpose by a change of word, phrase or tone. For instance a parody of a gospel hymn might be:

> Like a mighty *turtle* moves the Church of God,
> Christians, we are treading where *we've always trod*.

Sometimes I parody maxims of childhood such as 'Sticks and stones may break my bones, but words can *paralyze me forever*' or 'Children are to be seen, not *hurt*'. Betz ('Paul's Apology', p. 9) opines that 'The Socratic "I know that I know nothing" is the most abbreviated foolish discourse'. Certainly it is parodic, but it is hardly a 'discourse', abbreviated or otherwise. Betz correctly identifies Paul's 'Foolish Discourse' (2 Cor. 11.1–12.18) as parody. Paul, like the Platonic Socrates (cf. I.F. Stone), uses parody as an elenctic weapon to expose, convict, shame and convince someone of their fault or error (cf. Vlastos, esp. pp. 125-57). Thus, it functions more like invective epideictic than forensic discourse.

Polemo, who thought of parody as 'fun making', describes Hipponax as the inventor of parody (H.J. Rose, p. 93). Aristotle links parody with humor (*De Poetica* 5. 1449a) and Quintilian discusses parody as a form of jest (*Inst. Orat.* 6.3.53). Furthermore, Quintilian thinks of parody as 'the prettiest of all forms of humor' because it depends for its success on the subversion of anticipation (*Inst. Orat.* 6.3.84). In the same passage he cites an example from Cicero: 'What does this man lack save wealth and virtue?' Internal evidence in Aristophanes' *The Frogs* and *Clouds* demonstrates the relationship of parody with laughter, the upturned mouth of smile or laughter among the ancients (cf. Aristotle, *Poetics*, ch. 5). Since Plato, the philosophers, particularly in the Cynic tradition, have adopted parody as a form of philosophical dialogue.

Parody functions as ridicule, according to C. Stone (p. 8), who remarks that 'ridicule is society's most effective means of curing inelasticity... Truth will prevail over it, falsehood will cower under it'. Stone, D'Israeli ('Parodies' , pp. 510-11) and others have followed the French parodist, Louis Fuzelier (1738) that parody is an effective ruse for maligning falsity. Parody functions 'to expose opponents, and it employs irony' (Betz, 'Paul's Apology', p. 10). Conversely, Kreuz and Roberts (p. 104) contend that 'parody can be accomplished without irony', although they maintain that parody intends to ridicule. Definitional difficulties (see M.A. Rose, pp. 5-53) reveal that this genre is ambivalent and creates comic incongruity between the original and the parody.

Following a lengthy 'defense' Paul disclaims self-defense (12.19). Reiterating what he said at 2.17, Paul mocks self-defense saying he 'speaks in Christ before God'. Betz recalls that Windisch asked, 'Why does Paul not concede that he defends himself?' Responding to Windisch, Betz ('Paul's Apology', p. 2) explains that 'Paul considers an "apology" to be incompatible with "speaking before God". Self defense belongs in rhetoric; however, rhetoric belongs to this eon and the art of persuasion is not adequate for the proclamation of the gospel' (1 Cor. 1–2). Perchance Paul's refusal to 'concede' self-defense is because he makes no defense. Greek philosophy, beginning with Socrates, considers self-defense improper because it is the métier of the rhetorician and sophist. Plato and Xenophon comment on Socrates' rejection of self-defense. At the end of the letter, Paul's denial functions as a 'subversion of anticipation'. Parody subverts the form. Mimicking the form, parody satirizes and caricatures it. Iteration of 'speaking before God' (2.17) indicates the denial at 12.19 applies not only to chs. 10–13 but to the entire letter.

2. Some Contextual Considerations

a. Genre

There is a plethora of genres, figures and metaphors in 2 Corinthians. Autobiographical data abounds along with apologia, polemic, irony, foolish discourse, parody, anastasis, metastasis, hyperbole and synkrisis. Second Corinthians is a letter written in the form of judicial rhetoric but parody subverts the expectations and makes the letter function like epideictic. Paul becomes the consummate pastor and educator to the Corinthians.

Ancient writers exercised great freedom in mixing genres and organizing their discourse. As Leander Keck picturesquely remarks, 'In antiquity ideas did not flow in pipes' (p. 11). This study will refer to 2 Corinthians simply as parodic apostolic defense. Paul has no need to defend his apostleship; he is an 'apostle of Jesus Christ' (1.1). Although he wishes he could avoid the worthlessness of defense, it becomes 'necessary' (12.1) and the Corinthians forced his hand (12.10). Self-defense requires boasting which is 'not according to the Lord' (11.17). Paul's boast becomes parodic as he 'boasts in the Lord' (10.17). He boasts as a 'fool' (11.1-12.18) and under necessity he boasts only in his 'weakness' (11.30). Boastful self-defense is 'useless' (12.1) and Paul finally says he has not defended his apostleship (12.19). His 'defense' is parodic and his motive is 'all for your upbuilding, beloved' (12.19c).

To interpret 2 Corinthians correctly one must remember it is a smorgasbord of genres. It certainly seems on the surface to be a defense speech. Parody subverts the form and Paul becomes the accuser, not the defendant. Irony reigns supreme as Paul dons the mask of a fool. A foolish speech parodies boasting as Paul incredulously boasts in his weaknesses. Interpretation of 2 Corinthians on the literal level distorts and obfuscates Paul's intentions. Subversion of the 'defense' makes 2 Corinthians function more like an epideictic (i.e. 'blaming') speech. This subversion allows the apostle to be the educator instructing the Corinthians regarding 'Christian' criteria for apostleship.

b. Paul's Apostolate

Speaking autobiographically, Paul always identifies himself as an apostle. Awareness of his place in God's purpose finds its most poignant expression in his understanding of himself as an apostle. Except for Philippians, 2 Thessalonians and Philemon, the superscription of all his letters reveals that he wrote in the official capacity of an apostle. What an apostle does is preach the gospel (cf. 1 Cor. 15.9-11; Gal. 1.6). Apostolic authority is predicated on a call from God (e.g. Rom. 1.1).

Paul becomes the representative of the New Testament apostle so that it is difficult to tell how early Christians defined apostleship before and apart from Paul's letters (Beardslee, *Human Achievement*, p. 79). His interest was not in a doctrine of the apostolic office and he saw no reason to defend his apostleship. As an apostle whom God called, Paul thinks it is 'a small thing' (1 Cor. 4.3) that the Corinthians judge his apostleship. The apostle turned educator wants to 'build up' the Corinthians by helping them understand the true nature of apostleship.

Apostleship is a critical issue for Paul. Of the 79 fully attested occurences of 'apostle' in the New Testament, 80 per cent of them are found in Paul or in Acts. Interestingly, in Acts, the author never calls Paul 'apostle' and Paul, in his letters, never calls the Twelve 'apostles'. Even though he is 'nothing' (12.11), Paul refuses any concession of inferiority to the 'super apostles'. Corinthian criteria can never call into question Paul's apostleship. Forced to boast, he parodies boasting with a fool's speech, a parody of going over the wall, a rapture to heaven and a healing story.

c. Corinthian 'Opponents'

Scholarly hypotheses about 'opponents' are endless. Baur identifies the Christ Party of Judaistic Christianity. Lütgert sees representatives of pnematic Christology, but not Judaizers. Lake finds non-Jewish allegorizing pneumatics. Bultmann (*Exegetische*) and Schmithals (*Gnosticism*) think the 'opponents' are Gnostics. Käsemann (*Perspectives*, pp. 33-71) finds non-gnostic 'spiritual men'. Georgi (*Opponents*, pp. 301-305) thinks of Jewish-Christian missionaries. Kümmel (*Introduction*, p. 284) locates the opponents within the Corinthian community. Munck (p. 186) says the opponents are the Corinthians themselves.

'Mirror reading' is the method scholars have used to identify Paul's opponents. That is, from Paul's statements scholars try to reconstruct the other side of the conversation. Since Paul's autobiographical statements are uniformly 'apologetic in tendency' (Betz, *Galatians*, p. 68 n. 113; cf. p. 222 n. 30), the assumption is that Paul is defending himself against accusations. George Lyons (pp. 75-122) has called the validity of 'mirror reading' into question. He suggests that Paul's rhetoric, not outside opponents, is responsible for the 'charges'. Even Betz ('Paul's Apology', p. 3) says that one cannot 'conclude from words of defense that there must be a corresponding accusation'. Quite amazingly, however, Betz says he can 'divide up' the charges and defense in 2 Corinthians 10–13. Unless one begins with certain presuppositions, how is it possible to 'divide up' charges and defense in 2 Corinthians?

No one familiar with 2 Corinthians doubts that there was tension between Paul and his church. Clearly he intends this parodic defense for the Corinthians. An offending member of the church and Paul's failure to keep a promise and visit the Corinthians created the need for this letter. He wants to 'test' their obedience (2.9) and their love (8.8). Moreover, he wants them to 'test' themselves (13.5) to determine if they are really Christians. In his only two references to apostolic authority in 2 Corinthians, Paul affirms that his authority is 'for building you up and not for tearing you down' (10.8; 13.10). He is not sorry he wrote the lachrymose letter because it produced a 'godly sorrow' that led to repentance and salvation (7.10). Everything Paul does is for 'building up' the Corinthians (12.19).

Pastoral concerns permeate 2 Corinthians and Paul's focus is on the Corinthian church. He humbles himself so they can be exalted and asks if he sinned by preaching to them without charge (11.7). He follows his attack on the 'false apostles' (11.13-15) by pleading that he not be considered a 'fool' (11.16). However, he is willing to be accepted as a fool for the sake of his church. He feels a 'divine jealousy' for Corinth (11.2) and he wants to present them as a 'chaste virgin' in marriage to Christ (11.3). A great fear for the apostle is that Corinth, like Eve, will be deceived (11.3) and that when he returns to Corinth he will not find them 'as I wish and that you may not find me as you wish' (12.20). He prays that they may 'become perfect' (13.9).

If he is addressing the Corinthians as a pastor wishing to build them up, Paul cannot consider them 'opponents'. There is only scant reference to 'false apostles' and 'false brothers and sisters', but abundant reference to his concern for the Corinthians. There is no evidence that Paul considers that he has any 'opponents' in Corinth. They are a troublesome lot, even 'a thorn in his flesh' (12.7), but Paul's pastoral heart does not permit thinking of the congregation as 'opponents'. Perhaps it is time to close the door on discussions about opponents at Corinth.

d. The Fool's Speech

Taking the role of the 'fool', Paul wears the mask of the Greek *eirōn* ('fool'). The Greeks gave the name *eirōn* to persons who slyly pretended to be less than they were (Sedgewick, p. 7). Betz (*Der Apostel*, p. 75) incorrectly thinks of Paul as the *alazōn*, the person who vaunts oneself as more than one is. Paul is the self-depreciator, not the self-inflator. Columbo, the fictional detective, is a perfect example of the self-depreciator; the cartoon character, Donald Duck, the self-inflator. The 'fool' engages in 'foolish discourse', requiring the literary forms of irony and parody. The entire speech is a parody of self-praise and is ironic. Paul deplores boasting but when it is forced on him (12.1, 11), he parodies boasting by boasting in his weaknesses (11.30). When an audience does not wish to hear a speaker's message, indirect discourse is required and the queen of indirectness is irony which 'looks down, as it were, on plain and ordinary discourse' (Kierkegaard, *Irony*, p. 265). According to Quintilian (*Inst. Orat.* 9.2.46), it was the role of the 'fool' that brought

Socrates into disrepute. Socrates typified and later dignified the term *eirōn* ('fool').

As a fool, Paul will boast in his weakness. Knowing that he will offend his readers, he gives an advance justification (i.e. a prodiorthosis) for the speech (11.1-21a). 'Boasting in weakness' is a parody of boasting and is ironic (cf. Forbes, pp. 1-30). Paul has no desire to engage in boasting; it is not pleasing to the Lord (11.17). In his parody of boasting, Paul unwittingly follows Plutarch's rules for praising oneself inoffensively (Plutarch, *Moralia* 539A-547F). He becomes the Socratic 'mock-modest' person. Judge ('Paul's Boasting', pp. 37-58) thinks Paul's boasting is a parody of the forms of rhetorical self-advertisement current in Hellenistic society. Building on Judge's suggestion, Travis (pp. 527-32) argues that Paul was parodying Hebrew, not Greek, conventions.

With bold foolishness, to the point of insanity (11.21) he boasts of his pedigree (11.22-23). He declares himself a superior servant of Christ (11.23) and argues that he suffers better than any who might disparage him (11.23-29). His parodic boast of suffering includes 30 specific instances of suffering in which he claims pre-eminence. Particular instances are not as important as the pleonastic effect of the catalog of sufferings. Boasting in weakness continues (11.30) as he parodies an escape over the wall (11.31-32) and two parodical aretalogies: a heavenly rapture (12.1-5) and a healing story (12.7-10).

This study advances the hypothesis that 2 Corinthians is a parody of a defense speech. To accomplish his goal, Paul uses the well-known form of a defense speech but subverts the form with parody. Paul never believed he needed to defend his apostleship because God called him to be an apostle. In excellent parodic form, the apostle subverts anticipation by announcing in 12.19 that, despite what the Corinthians think, he has not been defending himself. They have forced him to be a 'fool' (12.11) but they have not disqualified him as an apostle of Jesus Christ. They cannot decide whether or not he is an apostle. As an apostle of Jesus Christ, he writes to 'build up' the Corinthian church.

3. Previous Readings of the Text

No Pauline letter creates more perplexity for the interpreter than Second Corinthians. Jülicher (p. 87) calls it 'the most personal of the extant letters of Paul'. One of Paul's most autobiographical letters, it reveals an apostle writing earnestly of his sorrows and joys, of his anxieties and hopes, of his doubts and confidence. One hears him speak in anguish of a short, painful visit to Corinth, of the tension over his failed promise to visit the church, a lachrymose letter and an offending member in the

Corinthian congregation. Intensely emotional, Paul responds to a challenge to his apostolic authority. By their criteria, the Corinthians apparently deemed Paul unworthy of the apostolic office.

There is 'strong and early attestation' of 1 Corinthians; for example in 1 Clement and the letters of Ignatius and Polycarp (Moffat, p. 87) but one cannot say the same for 2 Corinthians. Marcion's Canon (c. 140–50 CE) provides the earliest certain attestation (Tertullian, *Against Marcion* 5.11.12) and later it appears in the Muratorian Canon, probably no earlier than the fourth century (Sundberg, pp. 1-41). Most surprising is the lack of any certain knowledge of 2 Corinthians in 1 Clement, a letter from the Roman church to the Corinthian church in the late first century, although the Clementine letter broaches the same issue, namely a challenge to authority, as 2 Corinthians (J. Kennedy, pp. 142-53).

a. Authenticity and Integrity

Traditions dating from the middle of the second century, attest 2 Corinthians in the authentic Pauline corpus. This late date is not an adequate basis to challenge Pauline authorship. The style, form and content of the letter are thoroughly Pauline. Scholarly consensus, for good reasons, assumes the Pauline authorship of this letter. Commentaries on 2 Corinthians and Introductions to the New Testament usually bypass discussions of authenticity. That the Apostle Paul was the author of what is now known as the Second Epistle to the Corinthians is not a matter of dispute among reputable scholars (P.E. Hughes, p. xv).

If authenticity is not in dispute, the integrity of 2 Corinthians certainly is. In 1771, J.S. Semler, a professor on the theological faculty at Halle, was the first scholar to dispute the integrity of this letter. However, it was Adolf Hausrath, a century later, who engendered the partition theory that received the endorsement of a representative section of New Testament scholars. His theory became known as 'the four-chapter hypothesis', and identified 2 Corinthians 10–13 as Paul's 'tearful letter' (cf. 2.3-4; 7.8, 12).

Anton Halmel divided 2 Corinthians into nine segments that he rearranged to find three distinct letters. Walter Schmithals found a collection of letters in 1 and 2 Corinthians and concluded he could identify nine discrete dispatches from Paul to the Corinthians ('Die Korintherbriefe', pp. 263-88). With Betz's commentary on 2 Corinthians in the Hermeneia series, one has the impression that he has established the partition hypothesis as indisputable fact by his appeal to the rigorous application of rhetorical analysis. Betz traces the history of critical scholarship on this issue from Semler to Georgi and Bornkamm; Georgi and Bornkamm have refined Hausrath's theory (*2 Cor. 8 & 9*, pp. 3-36). Betz concludes that chs. 8 and 9 are separate 'administrative letters', neither of which originally appeared where they are now located in 2 Corinthians. He contends that if he is correct, then Semler's hypothesis can be 'regarded as proven' (*2 Cor. 8 & 9*, p. 36). Now, Amador has challenged Betz on Betz's rhetorical-critical turf and concludes:

> What for Betz was a method that helped to secure the fragmentary hypothesis could, in fact, overturn its very presuppositions and thereby throw open the question of multiple sources. Indeed, it is quite possible that rhetorical criticism can serve to secure a certain level of coherence in the letter's canonical structure, and thereby work in ways precisely opposite that of Betz (*Unity of 2 Corinthians*, p. 35).

Fragmentary hypotheses may not be as secure as they once seemed. Amador has made a convincing argument that rhetorical analysis points to the unity of 2 Corinthians.

Defenders of the integrity of 2 Corinthians may not be fighting a lost cause. Amador argues that:

> The difficulty with this [partition hypothesis] is that it is founded upon a particular and problematic notion of communicative dynamics, namely that communicative events such as letters are concerned with restricted coherence, focused consistency and unitary intentionality and context (*Unity of 2 Corinthians*, p. 2).

Indeed, he goes further and says:

> The fragmentation of 2 Corinthians into multiple sources is made possible only by a hermeneutic that assumes a logical, progressive development of events and circumstances that are not possible to address, or even to take shape, in a complex fashion. Instead each step of the correspondence must be strictly coherent (without multiple argumentative *topoi* or *dispositio*, consistent (in tone and approach within each document) and unitary (with respect to audiences and situations addressed by the rhetor) (*Unity of 2 Corinthians*, p. 37).

If Amador is right, the burden of proof shifts to scholars who espouse the multiple-source theory. We may no longer assume that communicative events, ancient or modern, function within such artificially restricted coherence, focused consistency and unitary intentionality.

There have been, and are, scholars who defend the integrity of 2 Corinthians (see Bernard, Lietzmann, Menzies, Kümmel, Goudge, Allo, Tasker, P.E. Hughes, Bates, Price, Danker, *et al.)*. Not only is the letter coherent, it provides many hints that point to its unity. At 1.17 and 10.10 Paul responds to the perception that he is fickle. He is not a 'peddler of God's word' (2.17) and refuses to accept monetary rewards from the Corinthians (11.7-12). Paul has conducted himself in Corinth 'in holiness and godly sincerity' (1.12) and refuses to practice 'cunning ways' (4.2); he has 'wronged no one, corrupted no one, took advantage of no one' (7.4). Furthermore, he seeks to avoid offense in financial matters (8.20) but thinks the Corinthians suspect deceit (12.16-18). He affirms his love for the Corinthians at 2.4, 8.7 and 11.11.

The apostle 'tests' the Corinthians' obedience at 2.9; he 'tests' their love (8.8) and he admonishes them to 'test yourselves' (13.5) because he has 'passed the test' (13.6). Catalogs of suffering appear at 4.8-9; 6.4-10; 11.23-29 and 12.10. Fitzgerald, (*Cracks*, p. 187) suggests that the hardship list in 6.4-10 presupposes the earlier list in 4.8-9 and prepares for the ones in 11.23-29 and 12.10. Paul hopes the Corinthians will receive benefits from his ministry (1.7, 15, 24; 3.2-3; 4.5, 12; 7.3; 8.16; 10.8; 12.19; 13.10). The term 'boast' (*kauchaomai*) occurs eight times in chs. 1–7, once in chs. 8–9 and 19 times in chs. 10–13. 'Commendation' language occurs at 3.1-3; 4.2; 7.11; 8.16-19 (including a letter of commendation, 8.22-24), 10.18 and 12.11. The author of 2 Corinthians refers to Titus in all three major sections of the letter (2.13; 7.6, 13, 14; 8.6, 16, 23; 12.18).

Bjerkelund (p. 149-55) observes that Paul's thanksgivings or doxologies customarily precede *parakalō* (appeal) periods as in Rom. 11.33-36; 12.1 and 1 Thess. 3.11-13; 4.1. Similarly Paul moves from 2 Cor. 9.15 to 10.1. Thus, we should no more sever 2 Cor. 10–13 from 2 Corinthians 1–9 than Romans 12 from Romans 1–11 or 1 Thessalonians 4–5 from 1 Thessalonians 1–3. Paul's tone changes much more sharply between 10.18 and 11.1 than it does between 9.15 and 10.1. At 11.1, the tone shifts dramatically for the 'Fool's Speech', but scholars have not found sufficient reasons to separate 11.1–12.18 from ch. 10.

A comparison of 2 Corinthians 10–13 with Galatians 5–6 convinces W.H. Bates of the unity of 2 Corinthians. At 2 Cor. 10.1 Paul writes 'I myself, Paul, appeal to you' and at Gal. 5.2 he lapses into the first person singular: 'Listen! I, Paul, am telling you'. In both 2 Corinthians 10–13 and Galatians 5–6 the syntax is more abrupt and the style more violent than in the main body of the letters. In both sections there is more frequent use of the first person singular. His approach is more personal in both sections than in the earlier parts of the letters; Paul states his position more dogmatically and less diplomatically in 2 Corinthians 10–13 and Galatians 5–6. Galatians 5–6 adds nothing of substance to chs. 1–4; Bates argues the same is true with 2 Corinthians 10–13 (p. 67). Bates concludes: 'The last four chapters [of 2 Corinthians] are the recapitulation of the arguments of the first nine, perhaps in Paul's own hand, as he had done in Gal 5–6'. To account for the change in tone and atmosphere at ch. 10, it is not necessary to maintain that they constitute a *peroratio*, a rather tenuous position at best. Fitzgerald thinks chs. 10–13 represent Paul's attempt to persuade the Corinthians so he can avoid another painful visit to Corinth for the purpose of discipline ('2 Cor. 10–13', p. 200).

Danker thinks of 2 Corinthians as one letter. 'If 6.14–7.1 is an interpolation, the early editors of what is now 2 Corinthians did a skillful job in mending the seams, for vv. 11-13 constitute an appropriate transition' ('II Cor.', p. 96). Commenting on 8.2 he observes: 'The link between chap. 8 and what precedes is strongly forged by the affliction-joy contrast' (p. 118). This contrast is consonant with Paul's experience (4.17-18; cf. 1.3-11) and the polarities of grief-repentance and anxiety-joy in ch. 7. The term 'joy' (*chara*) echoes the repeated use in ch. 7 of Greek cognate terms for 'rejoice' (*chairein;* 7.7, 9, 13, 16) and 'joy' (*chara*; 7.4, 13). There is evidence at 2.1-3, 12.21 and 13.1 that Paul plans to visit Corinth after the dispatch of the letter that includes chs. 10–13. Danker, like other scholars, hypothesizes a lapse of time between the writing of chs. 1–9 and 10–13, during which time Paul received new information from Corinth and argues this accounts for 'evident connections with chaps. 1–9 as well as for the discordant features' (p. 147).

One may certainly make a rational defense for the integrity of 2 Corinthians. However, one might wish to refrain from the dogmatic extreme that 'modern denials of its [2 Corinthians] unity are unsupported by any evidence of an objective nature or even circumstantial nature' (Witherington, p. 328). There is little warrant for Witherington's sarcastic remark that 'There are almost as many partition theories as there are commentaries on 2 Corinthians' (p. 328). However, it is noteworthy that no manuscript evidence supports a partition theory for 2 Corinthians. Neither Marcion nor the Muratorian Canon, the earliest sources referring to the letter, support a fragment theory. Kümmel offers a more mature response: 'Looking at the whole question, the best assumption is that II Cor as handed down in the tradition forms an originally unified letter' (*Introduction*, p. 292).

b. Paul's Corinthian Connection

Our primary sources for information about Paul's Corinthian connection are his Corinthian letters and Acts (18.1-17). From these data we are able to construct an approximate outline of his Corinthian mission. However, the Paul of the letters does not synchronize perfectly with the Paul of Acts. On the one hand, Acts does not tell us that Paul wrote letters and does not allude to the internal church problems Paul encountered; Acts does not describe the Corinthian challenge to Paul's apostleship. On the other hand, Paul's letters do not mention the 'Damascus road' experience. Paul, as we know him, is a composite, derived from Acts and the

Pauline letters. Even so, we know the historical Paul better than we know the historical Jesus because he wrote letters to his churches that are still extant. Usually he writes about problems in the churches. If Paul had not had problem churches, he might never have written any letters; at least they would be diffrent than the letters we have.

1. Roman Corinth

Dorian Greeks established Corinth in the tenth century BCE. Situated at the base of the Acrocorinth, it was on the isthmus that connected northern Greece with Peloponnseus, and boasted two harbors, Lechaeum to the west and Cenchreae to the East (Pausanias, *Description of Greece* 2). Periander (c. 625–585 BCE) built the five-foot-wide rock-cut track used for conveying ships across the isthmus. Apparently, by 400 BCE, Corinth was an illustrious and affluent city. Statistics indicate that the population may have approached 100,000 at that time. Most extant remains there date only from the fourth century BCE. Much of its wealth came from the commerce that passed between the Adriatic and the Aegean seas.

In 147 BCE Rome ordered the disintegration of Corinth. Leaders of the Achaian League resisted, but in 146 BCE the consul Lucius Mummius devastated and completely destroyed Corinth, massacring the men and selling the women and children into slavery. Mummius, with 32,000 troops, vanquished a motley Achaean army less than half as large and led by Diaeus (Cf. Pausanias, *Description of Greece* 8.16.7-8). For about a century, except for a few squatters who remained on the site, Corinth was desolate. There is, however, evidence that many of the public buildings and perhaps residences of Greek Corinth remained standing (Williams, pp. 21-23). In 44 BCE Julius Caesar undertook to lay the foundation for a new, Roman Corinth. Caesar named the new city Colonia Laus Julia Corinthiensis and imported Italian freedmen to populate it. Latin became the official language and dominated public inscriptions until well into the second century CE. Rome named Corinth the capital of the senatorial province of Achaia, the center of operations for the ruling proconsul. Despite setbacks, the city remained an important commercial center through the Middle Ages. The present village was rebuilt after an earthquake in 1928.

First-century Corinth, to which Paul ministered, was the leading commercial center of southern Greece. Paul's Corinthian correspondence addressed a congregation that resided in a Roman colony. The strategic geography allowed it to become the central crossroads for business going east and west. Strabo (c. 64/63 BCE–21 CE), refers to Corinth as 'wealthy' because of its fortuitous location and two harbors (*Geo*. 8.6.20a). Horace (*Odes* 1.7.2) uses the expression 'double-sea Corinth'. Production of Corinthian bronze and the manufacture of various decorative and utilitarian articles also contributed to Corinth's wealth. Throughout the empire, people valued Corinthian bronze 'before silver and almost before gold' (Pliny, *Natural History* 34.1.1). Ben Witherington (pp. 9-10) minimizes the data concerning Corinthian bronze in Corinth.

Most of the citizens must have spoken Greek by the time Paul arrived in Corinth (c. 50 CE) due to the influx of Greeks from neighboring areas. In the first century CE, the rhetor Favorinus addressed Corinth and described it as thoroughly Hellenized despite its status as a Roman colony (see Dio Chrysostom, 37.26). Of the names of Corinthians referred to in the New Testament, they are almost evenly divided between Latin and Greek names.

Corinth gained an unenviable reputation for licentiousness. Cicero (*On the Republic* 2.7-9) observes that 'Maritime cities also suggest a certain corruption and degeneration of morals ... [they] import foreign ways as well as foreign merchandise'. Strabo (8.6.20) reports that the Temple of Aphrodite at Corinth 'was so rich that it owned a thousand temple slaves, courtesans, whom men and women had dedicated to the goddess'. Aupelius (*Met.* 10.20-22) refers to sexual expression in some pagan religious festivals and temple precincts (cf. Mason, pp. 160-65). However, Conzelmann (p. 12) argues that Strabo's reference to temple prostitutes is anachronistic and refers to the pre 146 BCE period. Murphy-O'Connor (*Paul's Corinth*, p. 56) maintains that sacred prostitution was never a Greek custom and notes the silence of all other Greek authors on the subject.

Witherington (p. 14) charges Murphy-O'Connor with 'attempting to exonerate Roman Corinth'. However, Danker ('II Cor.', p. 14) asserts more decisively than O'Connor that 'Allegations of temple prostitution belong in the category of gossip rather than serious historical recital', and suggests that immorality in the contemporary church is perhaps even more serious than one finds in the Corinthian congregation. There is mixed evidence and it is uncertain whether sacred prostitution was a practice in classical Corinth. There is little doubt, however, that Corinth had a reputation for being home to many prostitutes (Saffrey, p. 373). First Corinthians leaves little room to doubt that there were sexual problems in the Corinthian church.

2. Paul and the Corinthian Church

According to Acts (15.36–18.22), Paul first arrived in Corinth after his mission to Athens and shortly after Aquila and Priscilla came to the city (18.2) as a result of the expulsion of Jews from Rome by Claudius. If the Jewish expulsion was in 49 CE and Paul was in Corinth while Gallio was proconsul (51/52 CE by the Delphian Inscription; cf. Jewett, pp. 38-40) and remained in Corinth for 18 months (18.11), Paul arrived in Corinth about 50-51 CE. Paul appeared before Gallio's tribunal (18.12-17) where the proconsul dismissed all charges against the apostle. While in Corinth, Paul established the first Christian congregation in southern Greece.

Paul wrote at least four letters to Christians at Corinth. His first letter, not extant, exhorted them not to associate with sexually immoral people (1 Cor. 5.9), but the Corinthians did not understand his instructions (1 Cor. 5.10-13). In the second letter, the canonical 1 Corinthians, he seeks to correct their misinterpretation and responds to reports from 'Chloe's people' (1.11) and answers questions the Corinthians had submitted in writing (1 Cor. 7.7a). With the formulaic *peri de* ('now concerning'), Paul explicitly refers to matters about which the congregation had inquired (see 7.7, 25; 8.1, 4; 12.1; 16.1, 12). A third letter, probably not extant, is one Paul describes as a lachrymose letter (2 Cor. 2.4; 7.8). Some scholars still identify 2 Corinthians 10–13 as the lachrymose letter, but that is not likely. Second Corinthians is Paul's fourth letter to Corinth. With confidence, we may speak of four letters from Paul to Corinth; to claim more is to intrude into the mucky waters of speculation.

Without recourse to 'mirror reading', one may draw some conclusions concerning Paul's Corinthian connections. 'Chloe's people' (1 Cor. 1.11) report ecclesial disunity (1 Cor. 1.11-17) and partisanship (1.18-4.21). However, 4.1-6 indicates that the dilemma is not so much about 'party strife', as opposition to the apostle. The Corinthian predicament includes incest (ch. 5) as well as sexual immorality and civil suits (ch. 6). From a written communication to Paul (7.7a), we learn of questions respecting marriage, conjugal rights and divorce (ch. 7), eating food offered to idols (chs. 8, 10), opposition to Paul (ch. 9), worship (ch. 11), charismata (chs. 12–14) and the resurrection of the saints (ch. 15). Corinthians boasted of their knowledge (1 Cor. 1.5; 8.1, 7, 10, 11; 12.8; 13.2; 14.6; also, see 2 Cor. 2.14; 4.6; 8.7; 10.5; 11.6) and spiritual status. The term 'spiritual' (*pneumatikos*) occurs 14 times in 1 Corinthians, but only four times in other undisputed Pauline letters. In 1 Corinthians Paul depicts the most 'spiritual' and most 'immoral' church in early Christianity.

Obviously, Paul encountered relational tautness in Corinth. Already, the Apostle offers parodic defenses of apostolic credentials in 1 Corinthians 4 and 9. Thus, with a high degree of probability, it is possible to reconstruct the contours of this relationship. Around 50–51 CE, Paul begins a mission to Corinth and planted a church (Acts 18.1-11); he remained for 18 months (18.11). Leaving Corinth, he goes to Ephesus (Acts 18.18-19) where he writes his first letter to Corinth, which we do not possess (1 Cor. 5.9), receives a vexatious report from Chloe's house (1 Cor. 1.11) and an inquiry from the church soliciting advice on diverse subjects (7.1). He informs that he will send Timothy to Corinth on a special mission (4.17; 16.10), requests their participation in an offering for poor saints at Jerusalem (1 Cor. 16.1-2) and promises to visit them (16.5-7).

Subsequently, a crisis arose and Paul made a 'painful visit' (2 Cor. 2.1) at which time, apparently someone offended him (2 Cor. 2.5). Rampant partisanship caused Paul to cancel a proffered visit and write a lachrymose letter (2.4; 7.8). Paul departed Ephesus expecting to meet Titus at Troas. Not finding Titus, Paul is so distraught he waives an opportunity for evangelism (2.12-13; 7.5-7). He advances to Macedonia where Titus appears with good news from Corinth (7.5-16). He writes 2 Corinthians and promises to visit 'the third time' (13.1). With 2 Corinthians, our information of Paul's Corinthian connection ceases. However, the information available is sufficient to provide an historical context for understanding 2 Corinthians.

A Parodic Defense of Behavior (2 Corinthians 1–7)

Paul presents a parodic defense of his apostolic behavior in 2 Corinthians 1–7. His boast comes early in the letter that he has 'behaved in the world, and especially toward you, with frankness and godly sincerity' (1.12). It is this proposition that will control the entire letter and reveals the parodic nature of the 'defense' he will make. With the triple anaphoric 'no one' (anaphora is a literary device that uses repetition for emphasis) Paul amplifies his deposition that he has 'wronged no one' at Corinth (7.2).

1. Epistolary Greeting (1.1-2)

Adapting the customary opening formula of a Greco-Roman letter, Paul greets the 'church of God which is at Corinth' (1.1). He identifies himself as 'an apostle of Jesus Christ through the will of God'. Naming 'Timothy, the brother', as a co-sender of the letter is Paul's way of strengthening his authority at Corinth (see also Phil. 1.1; 1 Thess. 1.1; Phlm. 1; Col. 1.1; 2 Thess. 1.11). That 2 Corinthians is not a circular letter is established by Paul's words 'I have spoken frankly to you Corinthians' (6.11; contra Witherington, p. 354).

The salutation almost becomes benediction with the words 'Grace to you and peace' (1.2). Instead of the anemic 'Greetings' (*chairein*), Paul uses 'grace' (*charis*), a decidedly richer theological term. 'Peace' is a stylized greeting derived from the Hebrew *šalōm*. 'Grace and peace to you from God our Father and the Lord Jesus Christ' is identical with that in every other genuine Pauline letter except 1 Thess. 1.1b which has only the invocation of 'grace and peace'. Pronouncing a benediction already requires the assumption of Paul's apostolic authority.

2. A Congratulatory Benediction (1.3-7)

In this section of the letter, Paul normally expresses thanksgiving to God for his readers, for aspects of their lives and the grace given to them (1 Thess. 1.3; 2 Thess. 1.3; 1 Cor. 1.7). With a subtle shift, Paul replaces the thanksgiving with a benediction in which all the items usually referring to addressees become self-referential. God comforts Paul and he becomes the apostolic conduit of God's comfort to others (1.4). He comforts 'through the comfort' with which God has comforted him. The 'sufferings of Christ' are abundant in the apostle (1.6) and his consolation is abundant 'through Christ'. Whether Paul experiences affliction or comfort, the purpose is the comfort and salvation of the Corinthians (1.6). Paul leaves no doubt that he is the one for whom the Corinthians should be grateful; God channels blessing to them through an apostle God has appointed.

That Paul begins with praise to God is not surprising. In defense speeches, the orator often begins by addressing the judge. Paul's parodic defense robs the Corinthians of their rank as jurors. Their opinion can have no bearing on Paul's apostolic status. Paul believes that only God is his judge, as he affirms in 1 Cor. 4.4-5 and repeats at 2 Cor. 12.19 (also see 13.3-7). However, Paul clearly has a vested interest in the opinion of the Corinthians (cf. 1.12; 8.20-21; 12.11). 'Consolation' language (*paraklēsis, parakalein*) is anaphoric in this passage. Different forms of the noun and verb occur ten times in seven verses. Like a series of hammer blows, Paul repeats the same word for emphasis. 'Blessed be God' (Bultmann, *2 Corinthians*, p. 21, reads it as imperative, but Furnish, (p. 109, as indicative) appears to be a Jewish formula (cf. LXX Ps. 40.14; 65.20; 71.18; 105.48). This formula appears anaphorically in the Eighteen Benedictions. Dahl ('Benediction', p. 5) has shown that one function of the formula is congratulatory.

Congratulatory benedictions do double duty: the speaker praises God as the giver of the blessing while congratulating the recipient of the gift. When Jethro exclaims to Moses, 'Blessed be the Lord who has delivered you out of the hand of the Egyptians and out of the hands of Pharaoh' (Exod. 18.10), he is praising Moses on his escape just as much as he is praising God for the miracle of deliverance. Benedictions often contain an element of self-congratulation (Dahl, 'Benediction', p. 7). Self-congratulation is explicit in Zech. 11.5, 'Blessed be the Lord, for I have become rich!' The morning benediction, 'Blessed be He who has not made me a Gentile...who has not made me a slave... Who has not made me a woman', shows that self-congratulatory benedictions were a daily practice.

From ancient times, self-praise has been offensive. Demosthenes (*De Corona* 4) coined the term periautologia for such self-praise. Aristotle (*Rhetoric* 2.17.16) suggests that one should state self-praise in the third person. Quintilian (*Inst. Orat* 11.1.22) counsels 'leave it to others to praise us'. Plutarch (*Moralia* 542E-543A) suggests that a person may praise oneself if one 'assigns part of their deeds and success to chance and to God'. Paul's use of a congratulatory benediction, perhaps unwittingly, respects the constraints Plutarch recommended.

3. An Emotional Appeal (1.8-11)

This paragraph plays on the emotional strings of the Corinthians. With the conjunction *gar* ('for') Paul connects his personal sufferings with the congratulatory benediction. Its function is not so much to inform his readers as to confirm what he says in vv. 3-7. Paul permits them to see him as the suffering and comforted one, and that by this means he mediates comfort to them. Verse 8, with the address, 'brothers and sisters', and the introductory formula 'I do not wish you to be unaware' (Cf. Phil. 1.12), marks a new beginning but the conjunction connects it to vv. 3-7. Verses 8-11 lack the liturgical style of vv. 3-7. Paul turns from addressing the judge (vv. 3-7) to speak directly to his partners at Corinth (vv. 8-11).

Paul's rescue from death must be a matter of great consequence to the Corinthians and the apostle invites them to give thanks for God's gift to him. At v. 3 Paul already insinuates self-congratulations as one God has blessed and made a channel of comfort to them. In the end he asks them categorically to give thanks to God for the apostle (v. 11). Verses 12-14 make explicit the implicit boasting and self-congratulations in vv. 3-11. From praising God, Paul quickly insinuates praise for himself.

A disclosure formula, 'for I do not wish you to be unaware', at v. 8 reveals that Paul's afflictions will be a major topic in his parodic defense. He informs the reader of his hardships in Asia, although he provides no details. His focus is on the effects of the tribulations on him. In v. 4 he has already amplified the topic with the phrase 'in all our afflictions' ('in any affliction', in NRSV is too weak). His suffering is for their 'consolation and salvation' (1.6). Verse 5 provides further amplification of Paul's suffering with the phrase 'the sufferings of Christ are abundant in me'. He begins a new paragraph by further magnifying his hardships in Asia (1.8). Hyperbolic language serves the same function as he describes his affliction literally as 'excessive beyond power'. So excessive was the burden that he 'despaired of life itself'.

The apostle envisioned no deliverance from death (v. 8) but he found meaning in his afflictions (v. 9). He had received 'the sentence of death' (1.9) and again magnifies the situation by making it literally 'so great a death' (1.10). Having accepted death, he can now amplify God's deliverance as a resurrection from the dead (1.9). The key to Paul's success is God. By enlarging on his tribulations, he can amplify God's deliverance. Praise to God makes the self-congratulation less offensive. The Corinthians share in the praise as he says they have 'cooperated together' in prayer on his behalf and this will result in many persons giving thanks to God for what God has given and will continue to give to Paul (v. 11).

There is enough praise for everyone in the thanksgiving. There is insinuated self-congratulation throughout and at v. 11 the self-praise becomes blatant. He remembers to praise the Corinthians and assure them of their mutuality with him. In this emotional appeal, he seeks the sympathy of the Corinthians. Paul hopes the emotional appeal combined with praise for the Corinthians will strengthen his apostolic authority at Corinth. Giving praise to God mollifies the odium of self-praise. He builds on the topics of his suffering, God's consolation and his desire to comfort others in their adversities.

4. Paul's Side of the Story (1.12-2.17)

Although Paul appealed for sympathy in vv. 8-11, in v. 12 he comes to the issue in dispute: apostolic behavior. Unfortunately, we do not have a record of the Corinthians' side of the story. Interestingly, Paul begins his 'defense' with a boast: his conscience. His 'conscience' is his witness that he has behaved properly 'in the world' and 'all the more toward you' (1.12). An unimpeachable witness, his conscience, testifies that Paul has behaved with 'frankness and godly sincerity'. The two nouns translated 'frankness' and 'sincerity' form a hendiadys; that is, both nouns connote purity and sincerity. At 2.17, Paul returns to 'sincerity' and at 6.11, the idea of 'frankness' recurs.

Apparently Paul thinks that some Corinthians believe his behavior is not becoming to an apostle. Verses 13-14 reveal that the opprobrious behavior concerns a letter he wrote to the church. He assures the community that his letters do not equivocate; he writes only what they can read and understand. He says what he means and means what he says (v. 13). Unfortunately the Corinthians understand Paul now only 'in part', but at the Parousia Paul hopes they will understand that he is their cause for boasting and they are his cause for boasting (v. 14). 'Boasting' language is prominent in 2 Corinthians The infinitive appears at 7.14; 5.2; 9.; 10., 13, 15-17; 11.2, 16, 18, 30; 12.1, 5-6, 9. The noun for boast (*kauchēsis*) is at 1.12; 7.4; 14; 8.24; 9.4; 11.10, 17 and another noun (*kauchēma*) at 1.14; 5.12 and 9.3. As Aristotle advises (*Rhetoric* 3.14.7), Paul seeks to remove all suspicion.

We do not know if the Corinthians had openly expressed suspicions, but Paul may have perceived that they had misgivings about him. It is also possible that Paul's rhetoric creates suspicions so he can instruct them on apostolic criteria. Paul indicates that the Corinthians were upset by his canceled visit and the painful letter he wrote in lieu of the visit (1.15-22). Paul makes no effort to deny the charges; the facts are clear. He does not challenge their understanding of the facts. The case, then, turns on Paul's motives in these actions. Motives are crucial in a 'defense speech'. He will argue that his actions were honorable and beneficial (cf. Aristotle, *Rhetoric* 3.15.12).

Declaring that he does not prevaricate in his letters (vv. 17-18) Paul calls on a second unimpeachable witness. God will testify that Paul's motive for canceling his visit was to spare them further pain (1.23). This same God has 'sealed' Paul and given to him the Holy Spirit as 'a first installment' (1.22). With insinuation of the patronage issue, Paul assures the Corinthians that he does not wish to 'lord it over' their faith; indeed, he considers them to be 'co-workers' (1.24). He had wanted to visit them twice as a 'double favor' (1.15). Because of painful memories of a previous visit, Paul says 'I made up my mind not to make you another painful visit' (2.1). Since his motive was to spare them (1.23) and himself (2.2-3), it was a beneficial action.

Having called two unimpeachable witnesses, Paul now returns to the letter he last mentioned at 1.13. His motive was not to cause pain but 'to let you know the abundant love I have for you' (2.4). Pulling on their heart strings, Paul says that he wrote 'out of much affliction and anguish of heart and with abundant tears' (2.4). It is hardly an accident that Paul uses the same word 'affliction' (*thlipsis*) as he used to describe his 'affliction' in Asia (1.8). Now he transfers responsibility for the pain to an offending member at Corinth (2.5) and to Satan who motivated the offender (2.11).

With this strategy, the defendant has become the prosecutor. For the sake of the Corinthians, Paul forgives the offender (2.10) who caused pain not only to Paul, but 'to all of you' (2.5). His 'co-workers of joy' have suffered with him. By making them partners in his pain, Paul makes the Corinthians witnesses for his defense. He seems to commend the 'majority' for punishing the offender but in the same breath urges them to reaffirm their love for this person (2.8). Paul is not on trial; the defense is parodic and his motive is to instruct them on God's criteria for apostleship.

At 2.12-13 Paul again plays on the strings of emotion by relating his distress at Troas where he could not find 'my brother Titus' (2.13). He has suffered afflictions in Asia (1.8), when he wrote the lachrymose letter (2.4) and while he was in Troas (2.13). We have no details of his ministry at Troas except that there was an 'open door' for evangelism. However, anxiety over Titus not being there with a report from Corinth (7.5) caused him to abandon the evangelistic opportunity and proceed to Macedonia. His reference to Titus as 'my brother' shows Titus's importance to him and appeals to the gentler emotions of the Corinthians (Windisch, *Korintherbrief*, p. 94). There is no mention of Titus in Acts or 1 Corinthians but there are several references in 2 Corinthians (2.13; 7.6, 13, 14; 8.6, 16, 23; 12.18), encompassing all three major sections of the letter.

Expressions of anxiety over the Corinthians (2.13) and love for them (2.4) reveal his pastoral commitment to his converts. He does not take expensive ego trips at the expense of the community. Appropriately now he turns to thanksgiving: 'Thanks be to God' (2.14). This expression usually refers to what directly precedes it. Windisch calls 2.14 'a little hymn' (*Korintherbrief*, p. 96). Paul concludes his narration of the story on a triumphant note. Turning from anxiety (2.13) to an exclamation of gratitude (2.14), he makes a transition to a self-depiction of his apostleship and introduces a new train of thought that he will pursue from 2.14 to 7.4. Typically he shifts from the topic of his activities to what God has done through him.

Parodically he describes his never-ending journey as a triumphal procession (2.14; cf. Seneca, *V. B.* 25.4 for a similar portrayal). In this triumphantal procession, Paul becomes a slave of Christ, spoils of war, for a triumphant victor (Egan, pp. 34-62). Lexically, the phrase 'to lead in triumph' in v. 14 describes a victory parade in which the vanquished enemy soldiers and generals are led about as prisoners (Windisch, *Korintherbrief*, pp. 96-97). Paul uses the term as a metaphor of shame (Marshall, 'THRIAMBEUEIN', p. 304). He can never forget that he is always on exhibit as a slave of Christ. Parodically and paradoxically, he asserts his apostolic authority by depicting himself as servant under God in Christ. Subtly hinting at the patronage issue, Paul indicates he is a client with God, not Corinth, as patron. On exhibit as an apostle, he has been made a 'spectacle' for Christ (1 Cor. 4.9).

On the day of the victorious procession, captives were normally somber and sullen (cf. Ovid, *Tristia* 4.2.19-24, 29-34). Glory went to the conquering commander and the display of spoils was the essence of victory (Rushford, p. 894). Parody makes the 'prisoner of war' triumphant as he verbalizes thanksgiving to God. Paul is not in the depths of depression nor is he filled with bitterness and resentment. He parodies the procession because although God has conquered him, he is no longer a foe. Through this slave God is spreading 'the fragrance that comes from knowing God' (2.14). He has become 'the aroma of Christ to God' (2.15). Being God's 'prisoner of war' is a cause for praise, not shame. His parody is subversive because it inverts the patronal system so that all persons are clients and only God is patron.

With the metaphor of 'fragrance' (*osmē*) the imagery of the triumphal procession continues (2.14b). At the procession, incense crackled and smoked on every altar (Ovid, *Tristia* 2.4; Plutarch, *Aem.* 32). The Greek *osmē* may refer to a pleasant (e.g. Jn 12.3; Plutarch, *Alex.* 20.13) or an unpleasant (LXX, Tob. 6.17; 8.3; Job 6.7) odor. Here and in v. 16b, it is a fragrance. Through Paul, God reveals the fragrance of the gospel in every place (2.14b). Paul is the 'fragrance' (*euōdia*) of Christ; *euōdia* refers only to pleasant odors. The aroma of Paul is Christ; placing 'Christ' first in the text makes this clear (P.E.Hughes, p. 79 n. 12). Attributing the 'fragrance' to Christ mitigates effectively the odium of self-praise.

There is a mixed response to Paul's aromatic presence. Persons who do not accept Paul's Gospel smell the 'stench' of death; believers smell the sweet scent of life (2.15-16). Similarly in 1 Cor. 1.18, the message of the cross is the power of God to believers but to unbelievers it is moronic. Paul's phrase 'stench of death' suggests the putrefied odor of a corpse (Sophocles, *Ant.* 408-13; Josephus, *War* 6.2). It also anticipates 4.10 where Paul carries about in his body 'the dying (*nekrōsis*) of Jesus'. Through Paul God spreads the 'fragrance that comes from knowing him' (2.14). Paul boasts only in weakness because he has learned that 'power is made perfect in weakness' (12.9b). His notion of 'power in weakness' is a subversion of Greco-Roman patronage as the Corinthians know it.

After his parody of self-praise in 2.14-16b, Paul poses a rhetorical question: 'Who is competent for these things?' (2.16c). The inferential 'for' (gar) and Paul's distancing himself from 'the many' in v. 17 assures that the anticipated answer is 'Of course, Paul is!' Tasker (p. 58) apparently tries to protect Paul from boasting by arguing that the expected answer to the rhetorical question was 'No one!' Against the effrontery of claiming 'competence', Paul guards himself by saying God made him competent (literally the verb is 'compented') to be a minister of a new covenant (3.5-6). These checks against the distastefulness of self-praise indicate that Paul is boasting in 2.16c-17 (Lenski, *Interpretation*, p. 902), but the boast is parodic.

An enslaved apostle, Paul rejects the status-maintaining leadership of patronage (cf. H.B. Martin, p. 135). Through his parodic boast of participation in the triumphal procession, he portrays himself as a shamed individual. By boasting of humiliation, Paul subverts patronage and the Corinthian criteria of apostleship. Subversive metaphors in vv. 14-16 attest that Paul wants to persuade the Corinthians of his view of apostleship. That the adjective 'competent' (*hikanos*) in 2.16 is repeated in 3.5, along with the cognate noun (3.5) and verb (3.6) shows that the key question in what follows will be apostolic competency. In 2.14-16 Paul applies to himself the analysis of the message of the cross in 1 Cor. 1 (Fitzgerald, *Cracks*, p. 163). By parodically describing his authority as servanthood, he hopes to undermine powerful patrons in Corinth and save the community for Christ and the gospel.

With seeming effrontery, Paul answers the question in 2.16b with 'I am' as 3.1 and 3.5 attest. Verse 17 is Paul's justification for his presumed answer to v. 16c, as the inferential 'for' indicates. He argues that he is different from 'the many' who peddle an adulterated gospel for profit. Unlike 'the many', he does not 'huckster' God's word. Paul's term 'the many' is an equivalent for the general public or the masses (cf. Dio Chrysostom 32.8). Epictetus (1.3.4) contrasts 'the many' (*hoi polloi*) with 'the few' (*hoi oligoi*). The Greek term that we translate by 'peddle' appears in LXX Isa.1.22 with the allusion to mixing water with wine to increase profits (BAGD, *s.v.*). Paul has in mind persons who teach for gain, and in the process, 'water down' the word of God. 'The many' is general rather than specific and cannot refer to intruders at Corinth. It is a device that tells us more about Paul than others, if indeed, there are others. The contrast is rhetorical and emphasizes Paul's integrity. It is fanciful interpretation to connect the term 'peddle' in 2.17 with chs. 8 and 9 and 12.13 and claim that money matters 'lie at the heart of the grievance some Corinthians have against Paul' (contra Witherington, p. 372).

While Paul mentions finances, there is no evidence that money was the heart of the problem. Succinctly Paul characterizes his ministry as (1) in Christ I speak as a person of sincerity; (2) in Christ I speak as a person commissioned by God; and (3) in Christ I speak as a person in the presence of God.

Paul's parodic defense ultimately says, 'With me it is a very small thing that I should be judged by you' (1 Cor. 4.3). Paul does not judge himself but leaves judgment with God. 'It is the Lord who judges me' (1 Cor. 4.4). He is not under Corinthian jurisdiction; only God may judge him. His whole ministry is in the presence and under the judgment of God. At 12.19 where Paul denies having given a 'defense', he repeats from 2.17, 'We speak in Christ before God'. After exhorting the Corinthians, 'Examine yourselves' (13.5), Paul announces that he has 'passed the test' (13.6), reflecting what he said at 1.12.

5. Letters of Commendation (3.1-6.13)

Boasts of being God's aroma, self-praise of competence and setting himself apart from the 'hawkers' leads to the question of self-commendation. After substantial self-praise in 2.14-17 (Knox, p. 129-33), Paul asks, 'Am I beginning to commend myself again?' (3.1). He has been commending himself, albeit parodically, and he will do it 'again' (3.1). Apparently the question in 3.1a intends to expose the reproach of self-commendation.

However, he will now commend himself amply, as he later will boast after declaring that it is not according to the Lord (11.16). With another rhetorical question he asks, 'Do I need, as some do, letters of commendation to you or from you?' (3.2b) The negative particle (*mē*) shows that Paul expects a negative answer to this question. He can adequately commend himself (3.2; 4.2).

Paradoxically, Paul says he needs no letter of commendation from the Corinthians and then declares the Corinthians to be his letter of commendation. At 4.2 he says he does commend himself and at 12.11 he remonstrates: 'Indeed you should have been the ones commending me'. It is as if the Apostle is saying, 'If you want commendation, I will give you self-commendation'. He proceeds to parody commendation to show that it is ludicrous. God has commended the apostle and so he cares little how the Corinthians judge him (1 Cor. 4.3).

Christ has written Paul's letter of commendation: the Corinthians. Chiastic antithesis clarifies the metaphorical language in 3.2-3. Christ wrote the letter 'not with ink but with the spirit of the living God...not on tablets of stone but on tablets of human hearts' (3.3).

not with ink		not on tablets of stone
	BUT	
on tablets of human hearts		with the Spirit of the Living God

Commendation does not come from the Corinthians; they are his commendation. The commendation comes from Christ. This strategy exalts Paul to his rightful place and puts the Corinthians 'in their place'. They do not have the authority to commend him; that authority belongs to Christ.

a. Commendation by Comparison (3.4-4.1)

Since 2.16c, apostolic competence has been a major theme. Gospel hawkers are not competent but Paul is because of his sincerity, his commission from God and his ministry in God's presence (2.17). Paul does not need their letters of recommendation but they need to be his letter of commendation. His commendation is from Christ; he led the Corinthians to Christ. Paul's confidence does not spring from human recognition but from God's commendation. Paul assuages the offense of self-praise by saying his confidence comes from God who has made him competent to be a minister of a new covenant, not of the law but of the Spirit (3.6). R.P. Martin (p. 53) demonstrates that 3.6 is in tandem with 2.16c as the following diagram will show.

3.6		2.16c
'Competented'		'Competent'
I	Paired with	Who?
Minister		These Things
New Covenant		

These key terms go to the heart of Paul's self-definition. Shunning every claim to self-sufficiency, he can say without shame, 'I am not worthy to be called an apostle' (1 Cor. 15.9). Since *diakonos* (minister) may also translate 'servant', there is irony in Paul's claim that God has made him competent to be a servant. His inversion of patronage continues to be subversive.

Antithesis is Paul's native tongue. He contrasts the 'new covenant' (3.6) with the 'old covenant' (3.14). The old covenant is according to the 'letter' and kills while the new covenant is according to 'the spirit' and gives life. In 3.3 he has already alluded to Jer. 31.31-34 and it is no surprise that he now considers the new covenant in contrast to the old. The accent falls on 'new' as Paul appeals to the 'newness' of his gospel. Paul's invocation of Jeremiah's promise shows that he is overstating his case when he says the old is 'fading away' (3.13). Käsemann (*Perspectives*, p. 150) misses the parody when he writes that the new is not a sign of a renovated Judaism but a new redemptive order. Paul was a Jew who shared Jeremiah's vision; he calls himself a Jew and never calls himself a Christian. He hoped for a renewal in Judaism of the covenant written on the heart. Paul sees himself as a minister of a covenant 'in the Spirit' not 'a written code'.

Using Lucian's convention of 'overlapping' (*On the Writing of History*, 55), 3.6 concludes what went before and introduces what follows. Everything from 3.7 to 4.1 is midrashic exegesis of Exod. 34.29-35 (cf. Dunn, pp. 309-20) with Jer. 31.31-34 clearly in view. In Romans and Galatians, the Law is an interim covenant in God's plan (cf. Talbert, p. 150). Likewise, both letters assert the priority of the Abrahamic Covenant over the Mosaic Covenant, which is temporary. There is also agreement in Romans and Galatians that Jew and Gentile alike receive the inheritance through faith. His concern with the Abrahamic and Mosaic covenants is soteriological and he works with Jeremiah 31 to tie the 'new covenant' with the Abrahamic covenant.

Self-commendation is the primary theme of 3.7–6.13 as references in this section demonstrate (cf. 3.1-3; 4.2; 5.12 and 6.4). One might even call this passage 'a letter of self-commendation'. That his self-commendation is parodic becomes especially evident at 10.18: 'For it is not those who commend themselves who are approved, but those whom the Lord commends'. He does not need letters of commendation (3.2) but he commends himself (4.2). He commends himself so the Corinthians can take pride in him (5.12) and as a servant of Christ he commends himself 'in every way' (6.4). Ironically, the basis of his commendation would argue that the Corinthians are correct when they challenge his credentials.

A comparison of 'ministries' clarifies the quality of the 'ministry of the new covenant'. He uses the topic of 'the more and the less', a strategy known both in Hellenistic rhetoric (*Inst. Orat.* 8.4.9) and rabbinic exegesis (*a minori ad maius*). Such comparison (*sunkrisis*) always intends to criticize. Paul's midrash on Exod. 34 interprets the 'fading glory' on Moses' face differently than the original author. Jeremiah gives Paul the language of a 'new covenant', a 'broken covenant', and a law written 'on their hearts' (31.31-34). Paul thinks of the Mosaic covenant as an interim covenant and the Abrahamic covenant as 'the everlasting covenant' (Gen. 17.7).

There is an implicit comparison of covenants but the explicit comparison is of Moses and Paul. That Paul intends to compare himself with Moses becomes clear when he declares that he is 'not like Moses' (3.13). Through his ministry the veil has been removed (3.14) at Corinth and he and persons to whom he has ministered 'are being transformed into the same image from one degree of glory to another' (3.18). The topic of 'the more and the less' allows Paul to engage in self-praise. That his confidence is 'through Christ toward God' (3.4) who has made him competent (3.6) Paul escapes the distastefulness of self-praise. Paul's ministry is 'much more' glorious than that of Moses (3.11). Not only is the new (Abrahamic) covenant superior to the Mosaic covenant, but God has qualified Paul to be a minister of the new (renewed?) covenant. He characterizes his ministry as one of 'boldness' (3.12) and 'freedom' (3.17) and in contrast to Moses, he appears with 'unveiled face' (3.11).

If Paul's audience understood this passage, we must assume more than a passing acquaintance with the Septuagint. We probably must also assume a Jewish presence in Corinth. To imagine Paul, a faithful, practicing Jew, defending himself with Jews in the audience, as superior to Moses is incredulous. It is difficult to imagine a first-century Jew who would denigrate Moses. Since, by God's mercy he has 'this ministry' that is superior to Moses, Paul does not 'lose heart' (4.1). Apparently, when Titus came, he had to report residual problems even if the 'majority' (2.6) had punished the offender (2.6). Beginning at 2.14, it appears that Paul needs to tackle the issue of apostolic commendation. Thus, as Paul can boast when it is necessary ('Since many boast according to human standards, I will also boast', 11.18), he can also commend when it is necessary. Just as his self-boasting is a parody of boasting, his self-commendation is a parody of commendation. The only commendation worthy of mention is the commendation of God (10.18) and Paul has a letter of commendation (the Corinthians) that Christ has written on his heart, but the Corinthians do not commend him well (12.11).

b. The Glory of the Gospel (4.2-6)

At 4.1, Paul again uses 'overlapping' so that 4.1 both concludes the previous section and introduces a new section. Links between 4.2-6 and 2.14-17 suggest that Paul is employing a literary device known as 'ring composition', that is, his closing thoughts revert to his earlier statements and complete the circle of ideas (R.P. Martin, p. 75). Persons who reject Paul's Gospel are 'the ones who are perishing' (2.15) and the ones to whom the gospel is veiled are 'the ones who are perishing' (4.3). 'The many' (2.17) are the ones who practice 'the hidden things of shame' (4.2). Paul conducts his ministry with transparency (3.12) and he does not practice 'craftiness' (4.2). He does not 'peddle the word of God' (2.17) and he does not 'adulterate the word of God' (4.2). His ministry is one of 'sincerity' (2.17) and he manifests the truth (4.2). Paul's ministry is always 'in the sight of God' (2.17) and he commends himself to everyone's conscience 'in the sight of God' (4.2). The substance of Paul's gospel is 'the knowledge of God' (2.14) or 'the knowledge of the glory of God' (4.6). There is little reason to doubt that here we have an echo of 2.14-17.

Ring Composition

Persons rejecting gospel are perishing (2.15)	Ones with veiled minds perishing (4.3)
The many adulterate God's word (2.17)	The many adulterate God's word (4.2)
Paul's ministry one of transparency (3.12)	The many 'things of shame' (4.2
Paul's ministry one of sincerity (2.17)	He manifests 'the truth' (4.2)
Paul's ministry 'in the sight of God (2.17)	Commends self 'in the sight of God (4.2)
Gospel is 'knowledge of God' (2.14)	Gospel the 'knowledge of God's glory' (4.6)

Earlier Paul denies any need for commendation (3.1), but now he commends himself to 'the conscience of everyone in the sight of God' (4.2). This startling self-commendation depicts Paul in stark contrast with persons who practice 'the shameful things that one hides' (4.2). Paul boasts that his conduct is an open book that he invites everyone to critique because the unimpeachable witnesses of everyone's conscience would acquit him. Like Epictetus (*Diss.* 3.22.13-18), Paul lives 'out in the open'.

His 'openness' (3.12) makes it unnecessary for him to practice 'craftiness' (4.2).

The 'truth' (4.2) is not Paul's personal probity, but the 'word of God' (2.17). This is the gospel he does not 'adulterate' (4.2) and does not 'peddle' (2.17). His gospel requires no 'veil' (4.3) because it is 'the aroma of the knowledge of God' (2.14), 'the light of the knowledge of the glory of God in the face of Jesus Christ' (4.6). Only persons who are 'perishing' can fail to grasp his gospel just as his 'aroma' is the stench of death to the 'perishing' (2.14). Paul's proclamation of truth confirms his 'sincerity' (2.17 and his sincerity confirms his apostolic competence (2.17; 3.5-6). Thus, he is bold to commend himself 'in the sight of God' (2.17; 4.2). Paul is 'well known' to God and should be 'well known' to the conscience of everyone at Corinth (5.11).

'Veil' becomes a many-splendored metaphor, applied first to Moses' face, then to the text of the Torah, and now to Paul's gospel (4.3). However, Paul transfers the blame for a 'veiled gospel' to 'the god of this age' who has blinded the minds of unbelievers so they cannot see 'the light of the gospel of the glory of Christ, who is the image of God' (4.4). 'Image' suggests that Christ is the coming-to-expression of the nature of God. This is so because Paul preaches Christ, not himself (4.5) He is a slave of the Corinthians, not their Lord (cf. 1.24). Although he is their servant, they are not his masters; he is their slave for Jesus' sake and his master is the Lord.

c. Boast of a Treasure in a Clay Pot (4.7-18)

After a lavish depiction of the glory of the gospel, Paul uses the derogatory metaphor of a 'clay pot' to characterize himself (4.7). His thetic statement with the inferential 'for' postulates a correlation between tribulations and frailty and their compatibility in an agent of the gospel. As a 'clay pot', the apostle has no nimbus of glory. At 3.10 Paul describes his ministry (cf. 3.6, 8) as a ministry of superlative splendor, but in 4.7 he emphasizes the superlative power in a clay pot. A 'clay pot' more adequately displays God's majestic power.

Note the parallels in 4.7 with 3.4-6. Paul has 'such confidence' (3.4) and he has 'this treasure' (4.7a). After each description of what he 'has', he immediately affirms dependence on God (3.5-6; 4.7b). In 3.6 and 4.6, he is a servant. His competence is the issue in 3.4-6, and at 4.7 the issue is 'this treasure'. He amplifies his thesis with an antithetical catalog of suffering; God's power is on display in Paul's triumph over adversity. God is the 'power' (*dunamis*) in his ministry and Paul magnifies God's power by denigrating himself to the status of a 'clay pot'.

What is this treasure stored in a clay pot? The antecedent of 'this treasure' is ambiguous. Commentators most frequently seek an answer in 4.1-6 and include: (1) 'this ministry' in 4.1; (2) 'the word of God' in 4.2; (3) 'the truth' in 4.2; (4) 'the gospel of the glory of Christ' in 4.4; (5) 'the knowledge of the glory of God in the face of Jesus Christ' in 4.6 (Fitzgerald, *Cracks*, p. 168). Certainty is not possible but there are clues one should not overlook. 'The knowledge of the glory of God' (4.6) = 'the light of the gospel of the glory of Christ' in 4.4 = 'our gospel' (4.3) = 'this ministry' (4.1). Differentiation between these metaphors is difficult; indeed, they appear to be synonymous. The treasure is his ministry, which is one of glory; his ministry is preaching the gospel of the glory of Christ. There is a grammatical connection between 'this ministry' (4.1) and 'this treasure' (P.E. Hughes, p. 135).

One may find a more compelling argument in 4.8-12 where Paul elaborates on the idea enunciated in v. 7. He emphasizes the fragility of the 'clay pot' to amplify the 'treasure;' the 'power' of his ministry is from God. To all appearances, Paul is a cheap, earthenware pot; his life did not appear to be one of glory to any unbiased observer. For Paul a correlative of human weakness is always the power of God (4.7). At issue is how one who exhibits so much human frailty can be a minister of the gospel of God's glory (cf. 10.10; 12.12). In 4.8-10 Paul responds that his weaknesses are his credentials. As in other passages where catalogs of suffering appear, the subject is Paul's ministry (Georgi, *Remembering*, p. 244). His weaknesses allow the demonstration of the extraordinary power of God in his ministry. The weakness of Christ's apostle is the weakness of Christ.

In the Hebrew Bible, the term 'earthen vessel' is often a metaphor for a human (Isa. 29.16; 30.14; 45.9; 64.8; Jer. 18.6; 22.8; Ps. 31.12; Job 10.9; cf also 2 Esd. 4.11; LXX Lev. 6.21; 11.33; 15.12). The striking Pauline paradox is similar to that found in *b. Ned.* 50b and elsewhere to speak of wisdom in an ugly vessel. Paul uses a metaphor of contempt to refer to himself in contrast to the power that is beyond comparison. Earthenware, in contrast to glass, is expendable when broken (*Gos. Phil.* 63.5-11). Sometimes people stored valuable treasures in earthen vessels (Plutarch, *Amelius* 32; cf. also Jer. 32.14). Although it was a 'throwaway' vessel, it sometimes contained precious treasure. Herodotus (3.96) knows the metaphor of 'treasure in clay pots'. Since he lists psychic (4.8) as well as physical distress and since Paul never bifurcates the body and soul, he probably intends the metaphor to refer to the whole person.

That Paul's ministry of such glory as one finds in 4.1-6 can now become a treasure in a clay pot reminds the reader that Paul's boasting is parodic. Certainly boasting about his weakness is not a convincing argument for Corinthians who apparently have already discredited his apostleship because of his weakness. Paul is boasting that the extraordinary power of God characterizes the ministry of a clay pot. The denigrating metaphor of the apostle does not extend to the 'treasure'. Seneca's sage (*Ep.* 71.26) 'knows his strength' and is full of self-confidence but Paul knows God's power and is full of self-confidence. He is not 'a man of steel', like the Stoic sage (Plutarch, *Moralia* 1057E; 541B). Rather, Paul has learned that 'power is made perfect in weakness' (12.9).

Parodically, a catalog of affliction becomes evidence of his apostolic competence. From his paradoxical 'treasure in earthen vessels', Paul amplifies the 'clay pot' metaphor with a catalog of tribulations. Pleonasm (redundancy) amplifies his suffering which 'shows a carefully controlled ability to arrange words to express emotion' (G.A. Kennedy, *NT Interpretation*, p. 155). With a strong emotional tone, Paul seeks to persuade (5.11). By shifting the focus from himself to God, Paul transforms the imagery in his catalog of suffering. He is a shattered vessel that remains unbroken (4.9). Without this shift, Paul would be like Seneca's sage who 'even if he falls...still fights upon his knees' (*Prov.* 2.6), and 'as often as he falls, rises again with greater defiance than ever' (*Ep.* 13.2-3). It is Plato (*Ion* 534D-E) who says that: 'The god of set purpose sang the finest songs through the meanest of poets to be a sign that...these fine poems are not human or the work of men, but divine and the work of gods ...that it is God himself who speaks and addresses us through them'. The weak and lowly instrument reveals divine power.

Four antithetical statements recite how Paul suffers 'in every way' (4.8). He structures the list so the contrast comes with an adversative and a negative particle ('but not').

afflicted	but not	crushed
perplexed	but not	driven to despair
persecuted	but not	forsaken
knocked down	but not	knocked out

There are four pairs of antitheses with eight present tense participles; except for the second pair, all verbs are in the passive voice. Paul constructs his catalog of suffering in 4.8-9 as four sets of paired participles in which the first affirms and the second denies something. Paul uses the negative particle 'not' (*ou*), not the more correct Greek *mē*. Perhaps the best explanation is that he is negating a single idea (BDF, §430.3). 'In every way' (*panti*, v. 8) and 'always' (*pantote*, v. 10) form an inclusio around this asyndetic (i.e. not joined together, lacking particles or conjunctions) catalog of contrasting participles and thus amplify the tribulations. Present participles indicate that the action is continuous and amplifies 'in every way'. The benefit of antithesis is its attentional novelty, and that it allows paired elements to be mutually interpretive and encourages assent by the hearer (Plank, pp. 78-80).

Antithesis appeals to the emotions. Antithesis is primarily a syntactical juxtaposition of semantical contraries, that is, antonymical juxtaposition. One understands things best when 'opposites are put side by side' (Aristotle, *Rhetoric* 3.19.1409). It infuses 'vehemence and passion into spoken words' (Loginus, *On the Sublime* 15.9). On the persuasive function of antithesis, Kenneth Burke says:

> Once you grasp the trend of the form, it invites participation regardless of the subject matter. Formally, you may find yourself swinging along with the succession of the antitheses, even though you may not agree with the proposition that is being presented... But in cases where a decision is still to be reached, a yielding to the form prepares for assent to the matter identified with it (Cited by Carpenter, pp. 434-35).

Antithesis is the most distinctive characteristic of Paul's style of writing (Weiss, II, p. 11).

Two paradoxical metaphors bracket this catalog in 4.8-10: 'treasure in clay pots' (4.7) and 'not dying, yet carrying around the dying of Jesus' (4.9b-10a). The movement from v. 7 to v. 8 forms a chiasmus:

A Power belongs to God (v. 7)
  B Not to Paul
  B' Paul is afflicted and weak (v. 8)
A' Paul is not crushed because of God's power (v. 8)

Adversity may serve as proof of the righteousness of the vessel. 'A potter does not test defective vessels, because he cannot give a single blow without breaking them. Similarly the Holy One, blessed be He, does not test the wicked but only the righteous' *(Gen. Rab.)*. Paul is not the power house but the 'clay pot' through which God exhibits extraordinary power and his afflictions validate his ministry.

The first pair contrasts 'affliction' (*thlipsis*) and 'distress' (*stenochoria*). The two terms are essentially synonymous. The word 'affliction' appears 12 times in 2 Corinthians 1–8. It is the most comprehensive term in his catalog. Both of the words in this pair mean to be pressed in, constricted or put under pressure. Since 'in every way' introduces all four sets of antitheses, Paul is saying 'In everything I am under pressure, but because of God's power, I am not crushed'.

Word play shapes the second antithesis in the Greek and no English translation does it justice but it means something like 'despairing but not utterly desperate'. Perhaps one may express the assonance by paraphrasing 'Sometimes at a loss, but not a loser'. Both words mean to be without means or resources, and so to be at a loss, be in doubt. In the Greek, the prepositional prefix intensifies the meaning: 'desperate to the nth degree'. When he was in Asia, Paul was 'desperate to the nth degree' (1.8). Paul wants to communicate that because of the amazing power of God all suffering loses its desperate character. In the third antithetical pair, Paul is 'persecuted but not forsaken'. The first word in the pair translates 'pursue' or 'persecute'. Since it appears in a tribulations catalog, it probably has the full sense of 'persecute'. 'Forsake' in the LXX is associated with God's promise never to forsake Israel (Gen. 28.15; Deut. 31.6, 8; Josh. 5.1 *et al.*). He is being persecuted but God is not forsaking him.

In the last pair, the apostle concedes that he is always being 'struck down' but 'not destroyed'. J.B. Phillips catches the sense of the word play with the paraphrase, 'knocked down but not knocked out'. The first term suggests being thrown to the ground, overthrown, abused, cast down or even killed. 'Destroyed', the last term in the catalog, is the strongest term in this list. He is being killed but he is not dying. It serves as a transition to carrying around 'the dying of Jesus' in 4.10. In this way 4.9b merges with 4.10 to form a paradox: He is not dying but he always carries in his body 'the dying of Jesus'.

Although the formulaic 'but not' discontinues, the antithetical constructions go forward and 'in order that' reveals the paradoxical concept. Paul 'always' carries in his body 'the dying of Jesus' (4.10). which is antithetical to 'not being destroyed' in v. 9. He carries about 'the process of the dying of Jesus' (BAGD, *s.v.*) in order that antithetically 'the life of Jesus' might bc madc visiblc in his body. As in vv. 8 and 11, thc adverb 'always' stands first to make it emphatic.

The verb translated 'being delivered up' (v. 11) is intimately linked with the passion narrative. Paul can testify 'I have been crucified with Christ' (Gal. 2.20; cf. Rom. 6.6). Here he most probably refers to the 'dying' of Jesus: 'I am always bearing the dying of Jesus in my body' and 'I am always being delivered up to death'. The 'dying' entails mortification (4.12) and death is at work in him so that his 'outer person' is being destroyed (4.16). The putrid pungency of the 'dying of Jesus' is like the 'smell of death' for unbelievers (2.16) but a 'fragrance of life' for believers (2.16). This 'dying of Jesus' in his body reveals the 'life of Jesus in his mortal flesh' (4.11). He endures all of this 'on account of Jesus'.

Anaphoric (i.e. repeated use of a word) use of 'but not' emphasizes that although afflicted, Paul has endured and survived by the power of God, indicated by participles in the passive voice. Atypical for Pauline letters, there is anaphoric use of the name 'Jesus'; the name occurs six times in vv. 10-14. This repetition shows Paul's solidarity with Jesus in his suffering and dying. Jesus is Paul's model of the Suffering Servant (cf. 4.5). A rhythmic pattern and repetition infuse passion into the discussion and compel the audience to hear what Paul says.

Antithesis in this passage provides an arresting contrast between dreadful situations and the surprising outcomes. Using repetition, Paul wants to tease his audience into wondering why, in such situations, the dreadful consequences did not occur. If he is always in such 'tight spots', why is he not 'hemmed in?' If he is always 'despairing', why is he not 'utterly distraught?' If he always 'shattered on the ground', why is he not 'broken?' Paul has already given the answer: 'the incredible power of God' (4.7). Both the death and life of Jesus are always present in his body. Paul begins with the phrase 'in every way' (v. 8) and reinforces it with two adverbs (*pantote* and *aei*), both of which mean 'always'. In this way, he radically transforms a list of specific afflictions into a description of Paul's entire ministry. The antithetical narration of suffering does not intend to communicate information about Paul. The particular incidents of suffering are not in view. Paul wants to persuade them that suffering characterizes his ministry just as it did the ministry of Jesus. Paul identifies his suffering with that of Jesus. He believes that Christ and the cross are the ground and cause of the suffering of the Christian. It is the 'death' in Paul that brings the gospel of 'life' to the Corinthians. The Corinthians are Paul's letter of commendation that Christ has written on his heart (3.3).

d. Looking to the Future (4.13-5.10)

As it did at 3.4, 12 and 4.1, 7, the participle 'having' (*echontes*) marks a transition to a new topic. Ironically, in this context of suffering, Paul weaves the theme of confidence into the narrative (2.14; 3.4, 12; 4.1, 13, 16; 5.6, 8). With the citation of LXX Ps. 116.10, Paul gives his first biblical quotation in 2 Corinthians verbatim: 'I believed, therefore I spoke'. Looking back to death working in him, the quotation supports v. 12. 'In accordance with Scripture' (literally 'according to the thing having been written') is a formula quotation and appears only here in the New Testament and it may be a juridical term. The relationship between 'to believe' and 'to speak' attracted Paul to the psalm. Having the same faith as the psalmist, he 'speaks' (i.e. preaches) because his sufferings guarantee his credentials. As a suffering servant who has survived all tests, apostolic status should not be in doubt.

Verses 13-15 is a transition from 4.7-12 to 4.16–5.10. Thus, he again employs the 'overlapping' technique. 'The same spirit of faith' (v. 13) points to the biblical citation that follows. 'Having' connects to 'we also believe' with a causal interpretation(A.T.Robertson, *Grammar*, p. 1134). Since 'but' (*de*) has adversative force, one might translate, 'Yet, because we have'. Paul's citation of Psalm 116 is apropos because it is a hymn of thanksgiving for deliverance from death. His 'speaking' ministry is a testimony to his faith in the triumph of life over death. He grounds his faith in the God 'who raised Jesus from the dead' (4.14). The first sentence (vv. 13-14) points back to 4.7-12 and forward to eschatalogical affairs in 4.16–5.10, especially the reference to the judgment in 5.10.

Paul commends himself as a suffering apostle despite perceived criticisms of his weakness (4.7-12; 6.3-10; 10.7-10; 11.16-29, 21-30; 12.9-29; 13.4, 9). It is God who has made him competent for ministry (3.5-6) and the power of his ministry is God (4.7). In this section he commends himself on the basis of his eschatological faith in God. With the phrase 'knowing that' (v. 14) he presumes a formulation familiar to the reader (v. 14). Ironically, death is at work in him (v. 12) but his confident self-commendation rests on the hope of the resurrection (v. 14). To the traditional formulation Paul adds the elliptical remark 'will present [us] with you' (v. 14b). The verb 'to present' has a broad range of possible meanings, one of which is to stand before a judge (Meyer, p. 500). With this remark, Paul adds judicial language and points to the judgment when both he and the Corinthians will stand before God, the Judge (cf. 5.10).

The conjunction 'for' in 4.15 connects it with vv. 13-14. 'All things' is a reference to his tribulations in 4.8-10 and 'to speak' in 4.13 in particular, but to everything in 4.7-14 in general. Pastoral concern comes to the fore as Paul declares, 'Everything is for your sake' (v. 15). Often he reminds the Corinthians of the benefits of his ministry to them (1.7, 15, 24; 3.2-3; 4.5, 15; 7.3; 8.6). Weakness and affliction, which Paul seems to think they belittle, have been for their sake. He makes a play on words with 'grace' (*charis*) and 'thanksgiving' (*eucharistia*) to say he suffers for the Corinthians so that abundant grace that increased 'through the majority' may cause 'thanksgiving' to increase to the glory of God (v. 15).

Pastoral and evangelistic aims merge in v. 15. Since Paul's suffering is 'for you', then 'through the majority' must refer to the 'majority' at Corinth as in 2.6 (cf. 9.2; 1 Cor. 10.5; 15.6; Phil. 1.4). 'To abound or overflow' is a transitive verb (i.e. 'cause to abound') with grace as the subject and thanksgiving as the object (Barrett, *Commentary*, p. 145). As he does in 1.11, Paul hopes that through the increase of grace in the majority, there will be increased thanksgiving for his ministry and that will be 'to the glory of God'. This is but another instance of self-praise that Paul softens by saying it is all for 'the glory of God'.

From 4.16 to 5.10 every statement, except 5.5, and 5.10, is antithetical. All antithetical pairs illustrate Paul's contrast of 'things seen' and 'things not seen' (4.18) which becomes a confessional statement: 'For I walk by faith, not by sight' (5.7). Outward appearances will not be Paul's standard for 'defense' or for self-commendation. He knows that God will raise him from the dead (4.14) and thus his commendation and defense now turns on eschatological hope rather than visible proof. He suffers afflictions now but God will vindicate him at the judgment. Paul is saying, 'I may not look like much to you now, but wait for the day of resurrection to pass judgment'. Surely, both the commendation and the defense are parodic.

An inferential 'therefore' (*dio*) connects v. 16 to the preceding passage and continues the idea begun in 4.13. Against all efforts by scholars to make 5.1-10 a 'theological soliloquy', and 4.13-18 a piece designed as a transition to 5.1-10, there is an essential unity in 4.13–5.10. 'Having' marks a new beginning at v. 13 and 'therefore' connects v. 16 to 4.13-15. After the 'therefore' at 4.16, Paul links his argument by using 'for' (*gar*) five times (4.17, 18; 5.1, 2, 4) with a causal genitive absolute at 4.18 before reaching another inferential 'therefore' (*oun*) at 5.5. This 'therefore' and the same vocabulary in 5.6-10 as in 5.1-5 assures the unity of the passage. Eschatological language and antithetical language continue in vv. 6-10 and 5.7 recalls 4.18.

Paul 'concedes' ('and if', M.E. Thrall, *Greek Particles*, pp. 36-39) that his 'outer person' is wasting away. However, what follows is fulfilled and not merely contingent (Burton, §284): there is continual renewing of the 'inner person'. The present tense of 'wasting away' points to an ongoing process; the passive voice to its inevitability. All that follows is a refinement of 4.16 which is a way to amplify what he is saying but states it differently and expands its meaning. He balances 'concession' of perceived weakness with eschatological hope.

At 4.16 apostolic confidence (or boldness) resumes, repeating 4.1 verbatim (but also see 3.12 and 4.13). The context (4.2-7, 10-13, 15-16) clarifies that Paul refers to boldness in preaching the gospel despite his weaknesses and the false interpretation of them. With the same faith of the psalmist (LXX 116.10), despite death being at work in him, he knows death is not the final word. The God who does not abandon him now (4.9) will raise him from the dead (4.14). 'Therefore, I do not despair' (4.16).

TEXT	THESIS	ANTITHESIS
4.16	The outer person	The inner person
4.17	Momentary light affliction	Eternal weight of glory
4.18	Things seen	Thing not seen
5.1	The earthly house being destroyed	Eternal house in the heavens
5.2	In this house we groan	Clothed with heavenly dwelling
5.3	Being naked	Will not be found naked
5.4	Not wishing to be unclothed	Mortal swallowed up in life
5.5	The Spirit as a 'pledge'	
5.6	Being at home	Being away from home
5.7	Walk by faith	Not walking by sight
5.8	Away from home in body	At home with the Lord
5.9	Being home	At home with the Lord
5.10	The judgment seat of Christ	

Antithetical parallelism amplifies Paul's claim that he does not 'lose heart' (4.16). Despite the deterioration of the 'outer person', the 'inner person' experiences daily renewal. 'Light affliction' (v. 17) is oxymoronic and over against 'glory beyond comprehension' (literally, 'excessively to excess') and perhaps Paul's greatest understatement. 'Eternal weight of glory' has a built-in word play because 'glory' on its Semitic groundplan speaks of heaviness, burden or weight. A conjunction, 'for', explicates what precedes and anticipates what follows suggesting that the 'things seen' and 'things not seen' is pivotal in 4.16 to 5.10. Paul does not see 'things seen' but 'things unseen', which is oxymoronic, paradoxical and antithetical.

Two verbs for 'to see' appear in the Greek of v. 18. The verb *blepein* is lackluster and simply means 'to look at something' while *skopein* means 'to set one's sight on' (Fuchs, *s.v.*). Seneca (*Moral Epistles* 58.27) echoes the Platonic distinction between things perceived by the senses and things 'that really exist'. Paul does not question the reality of things seen but neither does he orient his life around them. He lives by faith, not sight.

Plain speech cannot accomplish Paul's goals, so he moves to symbolic, metaphorical speech. His earthly tent-like house is falling down; his heavenly house is not made with hands and is eternal (5.1); 5.1 repeats the 'eternal' in 4.18. The antecedent of 'this' in 5.2 is 'tent' (5.1). In his tent Paul 'groans' and desires his heavenly building (5.2). The verb translated 'to groan' means to sigh or moan as the result of deep concern or stress (Louw *et al.*, §25.143). Verse 2 retains the parallelism of the earthly tent and heavenly building, but results in a hopelessly mixed metaphor. Clothing oneself with a building is a bizarre metaphor, but the context clarifies the intent. Paul is being 'stripped', but he will not be found 'naked' at the judgment (5.3). 'Being clothed' is better attested than 'being unclothed', but Bultmann (*2 Corinthians*, p. 137) correctly notes that only 'being unclothed' makes sense in this antithetical statement.

The term translated 'to find' often refers to the results of a judicial investigation and points to the judgment in 5.10. The 'even if' introduces a point one should presuppose and expresses confidence rather than doubt (M.E. Thrall, *Greek Particles*, pp. 86-91). English has preserved the figurative and forensic connotation of 'to find'. A judge may ask a jury, 'How do you find?' A judge may say, 'The court finds'. Verse 4 restates vv. 2-3 apologetically but adds 'being burdened' to amplify 'groaning' in v. 2. Paul desires that 'what is mortal may be swallowed up by life' (v. 4). In Pauline letters the only other occurrence of the verb 'to swallow up' is 1 Cor. 15.54.

For the first time since 4.16, v. 5 is not antithetical; it summarizes 5.1-4 and prepares for a shift in style at 5.6. Hope is not a delusion; God has given the Spirit as a 'down payment' on things to come. Paul places 'God' at the end of the sentence, giving it an emphatic position. 'For this very thing' refers back to mortality being swallowed up by life in v. 4, as well as to all the counter theses in vv. 1-4. Groaning and good courage place Paul in what Wendland (p. 170) calls the *dialektic* of Christian existence.

At v. 6 there a shift in style and 'body' replaces the metaphors for body used from 4.16–5.5. 'Body' appears five times in vv. 6-10. 'Being of good cheer' (v. 6) replaces the 'I do not lose heart' of 4.16 and Paul adopts the 'at home' and 'away from home' metaphors. Note that Paul does not think life in the physical body is incompatible with life in Christ (v. 7; Gal. 2.20). Obviously, he was not happy with v. 6 and he discontinues the anacolouthic (the result of a shift from one construction to another in the middle of a sentence; a grammatical *non sequitur*) sentence to move to safer terrain in v. 7. Abandoning the syntax of v. 6, he creates a new formulation in v. 8 with more satisfactory results. Verse 7 abandons the 'home place' imagery but continues the antithetical style with a parenthetical correction of v. 6. Returning to the 'seen...not seen' in 4.18, he asserts that he conducts his life in the realm of faith, not the realm of sight.

In v. 8 a finite verb, 'we are of good cheer' replaces the participle 'being of good cheer' in v. 6. Paul reverses the order of 'being at home' and 'being away from home', adding 'I am resolved instead'. He omits 'from the Lord' (v. 6) and adds 'toward the Lord' in v. 8. He moves from the present tense of v. 6 to aorist tenses in v. 8. He has 'determined' (BAGD, *s.v.*) to 'get away from being at home' and 'be at home toward the Lord'. These changes transform the 'home place' metaphor from one of location to one of direction. One's present location is not as important as the direction in which one is moving.

An inferential conjunction ('therefore') with 'and' connotes a self-evident inference (Moule, *An Idiom Book*, p. 164) and alerts the reader that a logical conclusion is imminent. Only in v. 9 does Paul complete the idea begun in v. 6. Whether being at home or away from home, Paul aims to please the Lord (v. 9). A stylistic device 'whether...or' indicates a summary conclusion and has the force of 'under all circumstances, in every situation'. Paul has the ambition, which he considers an honor (BAGD, *s.v.*), to please the Lord. Concern to 'please the Lord' (v. 9) gives a forward glance to 'the judgment seat of Christ' (v. 10). In v. 10, 'appear' connotes being laid bare, stripped of every façade of respectability and openly revealed in the full reality of one's character. Paul is silent on the judgment of the wicked. His concern is judgment for Christians, especially Christians at Corinth. Judgment reveals deeds done 'through the body' and no one escapes scrutiny.

Commending or defending himself and his apostolic credentials at Corinth on the basis of what he hoped to become eschatologically must have brought raucous laughter in Corinth. They are interested in what he is, not what he will become in the sweet by and by. Paul knows quite well that he is not giving the Corinthians what they want to hear. More than anything, he is showing them how ridiculous letters of commendation and defense speeches are. He parodies boasting, commendation and defense speeches. His goal here, as in the suffering catalogs (4.8-9; 6.4-10; 11.23-29; 12.10) is to stir emotions. His emotional appeal indicates that Paul has no interest in giving information about himself or instructing the Corinthians on eschatology. He wants to compel the Corinthians to ask, 'Considering your weaknesses, what is the basis of your confident hope?' Everything in 4.16–5.10 intends to show why he does not 'lose heart' (4.16). Validation of his credentials is not found in 'things seen' but in 'things not seen'. Paul lives by faith, not by sight.

e. An Ambassador for Christ (5.11-6.13)

With 'therefore', a new section begins, but 'knowing the fear of the Lord' (5.11) casts a backward glance to the judgment in 5.10. The fear of the Lord is the 'judgment seat of Christ'. His motive for 'persuading people' is 'the fear of the Lord'. 'Persuading people' is a definition for rhetoric (Betz, *Galatians*, p. 54 n. 103). Paul wants to 'persuade' the Corinthians to his understanding of apostolic competence. I 'have been revealed (perfect tense verb) to God' shows that Paul considers approval by God an accomplished fact. In the previous verse he suggests that everyone will be judged at 'the judgment seat of Christ', but now he considers that God has already approved him. Appealing to God gives him an unimpeachable expert witness. He 'hopes' he has been revealed for what he is to the Corinthian conscience. That he has passed the scrutiny of God is a fact; that he has found approval in Corinth remains only a hope. This statement is similar to Paul's challenge: 'Test yourselves...I hope you will find out that I have not failed [the test]' (13.5).

God, not the Corinthians, is the judge and with insinuated threat, Paul denies to the Corinthians the status of jurors. At the same time, he is expressing deep pastoral concern. He believes that unless the Corinthians accept him and his gospel they may accept 'the grace of God in vain' (6.1; see 11.3-4; 12.20-21; 13.5-6). Before God and the Corinthians, Paul is an open book and before God he has passed the test. Here, as in 3.1-3; 4.2 and 6.4 he uses 'commending' language. At 3.1-3 and 5.12, Paul denies he is 'commending' himself; at 4.2 and 6.4 he says he is 'commending' himself.

'Now I am not commending myself again' (5.12) recalls 'Am I beginning to commend myself again?' (3.1). Rather than 'commending' himself he is giving the Corinthians an 'opportunity' to boast about him. In other words, he is not commending himself but giving them an opportunity to commend him. Reference to persons who boast 'in outward appearance and not in the heart' may be a blast against Sophistic teachers and preachers (Winter, p. 122). The Corinthians should give him the approval of their conscience and 'conscience' conveys the idea of a positive evaluation of behavior (M.E. Thrall, 'Suneidēsis', p. 123).

As the explicative 'for' shows, boasting 'in appearance' is still an issue (v. 13). The antithesis 'in appearance...not in heart' (5.12) becomes 'insane...sane'. A selfless individual, if Paul is 'insane' it is 'for God'; if he is 'sane' it is 'for you'. The verb 'to be insane' appears nowhere else in the Pauline corpus but in Mk 3.21, Jesus' family alleges, with this same verb, that Jesus is 'out of his mind'. In LXX Isa. 28.7 it is to be 'out of one's mind' because of intoxication. Philo (*On Drunkenness* 146-47) uses it to describe religious ecstasy mistaken for drunkenness. In the *T. Job* 39.10 it refers to 'being mad'. By contrast, Paul is 'in his right mind' for the Corinthians.

Since 'to you' is a dative of advantage in Greek, 'to God' would not be otherwise. If the latter is a dative of advantage, the verb cannot mean 'to be insane'. Possibly Paul is referring to what he has written about glossalalia being 'speaking not to people but to God', but prophecy is 'speaking to people' (1 Cor. 14.3). However, it is closer at hand to relate it to the ecstatic heavenly rapture in 2 Cor. 12.1-5 where Paul parodies ecstasy as a weakness in which he will boast. Here Paul is saying to the

Corinthians, 'My ecstatic experiences do not concern you; they are private'. Otherwise it would be boasting 'in appearance' and Paul's concern is to 'be in his right mind' and communicate the gospel. Thus Paul's 'ecstasy' concerns God and his 'sanity' concerns the Corinthians (Bultmann, *2 Corinthians*, p. 150).

Being in one's 'right mind' for others (v. 13) is being responsive to the claims of love under which life in faith always stands (v. 14; cf. Gal. 5.6). The 'love of Christ', exemplified by 'dying on behalf of all', controls Paul's conduct (v. 14). As he lives 'under the dominion of grace' (Rom. 6.14), so also he lives 'under the dominion of love'. With reference to Christ dying 'for all', Paul appeals to a shared credal statement (1 Cor. 15.3). After resolute deliberation, Paul has come to a firm decision that 'one died for all'. The terms translated 'convinced' and 'on behalf of' have juridicial connotations. Christological soteriology allows no place for 'boasting in appearance'. What Paul is, he is in service to others, as v. 15 states and v. 16 explicates. Persons who come to authentic existence by appropriating the merits of Christ's death should no longer live for themselves because they do not belong to themselves (cf. Gal. 2.20; 1 Cor. 6.19).

Paul no longer lives for himself but for the one 'who died and was raised for them' (v. 15). To live for Christ is to live for others (i.e. the Corinthians, v. 13) as v. 18 makes explicit. As an apostle whose ministry is 'in the sight of God' (2.17) and who has proleptically faced the 'judgment seat of Christ' (5.10-11), all 'boasting in appearance' (5.12) has ended. Apostolic service is 'for Christ' (5.15) which is to be 'in his right mind' for the Corinthians (5.13). Paul redefines the criteria for apostleship as living for Christ and others. External characteristics (v. 12b), even impressive ecstatic experiences (v. 13a), count for nothing. He serves Christ by serving the Corinthians.

People who live in the eschatological 'now time' (6.2), do not know others 'according to the flesh', or 'by appearance' (5.16; cf. v. 12). The transformed perception of others is so extreme that Paul no longer knows Christ 'according to the flesh' (Bultmann, *2 Corinthians*, pp. 155-57; Barrett, *Commentary*, p. 171). Perhaps this transformed standard of knowing extends to all Christians, but Paul is certainly reminding the Corinthians not to judge his apostleship 'according to the flesh'. Christ was 'crucified as a weakling' but lives 'by the power of God' and Paul is weak but he will live with Christ 'by the power of God' (13.4). This principle applies to all Christians because 'anyone' who is 'in Christ' has become a 'new creation' (5.17). As 'new creations', the Corinthians must judge Paul as a 'new creation'. He characterizes his apostolic service as established in the saving event of reconciliation (v. 18).

Paul seeks the reconciliation of his readers both to God and to Paul. He finally exhorts them, 'Be reconciled to God' (5.20). Since Paul is 'God's co-worker' (6.1), reconciliation with God entails reconciliation with God's ambassador (5.20). The old eon has passed from existence and 'everything has become new' (5.17). 'Behold' (v. 17) is an interjection writers use to mark an unusual moment or deed. Paul has described himself as a 'minister of a new covenant' (3.6), 'a minister of the Spirit' (3.6) and a 'minister of righteousness' (3.9). Now, God has given to him 'the ministry of reconciliation' (5.18) and has entrusted to Paul 'the word of reconciliation' (5.19). As an ambassador for Christ and a co-worker with God, he urges earnestly: 'Be reconciled to God' (5.20) and 'Do not receive God's grace in vain' (6.1).

Failure to become reconciled to God's messenger is tantamount to receiving God's grace in vain. The Corinthians need reconciliation with God's way of bringing reconciliation. Paul had to accept that God reconciled the world through a man from Nazareth. God works in such 'flesh hidden' ways to reconcile the world. As God's ambassador for Christ, Paul's apostleship is clothed with flesh by God. Here as in 1 Cor. 1.18-25, God works in 'foolish ways', even the folly of the cross. Paul's challenge 'Be reconciled' is first 'Be reconciled to God's foolish way of reconciliation'. All the time Paul is moving to say 'Be reconciled to me and the weaknesses of my ministry'. Otherwise, the Corinthians are in danger of removing themselves from the human arena of God's means of reconciliation.

Reconciliation to Paul is the equivalent of reconciliation to God. The 'right time' (*kairos*) for reconciliation to God and the ambassador for Christ is 'now' (6.2). With passion, Paul urges that 'now' is the acceptable time to become reconciled to Paul; 'now is the day of salvation' (6.2). The anaphoric exhortation 'be reconciled' appears five times in 5.18-20. It is clear that reconciliation has become of paramount importance to the apostle. Paul justifies the use of the official term 'ambassador' because the divine act of reconciling the world in Christ requires the institution of a 'ministry of reconciliation'. Such a ministry necessitates an 'ambassador' entrusted with a 'word of reconciliation' (5.18-19). Paul does not separate the 'ministry of reconciliation' from the 'message of reconciliation'. Preaching is not just reporting the good news of salvation; it is an essential part of salvation.

Authority for Paul's message rests on his being an ambassador for Christ; he is God's mouthpiece for the message of reconciliation. By repeating 'beg/exhort' Paul ties 6.1 to 5.20. In 5.20, God is the subject of 'beg', but in 6.1 Paul is the subject. God and Paul are co-workers and

Paul is Christ's ambassador. Paul's exhortation, 'Do not receive the grace of God in vain' is the same as God's exhortation. He forces on the community an 'either ... or' decision and he bases his announcement in 6.2 on Isa. 49.8. If they are not 'to receive the grace of God in vain', they must recognize that Paul's word encounters them as God's eschatological message.

Using pesher exegesis (R.P. Martin, pp. 168-69) Paul makes the word translated as 'grace' in Isa. 49.8 mean 'acceptable' in 6.2. Consonant with Rabbinic exegesis, he interprets the word as a prophecy of the eschatological saving deed of God. His coming to the Corinthians with the message of reconciliation provides the word of the cross that creates a crisis in the sense that one must respond to the demands of the new age initiated by the resurrection of Christ (5.16). 'Now' is the 'right time' to seek reconciliation with God and the ambassador of Christ.

At 6.3-4, Paul restates the essence of 5.12. After commending himself, Paul says he is giving the Corinthians 'an opportunity' to boast about him (cf. 1.14). Self-commendation is possible because Paul gives 'no offense in anything' so that no one may discredit his ministry (6.4). With the topic of avoiding blame he clears the way for yet another catalog of suffering. In 5.12 Paul does not commend himself but at 6.4 he does commend himself as 'a minister of God'. Fitzgerald (*2 Cor. 10–13*, p. 187) thinks there is no contradiction.

The placement of the pronoun is crucial. Every time in 2 Corinthians that Paul wishes to make a negative comment about self-commendation, he places the pronoun before the verb (3.1; 5.12; 10.12, 18). When he speaks positively, either of the Corinthians' self-commendation (7.11) or of his own (4.2; 6.4), he places it after the verb. Negative boasting is boasting 'in appearance'; positive boasting is boasting 'in the heart'. Paul's boast of being God's minister is boasting 'in the heart'. His behavior befits a servant of God as his catalog of afflictions and virtues will confirm. Thus, self-commendation is appropriate.

The hardship list at 6.4b-5 presupposes the one in 4.8-10 and anticipates the one in 11.23-29; the last three hardships in this list also appear at 11.27. After commending himself with a list of nine hardships (vv. 4b-5), Paul commends himself with eight virtues and gifts (vv. 6.6-7b), three vicissitudes (vv. 7c-8b) and seven antitheses (vv. 8c-10). The first item in the list of sufferings is 'endurance', but it is separated from the rest of the items and is at the head of the catalog. The terms 'endurance' and 'purity' (first in the list of virtues) frames his catalog of suffering. Paul has done more than 'endure' afflictions. Character and integrity attach to Paul's endurance, differentiating it from mere toleration of suffering. He has endured with the purest motives.

In a powerful rhetorical structure Paul uses the preposition 'in' with the 18 items in his catalogs of suffering and virtue (6.4-7a). There are 9 hardships and 8 virtues. He chooses the preposition 'through' for the 3 vicissitudes and closes with 7 antitheses using 'as' with the first item in each pair and the conjunction 'and' joins the first item to the second except in numbers 5 and 6.

TEXT	CATALOG	STRUCTURE		
6.4-5	HARDSHIPS	in much endurance		
		in afflictions	in hardships	in calamities
		in beatings	in imprisonments	in riots
		in labors	in sleepness nights	in hunger
6.6-7a	VIRTUES	in purity	in knowledge	
		in patience	in kindness	
		in holiness of spirit	in genuine love	in truthful speech
		in the power of God		
6.7b-8b	VICISSITUDES	through the weapons of righteousness		
		through honor and dishonor		
		through ill repute and good repute		

6.8c-10	ANTITHESES	as	imposters	and	true
		as	unknown	and	well known
		as	dying	and	alive
		as	punished	and	not killed
		as	sorrowful	but	rejoicing
		as	poor	but	making many rich
		as	having nothing	and	possessing everything

Isocrates says the most powerful way to be persuasive is to argue from one's life (*Or.* 15.278). Arguing from experience, Paul's *Vita* for commendation seems quite strange. It would persuade no one in Corinth that Paul met their criteria for apostleship. Paul wants to do nothing that would be 'a cause for stumbling' and discredit his ministry (6.3). Parody is the only way to make sense of what he is saying. Two things are quite clear: (1) Someone has already 'discredited' his ministry; (2) Paul believes he has done nothing to discredit his ministry. His claim of having done nothing to discredit his ministry would be antagonistic and polemical in this context.

In one of the most lyrical passages in the Pauline corpus, there are four distinct strophes providing lists of hardships, virtues, vicissitudes and antitheses. Anaphora embroiders the lyrical quality. Chrysostom calls this passage a frank, somewhat laconic, resumé of Paul's apostolic career a 'blizzard of troubles' (*Homily* 12.2). Verses 3-4a are introductory with the comment about 'giving no cause for offense' against his ministry and v. 3 complements 5.12 and Paul's desire that the Corinthians take pride in his ministry.

Boasting in 6.3-10 is 'in heart', not 'in appearance'. The first strophe stresses Paul's 'endurance' that characterizes his ministry. He presents nine tribulations in three triads. 'Endurance' heads the list but differs from what follows because it describes behavior rather than being an affliction. With 'purity' leading the list of virtues, 'endurance' frames the afflictions as sincere endurance. The first triad characterizes general hardship, what von Hodgson (p. 63) calls 'generic tribulations'. Nouns in this triad (afflictions, hardships, distresses) are in essence synonymous. In Greek the last item is the longest and thus creates a crescendo (Fridrichsen, p. 27). More significantly, it is the most severe affliction in this triad, as 4.8 and 12.10 confirm. All three terms are generic and give the image of an apostle who is always suffering.

The second triad specifies hardships other persons have inflicted on Paul. 'Beatings' refers to the blows of a whip that cause anguish. 'Imprisonments' recalls Acts 16.22-23 where Paul and Silas received 'many stripes' and were thrown into prison. Again, in Greek, the last item is the longest. It translates the word 'riots, commotions'. It means disturbance, disorder, unruliness, riot (BAGD, *s.v.*). According to Acts, Paul's ministry often precipitated riots, including Corinth (18.12-17; also 13.50; 14.5-6, 19; 16.22; 17.5-9, 13; 19.23-41). The second and third triads (v. 5) bear a striking resemblance to 11.23, 27. Except for 'calamities', found again in Paul's letters only at 12.20, all the terms of 6.5 reappear in 11.23, 27. Of the nine items of 'affliction', only 'calamities' does not appear in at least one of the other Pauline catalogs of adversities (cf. 4.8-9; 11.23b-29; 12.10; 1 Cor. 4.9-13; Rom. 8.35).

'Afflictions' arising from apostolic service form the last triad as 'occupational hazards'. Adversities in this triad are similar to hardships. In his discourse on virtue Chrysostom mentions 'calamities', along with 'hunger and cold', 'thirst', 'the lash', and so on (*Or.* 8.15-16). He adds that Stoics believe such troubles must be approached 'in a spirit of contempt', even 'cheerfully' (*Or.* 8.18). Paul takes seriously the adversities and believes he must endure them. All of the terms in this triad occur again in the same sequence at 11.27. As a matter of principle, Paul refused the financial support of the Corinthians. His situation was desperate enough at times that he had to rely on other communities to supplement his financial reserves (2 Cor. 11.8-9; Phil. 4.14-18). As a minister at Corinth, he also was a tentmaker in order not to be a financial burden. Evening hours spent in evangelism (Acts 20.7-12, 31) would only add to the weariness resulting from exhausting toil, sleepless nights and lack of food (v. 5c).

Refusal to accept Corinthian support condemned Paul to poverty, explicitly mentioned twice at 6.10, but already anticipated in v. 4 with 'hardships' and 'calamities'. 'Labors' refers to trouble or difficulty and one may translate it 'fatigue'; it implies toil to the point of fatigue (BAGD, *s.v.*) and it is the result of wearisome toil. Paul says he works 'with his own hands' (1 Cor. 4.12) and at 11.23 may refer to missionary labors. The second and third terms in this triad must also refer to deprivations associated with his craft. 'Sleepless nights' and 'hunger' are likely due to exigencies of his apostolic ministry. The context does not permit 'hunger' to refer to ritual or ascetic fasting, but to compulsory deprivation of food. In 11.27, he associates 'hunger' with famine, thirst, cold and nakedness.

Paul's catalog of virtues functions to describe the manner by which Paul responds to hardships and persecutors. The catalog of hardships give substance to the catalog of virtues. The 'power of God' refers to 4.7-12. In this way, Paul attributes his virtues to God and not his personal discipline and determination. After listing his hardships, he may boast inoffensively of his virtues because audiences are not inclined to resent persons who have earned their reputations at considerable cost to themselves (cf. Plutarch, *Moralia* 544D). Listing his virtues testifies that Paul has endured and overcome hardships with his integrity and moral excellence intact.

With the second strophe, the 'in' continues but now there are eight virtues arranged in pairs. Paul has endured with 'integrity' and 'knowledge'. Knowledge is a powerful ally of virtue and is one of the gifts of the Spirit (1 Cor. 12.8). 'Patience' and 'kindness' appear in the list of the fruit of the Spirit (Gal. 5.22; also cf. Rom. 2.4; 1 Cor. 13.4; Eph. 4.2; Col. 3.12). Paul describes himself as a kind, concerned and caring person. He has behaved with a 'holy spirit' and 'sincere love'. In Rom. 12.9, he requires love to be sincere (literally, 'unhypocritical') and here he claims to live what he preaches. With the final pair, there is a shift from personal qualities to his preaching ministry: 'the word of truth' and 'the power of God'. The 'word of truth' is a technical term denoting the Gospel (Col. 1.5; Eph. 1.13) and the 'power of God' is the dynamic of his preaching. Paul has not become 'a peddler of the word of God'; he has conducted his entire ministry 'in the power of God' (6.7b).

Having completed his catalog of virtues, Paul concludes the seemingly endless use of 'in' and introduces his catalog of vicissitudes (vv. 7c-8b) with 'through'. The Greek preposition *dia* with the genitive translates 'through', but here it functions to describe the attendant circumstances of apostolic commendation (GNTG, III.267; Bultmann, *2 Corinthians*, p. 173; BAGD, *s.v.*). The first vicissitude 'with the weapons of righteousness for the right hand and for the left' (6.7c) describes Paul as an 'armed soldier'. Two remaining phrases describe the paradoxical consequences of his apostolic ministry: 'honor and dishonor' and 'ill repute and good repute' (v. 8). These two antithetical phrases produce a chiasmus.

A Honor
    B Dishonor
    B' Ill repute
A' Good repute

Taken together, the first and last terms describe positive responses while the two middle terms are negative responses to Paul and he wants to emphasize A and A'.

A warrior for Christ, Paul is armed for battle (cf. Eph. 6.10-17). He fights with 'weapons of righteousness'. He does not wage war 'according to the flesh' (10.13) and his 'weapons of war' are not merely human'; they have divine power to destroy strongholds (10.4). With a sword in his right hand and a shield in his left hand, he demolishes arguments. Despite his righteousness, Paul has known both victory and defeat. Reminiscent of 2.16, Paul's ministry has had mixed responses. He has known 'honor' (or 'glory') and 'dishonor'. Paul has known honor (a good reputation), or even popularity (BAGD, *s.v.*) but he has also known dishonor and disgrace. His ministry has provoked both praise and slander. Changing circumstances have brought him both fame and infamy. Whatever the circumstances may be, Paul will continue to wage war with weapons of righteousness and he will do so with integrity.

In the fourth strophe (vv. 8c-10), the literary form differs from vv. 7b-8b. There are seven pairs of antitheses, each pair introduced by 'as' with 'and' separating the antithetical items in each pair. Items five and six vary slightly from the others because they have a light adversative ('but', *de*); however it may also translate 'and'. The alteration is more stylistic than substantive. The theses reveal what Paul believes are false perceptions of his apostolate by people who judge him by appearance (5.12) and according to 'human standards' (5.16).

The antitheses state what is visible to faith 'in the heart' and 'according to the Spirit'. Anyone who is 'in Christ' and has become 'a new creature' (5.17) will recognize Paul for what he is. Each thesis illustrates

Paul's 'ill reputation' and the antitheses, his 'good reputation'. Throughout 6.1-13, and especially in vv 8c-10, Paul is again pulling on the heart strings of the Corinthians. In written form, the antitheses seem a bit grotesque, but orally they draw dramatic power from the images they evoke and the rhythmical force of the phrases. Literary devices such as anaphora, chiasmus, and especially antitheses amplify the emotional tone.

Marshall (*Enmity*, p. 497) finds in vv. 8b-9c a 'poignant reference to mistrust and suspicion'. Persons who evaluate the apostle 'in appearance' perceive him to be a trickster, deceiver or impostor (1.15-2.2; 2.17; 4.2; 8.20-22; 12.16-18). Judged 'in heart', Paul knows he is true, sincere and worthy of merit (1.12, 23; 2.4, 17; 4.2; 5.11; 6.7). Some persons think he is 'an unknown' (3.1-3; 12.11-12), but he is 'well known' to God and the Corinthian conscience (1.13-14; 5.11). In his weakness, some characterize him as 'dying' (4.7-5.10; 1 Cor. 4.9; 2 Cor. 1.8-9; 4.8-9; 11.23-29). Paul can concede this perception in a way that he cannot for the first and second items; it has been in view since 2.4. The interjection, 'behold!' indicates that what follows the interjection is surprising (Filson, p. 350) 'Behold we are living'. This expression is one of joy and victory.

The third and fourth pairs of antitheses allude to LXX Ps. 117.18. However, the psalmist reflects a widespread view that suffering is a form of divine discipline (e.g. Prov. 3.11-12; Job). Contrarily, Paul believes suffering is a means of self-disclosure (4.7-12). He receives 'punishment', but he is 'not killed'. The apostle may be 'sorrowful', and yet he is 'always rejoicing' (e.g. 2.3; 7.4, 7, 9, 13). Of the 23 Pauline uses of 'sorrow' and 'to be sorrowful', 18 of them appear in 2 Corinthians. Paul appears 'as poor', but he makes many 'rich'. A similar statement in 8.9 about Christ indicates that here the logic is christological and represent Paul's *imitatio Christi*. Similarities in 6.10 and 8.9 lead Windisch (*Paulus und Christus*, pp. 166, 239) to characterize Paul as 'a second Christ'. Enriching others with the riches of the gospel of salvation is the essence of apostleship (2.14-16; 4.6; 5.13b). Paul is able to enrich others because he has a 'treasure in an old clay pot' (4.7). He appears 'as having nothing', and yet he 'possesses everything'.

To summarize, the function of the catalogs in 6.4-10 is not to communicate new information, but to reorient the Corinthians' view of apostleship. Listing various items is pleonastic (redundant) and strengthens his appeal to their emotions. In the affliction catalog Paul emphasizes the great endurance that characterizes his ministry and 'proves' his sincerity. Moreover, he endured much suffering with integrity, as his catalog of virtues demonstrates. With an obvious cross-reference to 4.7, Paul refers to 'the power of God'. That God has made him competent to face both victory and defeat in his battle for the gospel is the purpose of the vicissitudes. Antitheses (vv. 8c-10) argue that Paul is more than he appears to be when judged 'by appearance'. Endurance of great suffering coupled with God's deliverance asserts that his character is unassailable. The final pair of antitheses expands and amplifies the sixth pair. Paradoxically out of his poverty he enriches others and is their benefactor. Similarly he can say of the Macedonians that 'their extreme poverty has overflowed in a wealth of generosity' (8.2). Judged 'by appearance', Paul has nothing, but judged 'according to the Spirit', he has everything.

'I have spoken frankly to you, Corinthians' (6.11) describes what Paul has been doing in 6.3-10. More literally, it reads 'I have opened my mouth to you', which conforms to a common Hebraic idiom for 'speaking'. In this context it means to speak freely and candidly (LXX Judg. 11.35-36). Aeschylus (*Prometheus Vinctus* 609ff.) says, 'I will speak... not twisting up riddles, but in straightforward speech, as it is right to open one's mouth to friends (cf. Ezek. 16.33; 19.21; Eph. 6.19). Only here and in Gal. 3.1 and Phil. 4.15 does Paul address a congregation by naming their city or province. Each time, it is to personalize and emphasize feelings of great emotion. Chrysostom (*Homily* 13.1) thinks it is 'a mark of great love and warmth and affection'. Not only is Paul's mouth opened wide; his heart is opened wide (6.11). 'My heart is wide open to you' (6.11) is the same as 'You are in my heart' (7.3).

Amplifying the figure of 'open heart', Paul affirms he has no restriction in his affections for the Corinthians (v. 12). The Greek term, here translated 'restriction', means to crowd together in a narrow space. Here it means 'to be cramped in affection', as the term translated 'affection' in the next clause confirms. The 'in you' = 'in your hearts'. Paul does not balance the first clause with an antithesis because he is not complaining. He is simply contrasting their behavior with his. Paul can use 'affection' (*splanchna*; KJV, 'bowels') almost synonymously with 'heart', but the term translated 'affection' is confined to a narrower territory, namely, 'to denote the self as moved by love' (Bultmann, *Theology*, I, p. 122).

'Restriction' of the Corinthians' love is not a result of Paul's behavior but is self-induced. Paul challenges them to reciprocate with love for him 'with same widening as recompense' (BDF §54; also see P.E. Hughes, *Second Corinthians*, p. 240 n. 3). Paul speaks to them as to children (v. 13; cf. 11.12; 12.14b-15a; 1 Cor. 3.1-2; 4; 4.14-15; Gal. 4.19; 1 Thess. 2.7-8). In tender terms of endearment and pastoral concern he implores: 'Widen your [hearts] also', a conclusion drawn from v. 11. It is synonymous with 'Make room for us' in 7.2. This passionate appeal from the Apostle is 'I have made room for you in my heart; make room also in your hearts for me'. He wants unconditional love and acceptance.

6. A Digression for Shame (6.14–7.1)

Anyone with even a modicum of familiarity with scholarship of 2 Corinthians is cognizant of the swarm of critical questions surrounding 6.14–7.1. Since the nineteenth century, scholars have been raising issues about the authenticity and integrity of this passage. There are basically four arguments against authenticity: (1) Nine terms that appear nowhere else in the undisputed Pauline letters; (2) extreme exclusivism; (3) affinity with Qumran; and (4) the 'unpauline' use of 'flesh' and 'spirit' in 7.1 (Furnish, pp. 371-83; P.E. Hughes, *Second Corinthians*, pp. 241-44; Rensberger, '2 Cor. 6.14–7.1', pp. 25-49). R.P. Martin (p. 193) thinks there will never be a consensus on the authenticity of this passage. However, there are good reasons for considering it an authentic Pauline piece.

Moffat (p. 125) epitomizes the question of integrity by describing the passage as standing 'like an erratic boulder' in its present context (cf. Plummer, p. 204). Scholars argue that integrity is an issue because (1) 7.2 connects nicely with 6.13 when you remove 6.14–7.2; (2) this passage creates a marked interruption of the sequence of thought; (3) 6.14-7.1 is a self-contained unit. Most scholars agree that this passage is to some extent disruptive but beyond this, there is little consensus. Critics have offered various explanations: (1) An anti-Pauline interpolation; (2) a non-Pauline interpolation; (3) Pauline but belongs to a lost letter; (4) Pauline but misplaced; and (5) Pauline in origin and indispensable to the context of chs. 6–7.

Scholars have proliferated hypotheses to resolve the difficulties. Perhaps the most extreme is that of Betz ('2 Cor. 6.14–7.1', pp. 88-108) who argues for an anti-Pauline fragment that represents the views of Galatian opponents. Some scholars conclude that it is a scrap of Qumran literature interpolated into our text (Fitzmeyer, pp. 205-17). Kuhn (p. 203 n. 1) was the first to note the relationship between 6.14–7.1 and Qumran literature. He claims that more than any text in a Pauline letter, it contains terminological affinities found in Qumran texts. Other scholars argue that 6.14–7.1 is a Pauline letter that Paul mentioned as a 'previous letter' in 1 Cor. 5.9-11 (Strachan, pp. 3-6). Windisch (*Korintherbrief*, p. 220) believes it is Pauline but has been dislocated from its original position following 6.2. A majority of recent scholars believe 6.14–7.1 is essential to 2 Cor. 6–7 and regard it as Pauline in origin. No hypothesis has gone unchallenged and none has resolved all the difficulties surrounding this paragraph.

Betz ('2 Cor. 6.14–7.1', p. 95) thinks the passage is anti-Pauline because, among other things, it advocates Torah observance. One can hardly deny Qumran affinities (Rensberger, p. 26), but Bruce (*1 & 2 Cor.*, p. 214) observes that the features are not peculiar to Qumran. There is always the danger of 'parallelomania' (Sandmel, p. 13). No data have proved that this section requires an Essene or Jewish-Christian author (M.E. Thrall, 'The Problem', p. 138). Displacement theories, whether they posit Pauline or non-Pauline authorship, have not been helpful. At present, no one has located Paul's 'previous letter' (1 Cor. 5.9). Partition theories offer little help with this passage. Hypotheses cannot prove or disprove Pauline authorship because in this passage there are numerous Pauline as well as non-Pauline features (Furnish, pp. 375-78). Few interpreters would accept the radically unequivocal stance that 'There is, in short, no *prima facie* evidence this passage could not have been written by the Apostle Paul' (P.E. Hughes, *Second Corinthians*, p. 242).

Despite difficulties, there is evidence that this passage is authentically Pauline. Fee (p. 147) has identified 13 Pauline features in 6.14–7.1. There are nine terms in this passage that occur nowhere else in the indisputable Pauline letters (three of them in the testimonium), but Pauline outbursts with a high incidence of words he has not used before are not uncommon: 1 Cor. 4.7-13 has six and even 2 Cor. 6.3-10 has four. P.E.Hughes (*Second Corinthians*, p. 242) counts some 50 words in 2 Corinthians that Paul does not use elsewhere. M.E. Thrall ('The Problem', pp. 138, 144-48) argues that Beliar is the only term that provides any substantial evidence against Pauline authorship but she concentrates on data that joins the passage close to its context. One might argue that 6.1 anticipates 6.14–7.1 (J. Murphy-O'Connor, 'Relating', pp. 272-75). Placing 7.2 immediately after 6.13 creates redundancy and 7.2 is clearly resumptive.

M.E. Thrall ('The Problem', pp. 133-38) has demonstrated that every verse in this passage has a parallel in 2 Cor. 2.14–6.13. There is absolutely no textual evidence that 2 Corinthians ever existed without 6.14–7.1. Hypotheses against its authenticity and integrity have not explained how or why it appears in its present context if it was non-Pauline; it is an almost insurmountable task for any theory that claims it is anti-Pauline. Despairing of finding an explanation for its presence in this context, proponents of these hypotheses can only respond: 'difficult to answer', 'not clear' or 'remains unsolved'.

There is sufficient evidence to justify classifying this passage as a Pauline digression. However, one must read the text as it is and seek to understand its function in its present context. The context suggests that this paragraph is an epideictic digression, where Paul goes on the offensive, blaming the Corinthians for their behavior. Danker ('II Cor.', p. 96) opines that 'If 6.14–7.1 is an interpolation, the early editors of what is now 2 Corinthians did a skillful job in mending the seams, for vv. 11-13 constitute an appropriate transition'. Paranesis in this passage suggests that it is their behavior, not his, that has caused 'restricted affection' for him while his heart is 'wide open' to them (6.11-13).

A digression may occur anywhere in a discourse (Quintilian, *Inst. Orat.* 4.3.12). The digression may express greater vehemence and freedom of speech than the surrounding argument. After a 'defendant' provides a list of services rendered, there may be a digression to denounce the opponent or audience for ingratitude (*Inst. Orat.* 4.3.12, 15). A digression must be relevant to the case being argued. It adds distinction to the argument 'only if it fits well with the rest of the speech and follows naturally on what has preceded, not if it is thrust in like a wedge parting what should naturally come together' (Quintilian, *Inst. Orat.* 4.3.5).

The ethical digression in particular is a feature of the greatest speeches of Aeschines, Demosthenes, Lycurgus and especially Cicero (G. Kennedy, *Classical Rhetoric*, p. 44). Since Paul's suffering is for the sake of the Corinthians (4.15), the catalogs in 6.4-10 are 'services rendered'. Greater vehemence and freedom of speech characterizes the paragraph at 6.14–7.1. Certainly Paul is denouncing their behavior that has 'restricted their affection' for him. In Plato's Socratic Apology, there is a digression in which Socrates reveals his philosophy of life and explains why he cannot abandon it now, even to save himself from death (28a-34b).

Conflictual or adversarial language such as we find in 6.14–7.1 is characteristic of Hellenistic-Roman diatribe (Beardslee, 'What Is 1 Cor.', p. 11) and diatribe has emerged finally and essentially as epideictic (Stowers, *The Diatribe*, p. 11). The chief goal of epideictic is to strengthen adherence to a particular value. Most modern preaching is epideictic because it aims to strengthen Christian belief and induce a congregation to live the Christian life. A preacher who inveighs against some group for its irreligious or immoral actions is practicing invective or negative epideictic. Apparently, Paul is doing exactly that in this passage.

Structurally the paragraph at 6.14–7.1 consists of (1) a hortatory prohibition formulated as a direct, second-person plural imperative (6.14a); (2) five rhetorical questions (6.14b-16a); (3) an affirmation (6.16b); (4) a collection of testimonia, a catena of Scriptural allusions and quotations (6.16c-18); and (5) a closing exhortation using a hortatory subjunctive construction (7.1a).

Structure of the Digression

Rhetorical		what	for	partnership	righteousness	and	lawlessness
Questions	or	what		fellowship	light	and	darness
6.14b-16a		what	but	harmony	Christ	with	Beliar
	or	what		share	believer	with	unbeliever
		what	but	agreement	Temple of God	with	idols

Affirmation 6.16b	For we are the temple of the living God
Testimonia 6.16-18	
Citation Formula	As God says
Promise Lev. 26.12; Jer. 32.38; Ezek. 37.27	I will live in them and walk among them, and I will be their God and they shall be my people.
Exhortation	Therefore, come out from them and be separate.
Citation Formula	The Lord says And I will be to you a father and a mother
Promise 2 Sam. 7.8; Isa. 43.6	And you will be to me as sons and daughters.
Citation Formula	The Lord Almighty says
Exhortation 7.1	Since we have these promises, beloved, Let us cleanse ourselves of every defilement of the flesh and spirit

Paul has urged the Corinthians: 'Be reconciled to God' (cf. 5.20–6.10). Reconciliation with God necessitates reconciliation with God's ambassador (6.4-11). At 5.20 God appeals to them for reconciliation and at 6.1 Paul appeals to them not to 'receive the grace of God in vain'. Self-commendation precedes and follows the appeal in 6.1, indicating that failure to accept Paul's ministry is tantamount to receiving God's grace in vain. Anyone who judges Paul 'by appearance' (5.12; 6.4-10) risks receiving God's grace in vain. The appeal in 6.1 anticipates the exhortation in 6.14: 'Do not become unequally yoked with unbelievers'.

Previously, the apostle has expressed concerns about the 'peddlers of God's word' (2.14). He asserts that 'the god of this age' = Satan = Beliar, (6.15) has blinded the minds of unbelievers (4.4). In 11.3, Paul fears that as the serpent deceived Eve, so the serpent will seduce the Corinthians away 'from a sincere and pure devotion to Christ'. Twice he manifests fear that on his 'third visit' he will find them unrepentant (12.20-21; 13.2). Finally, he challenges them to 'test yourselves' to see if they are 'in the faith' (13.5). The relevant digression in 6.14–7.1 comes after a plea that the Corinthians open their hearts to the apostle (6.11-13). He resumes that appeal in 7.2 with 'Make room for me'. Thus, the exhortation 'Do not be unequally yoked with unbelievers' is the same as the appeal 'Do not receive the grace of God in vain' (6.1). The appeal and the exhortation take aim at persons who judge Paul's ministry 'by appearance'.

Having regaled the Corinthians with his heroic tales of devotion for others, Paul (6.4-10), declares his fervent love for them and pleads for reciprocity (vv. 11-13). The paranetic digression on defiling and compromising associations (6.14–7.1) becomes a buffer between passages that emphasize his integrity (6.4-10; 7.2-16). Methodius of Olympus (third century) notices Paul's proclivity for digressions when he noted that 'the sudden shifts in Paul's discussions, which give one the impression that he is confusing the issue or bringing in irrelevant material or wandering from the point at issues...[are part of Paul's] most varied style' (cited by Mussurillo, 'Rhetorical Criticism', pp. 55-56). Wüllner (1995, p. 46) believes Paul's digressions 'are an integral part of his rhetorical sophistication, and that they serve certain functions in his argumentation'. However, Wüllner's thesis is the antithesis of the more familiar scholarly notion that Paul 'at times will go off at a tangent, and interrupt his argument to discuss another matter in passing' (Beare, p. 17; Kümmel, *Introduction*, p. 278).

With a burst of oratorical power, Paul states his negative of prohibition, amplifies it with five antithetically formulated rhetorical questions supported with a catena of Scriptures and closes with an exhortation. Nine terms in this passage that appear nowhere else in the Pauline corpus, three of which are in his testimonia, may witness to its rhetorical power. This phenomenon may not be as great a problem as some scholars have thought. Demosthenes, in his speech *On the Crown*, uses a number of words that he uses nowhere else and he does so purely for rhetorical effect (e.g. 35, 49, 97, 119, 152). It could well be the echo of Paul the preacher: exhortation, a series of rhetorical questions, scriptural support and closing exhortation. This onrush of new vocabulary in this passage is consonant with invective as the preacher inveighs against the congregation. Six of the new words appear in vv. 14b-16a where we find five rhetorical questions. All six of the new terms are virtually synonymous and express the idea of associative relationships in antithetical form. Like any good orator, Paul wanted to provide variety of vocabulary and grammatical constructions in such a vehement passage.

This digression is a tightly knit argument. A metaphor from LXX Deut. 22.10 or LXX Lev. 19.19 provides the basis for Paul's primary prohibition: 'Do not be unequally yoked with unbelievers' (6.14). The present imperative 'Do not become', combined with a present participle (being unequally yoked), results in a periphrastic construction. Periphrasis (i.e. the use of a longer phrasing in the place of a shorter and usually plainer form of expression), may provide a more powerful rhetorical expression and emphasize the durative force of the verb. 'To become' with a present participle may connote the beginning of a state or condition. Thus, one may translate the prohibition 'Do not lend yourselves to becoming misyoked with unbelievers' (BDF, §§352-54). Rhetorical questions amplify the admonition in v. 14a. Each question anticipates a negative answer and reinforces the prohibition by essentially repeating it (Barrett, *Commentary*, pp. 195-97). Each rhetorical question asks essentially the same question and the antitheses illustrate the absolute antithesis between 'believers' and 'unbelievers' (Furnish, p. 372).

The 'for' in v. 14b suggests that the rhetorical questions explicate the exhortation and demonstrate the logical and obvious incongruity of being misyoked. A common practice in antiquity was to use rhetoric to reinforce moral exhortation (Epictetus 3.23.16; Philo, *Ebr.* 57; Ecclus. 13.2b, 17-18). Another 'for' ties the affirmation in v. 16b to the rhetorical questions. The affirmation, 'for we are the temple of the living God' (cf. 1 Cor. 3.16-17), functions to show why the questions are pertinent, add support for the stated (v. 14a) and implied (vv. 14b-16a) admonitions and prepare for an ethical appeal in the testimonia (vv. 16c-18). Testimonia support the affirmation with biblical quotations, one of which is admonitory (v. 17). A final exhortation (7.1) sums up the admonitions in vv. 14a, 17.

Considering the 'promises' in vv. 16c and 17c-18, Paul's style at 7.1 and throughout the paragraph is homiletical and the verb 'to cleanse' is a hortatory subjunctive. The admonition, 'Let us cleanse ourselves from every defilement of body and of spirit, making holiness perfect in the fear of God' (7.1) is virtually synonymous with 'Come out from among them and be separate from them' (6.17) and 'Do not be unequally yoked with unbelievers' (16.14). All three statements are hortatory. Far from interrupting the movement from 6.13 to 7.2, Paul preempts and counters any possible 'charge' that his plea in 6.11-13 is purely personal.

This digression argues that God's interests are at stake when Corinthians respond negatively to Paul's ministry (6.1). By stressing the theme of association with six words not found elsewhere in the Pauline corpus, all of which connote 'to have in common', Paul connects the parenesis to the 'apology' and prepares for the resumptive 'Make room for us' (7.2) and the reminder that he is willing to live and die with the Corinthians (7.3). Paul's goal is that instead of being 'yoked' with unbelievers, that the Corinthians will become 'yoked' with him. 'You are restrained in your affection' (6.12b) is especially relevant to this discussion. They have held back their affection for Paul because they are 'misyoked' with what is worldly and 'in appearance'. Thus, there is a need to 'cleanse ourselves' so that the Corinthians can make room in their hearts for Paul and his gospel. More than ever, in this paragraph, Paul is the prosecutor and thus in a 'defense', he parodies the form to subvert the notion that he needs a defense.

7. Report and Summation (7.2-16)

'Make room [in your heart] for us' (7.2) is resumptive, returning with renewed vigor to the appeal 'Open wide you hearts also' (6.11) and would be redundant if placed immediately after 6.13. Paul has pleaded with the Corinthians not to accept the grace of God 'in vain' (6.1). He wants them to express God's grace by widening their hearts to him (6.13), God's ambassador (5.20). In a paranetic digression Paul demonstrates that the loyalty and commitment he seeks is not purely personal, but is what God requires. Summarizing the digressive appeal, he exhorts them to 'perfect holiness in the fear of God' (7.1).

A triple anaphoric (i.e. repeated) 'no one', placed in an emphatic position, suggests that Paul is determined to maintain his oratorical momentum. Both the placement and anaphoric use of 'no one' function to emphasize the objects of the verbs, not the subject. The three verbs, 'wronged', 'corrupted' and 'taken advantage' are in the aorist tense. Aorist verbs preceded by a negative substantive 'no one' signify that in his last visit to Corinth there was not a single instance in which he has wronged, ruined or taken advantage of anyone at Corinth. Paul may be comparing himself to Corinthian leaders whom he believes have wronged, ruined and taken advantage of the Corinthians. This claim in 7.2 recapitulates his argument that his apostolic behavior is above reproach and the Corinthians need not be suspicious of him. Paul is still on the offensive in this conclusion to his first major argument. Parody is surely the best way to interpret such strange 'concluding arguments' by the defense.

In 7.2-3 Paul is litigating for trust. He protests that he is not guilty of any misconduct. With a compassionate, pastoral spirit he gently says his asseverations of innocence are not meant to condemn the Corinthians.

In light of what follows, his claim is assuredly ironic. Offering a literary figure, epidiorthosis (subsequent justification that intensifies what one has said; BDF (§495.3) does little to blunt the ironic thrust. Repeating what he has said before, perhaps in 6.11-13 (cf. also 13.2), he reminds the Corinthians that they are 'in my heart to die together and to live together' (7.2). His statement recalls the words of Electra to Orestes: 'I am prepared to join you in death or in life' (Euripedes, *Orestes* 307). The pledge to 'live and die' with the congregation describes an inviolable bond with them and affirms Paul's love in the strongest possible terms.

At 7.2-3 there is, again, an 'overlap at the edges' because it concludes what precedes and introduces what will follow. Then, at 7.4-16 Paul continues summarizing his argument, appealing again to the emotions. These verses reiterate Paul's claim to integrity (7.2) and polish off the argument by completing the narrative of Paul's experience since arriving in Macedonia (7.5-7). After pleading for the Corinthians' trust (7.2-3), Paul expresses his 'confidence' in them (BAGD, *s.v.*). The word translated here as 'confidence' may also mean 'boldness'. Furnish (p. 385) combines the two ideas and translates them as 'candor'—the freedom of speech one has when addressing persons one trusts. If Paul meant 'candor', his statement is certainly ironic and parodic.

A reference to 'comfort' renews a prominent theme in 1.3-7. In 7.4 Paul uses alliterative style and repeats the words throughout the text (see Lietzmann, p. 131) resulting in the following structure. Please note that the alliterative style is much clearer in the Greek than in an English translation.

v.4 *paraklesei* (comfort)	Paired with	v. 6	*parakalōn* (comforting)
			parekalesen (comforted)
		v. 7	*paraklesei* (comfort)
		v. 13	*parakeklēmetha* (we have been comforted)
v.4 *chara* (joy)	Paired with	v. 7	*charēnai* (to rejoice)
		v. 9	*chairō* (I rejoice)
		v. 13	*echarēmen* (we rejoiced)
v. 4 *thlipsei* (affliction)	Paired with	v. 5	*thlibomenoi* (being afflicted)

With the word 'comfort' at vv. 6 and 13, there is a 'ring composition' or inclusio. Verse 4 is determinative for topics in 7.5-16 and forms a close connection between 7.2-4 and 7.5-16.

'For even' (v. 5) introduces an explanation for the statements that immediately precede it. Here it explains Paul's being overcome with joy in afflictions (v. 4; vv. 7, 9, 13b, 16). Verses 5-7 provide no new information regarding his sojourn at Macedonia. What is new is the encouraging news Titus communicates to Paul and his joy at receiving the report. In 2.13 Paul says his 'spirit' had no rest; here he says his 'flesh' had no rest in Macedonia (v. 5; see 7.1 where he combines 'flesh' and 'spirit'). There is pleonastic use of 'comfort' here similar to 1.3-7. God 'comforted' Paul (cf. v. 4) and the Corinthians 'comforted' Titus who reported it to Paul, causing him to rejoice even more. Presumably, the Corinthians know Titus has related to Paul how they longed and mourned for their apostle and were filled with zeal for him (v. 7). The purpose is not to inform the congregation but to prepare them to give an offering for the saints at Jerusalem.

Paul revisits a previous topic (cf. 2.3-11) in vv. 8-13a. He had written a previous letter 'out of an exceedingly troubled, anguished heart... through many tears' (2.4). It is of more than passing interest that here Paul mentions the lachrymose (tearful) letter and Macedonia but never broaches the subject of the canceled visit. Here the subject is the effect the 'painful letter' had and its resulting joy for the Apostle. Even if the letter made them sorrowful, it led to repentance (v. 8). In this way Paul commends himself, shows the advantage of his action and clearly shows that it was Corinth, not he, who was at fault. This is hardly what one would expect in a defense or a commendation. Although he earlier wrote that he did not intend to cause grief (2.4), here he rejoices and has no regrets about the lachrymose letter.

Paul concedes that for a time he had regrets about the letter, but having learned the effects of the letter, he no longer has regrets (more literally, he does not repent). After all, their sorrow was temporary (v. 8). Moreover, its results indicates that his action was advantageous in that it led to repentance (v. 9). Interestingly, the repentance is remorse in the Christian life, not that of unbelievers (Bultmann, *2 Corinthians*, p. 55). On the topic of the tearful letter (vv. 8-13a), Paul speaks of the openness with which he speaks to them (cf. v. 4). Confidence in the radical integrity of his Corinthian ministry makes him bold to address such a sensitive subject as the painful letter. He has repeatedly affirmed his integrity in 2 Corinthians (1.12, 18, 23; 2.17; 3.1-3; 4.2; 5.11; 6.11; 7.2). A clear conscience allows the apostle to have no fear of absolute candor. Again, in a defense speech, he repeatedly commends himself, and calls them to repentance. Thus, he is the prosecutor and the defense is parodic. Pleonastic protestations reveal a certain self-consciousness about the troubling letter.

Godly sorrow that led to repentance means Paul caused no injury to them (v. 9); instead it was advantageous for them. The 'loss' in v. 9 is antithetical to 'salvation' in v. 10 and synonymous with 'death' in v. 10. If failure to accept Pauline leadership is tantamount to receiving God's grace in vain (6.1) and if their behavior has led to sinful practices (11.2-3; 12.20-21) so that he challenges them to 'test yourselves' (13.5), then, 7.9 suggests that salvation embraces their relationship to God and to the apostle, Christ's ambassador (5.20). He characterizes their repentance oxymoronically as a 'repentance of which one need not repent'. This 'unregrettable regret' or 'repentance of which one need not repent' is possible because it leads to salvation.

With a burst of pleonasm (redundancy) and anaphora (repetition), Paul displays an indubitably euphoric spirit. At 7.11, he explains the statement in v. 10 beginning with the attention-getting 'Behold!' before listing six nouns that verify Corinthian repentance. The interjection enlivens a narrative by arousing the attention of the audience (BAGD, *s.v.*). The anaphoric 'but', repeated six times in v. 11, reveals Paul's intense emotional state. The adversative use of 'but' introduces a new element in an emphatic manner to denote an idea reaching its climax (BDF, §488.6).

Paul's exhibit begins with 'See how much zeal [for me] it has called forth in you!' and then lists six forms in which their zeal has manifested itself. In the original, his anaphora and pleonasm looks like this:

See how much zeal [for me] it has called forth in you!

but	defense
but	indignation
but	alarm
but	longing
but	zeal
but	punishment

The repeated 'but', combined with the continued force of 'how much', with which 'zeal' connects suggests that the 'how much' attaches also to the six nouns following 'zeal'. The NRSV translates: 'For see what earnestness this godly grief has produced in you, what eagerness to clear yourselves, what indignation, what alarm, what longing, what zeal, what punishment!'

'Clear yourselves' in the NRSV is the noun *apologia* (defense) in Paul's statement. The Corinthians have defended themselves and Paul exonerates them. Paul brackets the list with the words 'defense' and 'punishment', both of which have explicit legal connotations. These two nouns are clearly forensic and are at home in a courtroom. The framing of the list with legal language surely intimates that they are the most important terms and suggests a judicial setting. In the following clause the terms 'innocent' and 'matter' (literally 'case') are also legal terms.

Therefore, Paul does not visualize his relationship with Corinth as personal, but as legal. (Bultmann, *2 Corinthians*, pp. 57-58). Note that they have 'commended' themselves to be 'innocent' in the 'case', but the 'clearing' of themselves is subsequent to repentance and defense.

Members of the congregation have expressed 'indignation', perhaps at the troublemaker of the painful letter. They exhibit appropriate 'fear' of Paul's punishment or of God or perhaps a reverential awe for Paul as God's ambassador (5.20). Moreover, they have demonstrated a 'longing and 'zeal' for Paul. The Corinthian Christians have shown a concern for 'justice' or 'punishment', perhaps for the offender mentioned in 2.3-11. Parody of parodies, the defendant has become not only the prosecutor but, now the judge whose verdict is 'In every way you have proved yourselves innocent in this case' (7.11). It is not that they had done no wrong but rather, they had made an atonement that rendered them not guilty. Immediately following the verdict, he refers again to the lachrymose letter and says its purpose was that their zeal for Paul 'might be made known to you before God' (7.12).

Reflection on the severe letter leads Paul to say 'it was not on account of the one who did the wrong, nor on account of the one who was wronged' (7.11). At 2.5, Paul said the wrong was 'not to me...but to all of you'. His purpose was to test 'whether you were obedient in everything' (2.9). Now 'in everything', they have proved that they passed the test (7.11). Plummer (p. 224) correctly notes that the construction 'not because of... nor because of' suggests the Hebraic mode of expression 'less because of' rather than 'not because of'. Paul wrote the lachrymose letter, less because of the offender or the injured party than that they might recognize him as their apostle. They do not have the authority to grant apostolic status, only to recognize it.

Paul may have forgiven but he had not forgotten the 'offender' and the apostle was most likely the injured party (cf. 2.5) but his greater concern is for the church. There is no way to identify the offender precisely but it was not the incestuous man of 1 Cor. 5 (contra P.E. Hughes, *Second Corinthians*, p. 277) because there the one wronged would have been the offender's father. The singular 'the one who has done wrong' here and 'such a one' in 2.7 makes it most probable that it was an individual. Paul's purpose is that the congregation might realize their zeal for him. That 'it might be revealed to you' suggests that Paul wants them to see for themselves that he is their apostle. 'In the presence of God' (cf. 2.17; 4.2; 5.12) clarifies that the court to which the Corinthians must answer is not the person of Paul, but God, whose apostle he is.

On account of Titus's report, the fact that Paul found 'comfort' (v. 13a) resumes the thought of 7.6 and serves as an inclusio, an 'envelope' device that brings two identical ideas together and echoes 1.3-7. Verse 13a closes the ring. Verse 13b revisits a thought implicit but undeveloped in v. 7. Paul finds comfort in the comfort accorded Titus at Corinth. Paul rejoices over the joy of Titus. In a hyperbolic construction, Paul rejoices 'beyond measure', showing that Titus' joy had increased his joy. 'Beyond measure' was sufficient, but Paul intensifies it with the redundant 'much more'. This overstated construction reveals Paul's elated emotional state, his appeal to the emotions at Corinth as well as his pastoral approach.

When Paul sent Titus to Corinth, he had boasted about the Corinthians and they did not make a liar of him or put him to shame (7.14). Obedience (to the apostle) at Corinth caused Titus to rejoice 'beyond measure' (v. 15; cf. 2.9). However, the hyperbolic 'you all' raises suspicions of euphoric over-optimism. The Corinthians received Paul's envoy with 'fear and trembling' because he represents Paul who is an ambassador with the authority of God (v. 15c; cf. Isa. 19.16; 1 Cor. 2.3; Phil. 2.12; Eph. 6.5). Verse 16 repeats from v. 4 that Paul can rejoice because he has complete confidence in the Corinthian community.

At this point, scholars often assume that serenity reigns at Corinth and that the Corinthians have satisfied Paul's concerns. However, pleonasm in chapter 7 hints that not all is well in the Corinthian paradise. Twice he must affirm his confidence in them. The pleonastic outburst in v. 11 catalogs the many good results of his painful letter that finally led to a 'Not Guilty' verdict for the Corinthians. Still, he mentions the lachrymose letter in v. 8 and returns to it in v. 12. Although he does not wish to 'condemn' them with his threefold anaphoric asservations of having wronged 'no one', he reminds them of their repentance following his tearful letter (v. 8).

There is no chance he will let them forget the pain they caused him at Macedonia (v. 5), not to mention at Troas (2.12-13) which the reference to Macedonia surely recalls. Although his lachrymose letter created chaos at Corinth (1.13–2.11), he does not repent (7.8). Use of four legal terms insinuates that Paul is dealing with 'legal' issues rather than personal preferences. That is, determination of his apostleship rests with God and thus the Corinthians have no jurisdiction in the case. Casting his relationship in legal terms does not diminish his pastoral role. 'In the presence of God' clinches an important point: the Corinthians are in God's courtroom and Paul is only acting as God's ambassador. While Paul announces the verdict, God is the judge. Apparently, Paul's optimism is parodic and it is no surprise that he will subsequently test their love (8.8) and explode in chs. 10–13, calling on the Corinthians to test themselves (13.5). They have passed one 'test' but there are two more 'tests'.

After v. 2, Paul does not utter a single word about his defense. In this courtroom, Paul, the defendant, has become Paul, the parodic judge. Parody has transmuted the Corinthian claimants into defendants before God and God's ambassador. Moreover, they have lost the judicial right to serve as jurors in the case. That Paul 'clears' their name does not diminish the parodic transmutation. Any need for reconciliation has always been that of the Corinthians, not of Paul, because his heart is open wide. He is prepared to live with them and die with them (7.1). This argument ends precisely where it began at 1.12.

At 6.18 God's promise is 'I will be a father to you'. As God's ambassador, Paul's goal is that the congregation will hear 'Paul says, And I will be a father to you'. Understood in this manner, 6.18 is an echo of 1 Cor. 4.15 where Paul asserts that he is their only father and that he became their father in Christ Jesus 'through the gospel'. There is no hint that Paul considers them 'opponents', but only as spiritual children whom he wishes to rescue from their self-imposed alienation from their founding apostle and spiritual father. Their 'repentance' provides reason for hope that they have abolished the wall of hostility that has separated them from their spiritual father.

A Parody of Benefaction (2 Corinthians 8–9)

For more than two centuries, critics have investigated the literary problems of 2 Corinthians. In 1776, Johann Salomo Semler wrote a commentary in which he proposed for the first time the hypothesis that 2 Corinthians consists of several letter fragments. Betz traces the history of this critical scholarship on 2 Corinthians from Semler to Georgi and Bornkamm (Betz, *2 Cor. 8 & 9*, pp. 3-36). Betz is particularly interested in Hausrath's partition hypothesis. It is now time, he says, to recognize that chapters 8–9 are two separate 'administrative letters', neither of which appeared originally where they are in 2 Corinthians. If Betz is correct, he argues that Semler's hypothesis can be 'regarded as proven' (Betz, *2 Cor. 8 & 9*, p. 36). Unfortunately for Betz, there is no textual evidence to support the hypothesis.

Against Betz's 'separate letters' hypothesis, 'grace' at 8.1 and 9.15 forms an inclusio, indicating that the chapters form a unit. Danker's opinion is that 'chap. 8 deals with details respecting the project, whereas chap. 9 concentrates on motivation for completion of the project' ('II Cor.', p. 19). Not only is there no textual evidence for partition theories, Marcion provides the first reference to the letter and he lends no support for partitioning. The Muratorian Canon, which may be as late as 400 CE, does not support partition hypotheses.

If chs. 8–9 did not originally appear in the letter following ch. 7, the editor(s) did an incredible job of hiding the seams. A reference to Macedonia at 7.5 anticipates 8.1 and becomes an overt link between chs. 1–7 and 8–9. Material in chs. 8–9 flows naturally from ch. 7 and continues Paul's parodic defense (cf. 8.20; 9.4). At 7.6, 14 the mention of Titus looks forward to 8.6, 16. Reference to Macedonia (7.5) prepares for 8.1-2, 24; 9.2-4. Paul boasts about the Corinthians (7.4, 14; 9.2). Similar ties are evident with the 'joy' and 'grace' of God (7.6-8, 13; 8.1), the earnestness and zeal of the Corinthians (7.11; 8.8; 9.2), Titus' concern for the Corinthians (7.13; 8.16-17) and the 'testing' of the Corinthians (7.12; 8.8). Against Betz (*2 Cor. 8 & 9*, p. 36), the precise purpose of the introductory formula 'I want you to know' (8.1) is to signal a change of topics (Allo, *2 Cor.*, p. 388). There is nothing strange about this transition to a new topic (Merklein, p. 178; BAGD, *s.v.*; cf. 1 Cor. 15.1).

Both chapters are replete with similar religious language such as 'grace' (8.1, 4, 6, 7, 16, 19; 9.8, 12, 15), 'partnership' (8.4; 9.13), 'ministry' (8.4; 9.1, 13), 'sign of love' (8.7), 'blessing' (9.5, 6) and 'liturgy' (9.12). Paul does not once refer directly to money (i.e. 'silver' or 'gold' coins); instead, he uses the word 'grace'. He endows the offering with a sacral-liturgical aura and not as a mundane enterprise. 'Money becomes more than just money within the Christian church; it attains an almost sacramental significance: A visible sign of an invisible grace' (Dahl, *Paul*, p. 31). Paul offers the Corinthians an opportunity to 'grace' the poor Jerusalem saints.

At 2.5-11 and 7.7-13 the Corinthians have passed their first test of obedience. An opportunity to pass the test of love and loyalty to Paul (8.8, 24; 9.4-5, 13) now presents itself. In the comparison of the Corinthians with the Macedonians (8.1-6), specifically that the Macedonians 'gave themselves to the Lord, and by the will of God, to us' (8.5). There is evidence of defective loyalty to Paul at Corinth. Paradoxically, Paul describes himself 'as poor, yet making many rich' (6.10). Macedonia becomes an *exemplum* (i.e. an example) for 'their abundant joy and extreme poverty have overflowed into a wealth of generosity on their part' (8.2). Christ is the supreme exemplum: 'For you know the generous act of our Lord Jesus Christ, that though he was rich, yet for your sakes he became poor, so that by his poverty you might become rich' (8.9). Paul becomes a 'second Christ' to the Corinthians and Macedonia exemplifies a Christlike church. Corinth should emulate the Macedonians who gave themselves to the Lord and to Paul.

Betz argues that 9.1 marks the beginning of a new letter (*2 Cor. 8 & 9*, p. 90). He cites Acts 28.22 for evidence, but there the phrase concludes a Jewish oral reply to Paul. The formula here is not an exact reproduction of 'now concerning' in 1 Corinthians (7.1, 25; 8.1; 12.1; 16.1, 12). Moreover, the formula in 1 Corinthians introduces new topics, not new letters (BAGD, *s.v.*). Paul is not introducing a new topic at 9.1 but is pursuing the same subject. More naturally, the 'for' connects 9.1 to 8.24 and 'indeed' links to the 'but' in 9.3. Grammatically, Paul is saying, 'On the one hand, it is superfluous to be writing this to you...but, on the other hand, I am sending the brothers...' If, as Betz says, chs. 8 and 9 are separate letter fragments, it is more than fortuitous that both 'fragments' begin with an exordium, that is the beginning of the speech in which the orator tries to gain the attention and good will of the audience (Cf. F.W. Hughes, p. 258 n. 1). Like 6.14–7.1, chs. 8 and 9 constitute a relevant digression in Paul's letter.

In this digression, Paul bases his argument on two standard topics: honor and advantage. A comparison (8.1-5) challenges the honor of the Corinthians by comparing their recalcitrance with the eagerness of the

Macedonians to raise an offering for Jerusalem. In vv. 6-9, he confronts their honor on several fronts as he asks for their participation in the offering. Advantage is the topic in vv. 10-15 and he directly introduces it in v.10 with the word 'to profit'. He does not ask the Corinthians to give beyond their means, although the Macedonians had done that (8.3). They are only to give according to their means so there would be 'equality' in the churches.

In vv. 16-23 Paul writes a letter of recommendation for Titus and two unnamed 'brothers' who will receive and secure the collection at Corinth. Verse 24 summarizes the exhortation to giving with another challenge to honor: proof of your love and our reason for boasting about you. Another challenge comes as a threat to shame (9.1-5). The appeal concludes with thanksgiving and the Corinthians are recipients of God's surpassing grace, an 'inexpressible gift' (9.15).

'Beneficence and reciprocity are dominant structural motifs in Paul's second letter to the Corinthians' (Danker, *2 Cor*., p. 116). Patronage or benefaction functions on the basis of gift and reciprocity. Paul opens (8.1) and closes (9.15) his argument with 'grace', a term that stresses the beneficence of God and thus forms an inclusio and indicates Paul's concern with patronage. Beneficence is a gift from a patron that places the recipient in the inferior role and establishes a patron-client relationship.

Acceptance of the gift obligates the beneficiary to respond with expressions of gratitude, praise and honor. Paul acknowledges the gifts of the Corinthians but now he wants them to excel in the 'grace' of giving (8.7). God is the Supreme Benefactor and Paul is God's envoy; both he and the Corinthians have obligations to God. However, in chapters 8 and 9, Paul offers them the advantage of becoming benefactors to the saints at Jerusalem. He takes precautions with the offering that he would provoke blame neither from God nor the church (8.20-21).

Perceived allegations of deceit (12.14-18) intertwine with Paul's refusal to accept payment at Corinth. At 11.7-11, the subject of refusal of patronage arises and ties chs. 10–13 with chs. 8–9. Apparently, Paul believes that at least some Corinthians want to be his patron, but he refuses to be their client. He offers them the opportunity to be patrons to Jerusalem but parodically notes that it will bring thanksgiving to God, not the Corinthians. God is the Supreme Benefactor who has called Paul to be God's ambassador (5.20).

At 8.14 Paul refers to the 'need' of Jerusalem Christians and at Gal. 2.10 he states, quite contrary to Acts 15, that 'they asked only one thing, that we remember those who are poor'. If helping the poor was the ultimate goal, it is strange that Paul only hints of 'needs' in this context. The ultimate goal of this parodic appeal for an offering becomes clear when Paul says, 'I am testing the genuineness of your love [for Paul] against the earnestness of others [the Macedonians]' (8.8). A comparison of persons (*sunkrisis*) usually serves the purpose of evoking shame and disgrace. Thus, Paul challenges the honor of the Corinthian congregation.

1. An Exemplum (8.1-5)

In 8.1-5, Paul presents what ancient writers called an exemplum (Lausberg, pp. 410-26). This exemplum is also an *encomium* (i.e. in praise of a person, place or thing) to Macedonia and forms the basis for a comparison (*sunkrisis*) with the Corinthians in what follows. The response of Macedonia in raising an offering for Jerusalem is praiseworthy and the exemplum is laudatory. An exemplum carries the force of immediate action (Quintilian, *Inst. Orat*. 5.11.6).

'I wish to make known to you' (8.1) is an introductory formula for a new section (Merklein, p. 178). From the textual evidence we cannot be sure how much of what Paul says in vv. 1-5 is 'new information' for the Corinthians. Furnish (p. 399) translates this phrase, 'I would like to inform you'. The exemplum functions as a challenge to Corinthian honor. The data in this factual exemplum implies a negative comparison of the Corinthians with the Macedonians. Such an implication would be an embarrassment to the Corinthians and the appeal to honor begins with an inducement to shame.

The appeal begins with emphasis on God's beneficence ('grace') that has generated a phenomenal profusion of benevolence ('grace') in Macedonia. In Pauline letters 'the grace of God' achieved the status of a technical term and encompasses God's salvation in Christ as a whole. The attributive participle ('having been given') reminds the reader of the ordinary meaning of *charis* ('grace') as 'gift'. At 8.1 'grace' refers to the willingness to contribute to the collection for Jerusalem and the same meaning applies at 9.14.

The Greek term, *charis*, is amenable to a wide range of meanings, all of which are important in chapters 8–9 (cf. BAGD, *s.v.*). Paul's strategy is to engage in wordplay and banter the Corinthians with the different meanings of the word. At 8.1 *charis* refers to God's grace to the Macedonians; at 8.4, 'benevolence;' at 8.6, it is 'this gift' (i.e. the collection); at 8.7, it is the act of giving; at 8.9, it is the 'grace' of Christ; at 8.16 it is 'gratitude' and in 8.19, it means 'benevolence'. At 9.8, it means 'benefit;' at 9.14, it is 'the grace of God;' and at 9.15, it translates 'Thanks'; as Paul closes this section with 'Thanks be to God!'

Use of the address 'Brothers and Sisters' is a 'style of preaching' (Jeremias, p. 151). With this address Paul emphasizes community and invites the Corinthians to hear what he has to say. Note, however, that he avoids 'friendship' language to sidestep the overtones of patronage (Judge, 'Paul and Socrates', pp. 191-203; Chow, p. 171). Paul wants to inform the Corinthians of 'the grace of God granted to the churches of Macedonia' (8.1). Paul speaks first of the grace of God to Macedonia, not Corinth. The implied negative comparison is the linchpin of the exemplum. The Macedonians have provided a model worthy of emulation at Corinth.

Significantly, Paul describes the Macedonian participation in the collection fundamentally as an act of divine grace. He attributes their generosity neither to his ministry nor to their selfless behavior, but to God's grace. It is God's grace at work in them, just as it will be when the Corinthians complete what they have begun (9.14). The Macedonians have done a wonderful thing, but it is a grace that the donors have experienced. Paul hopes the Corinthians will also experience that same grace. In a passage permeated with benefaction language, Paul makes it clear that God is the Supreme Benefactor.

Paradoxical language describes the Macedonians as paradigmatic of Christian experience: abundant joy in severe affliction (8.2). This portrait is oxymoronic: their abundance of joy and their down-to-the-depth poverty overflowed into a wealth of generosity. That the marvelous feat at Macedonia results from God's grace is clear from the paradoxical language. It is 'in a severe affliction' that their 'abundant joy' and their 'rock-bottom poverty' have overflowed 'into a wealth of generosity'.

Several terms in chs. 8–9 denote 'abundance': 8.2, 14; a verb, 'to have abundance' at 8.2, 7; 9.8; an adjective 'abundant' at 9.1; 'wealth' at 8.2; 'wealthy' at 8.9; 'be wealthy' at 8.9; 'make wealthy' at 9.11. Paul uses all these terms to refer to the general experiences of the Corinthians (cf. 1 Cor. 1.5; 4.8; 8.8; 14.12; 15.58). These allusions to wealth at Corinth may suggest a minority of wealthy members in the church. The 'offending brother' of 2.4 may be the leader of this wealthy, but recalcitrant minority at Corinth that has become 'a thorn in the flesh' for the apostle.

Whatever the 'affliction' of the Macedonians was, it almost certainly relates to their 'rock-bottom poverty'. Paradoxically they have an abundance of joy and out of their poverty wealth overflows. Joy in tribulation is a major theme in 2 Corinthians (1.3-7, 8-11, 15, 24; 2.3, 4, 7; 4.7-18; 7.4, 7, 9, 13-16; 11.23-29). For Paul, 'joy' is not just a happy feeling; it is the saving gift of God, part of the new creation brought by the Holy Spirit (Rom. 14.7; 1 Thess. 1.6; Georgi, *Remembering*, p. 71). In spite of oppressive affliction and austere poverty, the abundant joy of the Macedonians yields a 'wealth of generosity'. The word 'generosity' (NRSV) translates a Greek term that expresses the sophisticated good breeding of the *petite noblesse* (the noble few), those people whose interior does not contradict their exterior. Thus, the Macedonians have shown a 'wealth of open-heartedness' (BAGD, *s.v.*).

Association of joy with generosity is significant. Aristotle states that 'The liberal person will give with pleasure, or in any case without pain. For virtuous performance is a source of pleasure and painless' (*Nichomachean Ethics* 4.1.13). Seneca observes that one should part with a gift without delay lest one appear to be giving it in such a manner that one seems to be extorting from oneself rather than making a donation (*On Benefits* 2.7.1). The Macedonians gave with pleasure and saw grace transform their abysmal poverty into a huge profit. The Greek term translated 'overflowed' (NRSV) has commercial connotations of showing a profit (Danker, 'II Cor.', p. 119; BAGD, *s.v.*). By use of business terminology Paul projects an image of the Macedonians as benefactors in the ranks of a Croesus and a Herodes Atticus, who were the Kennedys of the ancient world.

Commercial language continues in v. 3 as Paul testifies through an oath that the Macedonians gave 'according to their means and even beyond their means'. Livy comments that the 'poor, out of fear of being despised, tend to extend themselves beyond their means' (34.4.15). There is no evidence that the Macedonians gave out of fear of being despised. Liberal persons are inclined to be so generous that they have little left for themselves. The Macedonians seem to have little concern for their welfare. Their generosity was one of grace.

Generosity depends, not so much on how much one gives, as on how much they have after they have given. It is not easy for generous people to remain rich because they see wealth as an instrument for helping others. Paul amplifies the generosity of the Macedonians by adding that they gave 'of their own free will'. It was not as if it were an extortion (9.5). 'Voluntary' has 'an almost technical connotation in this context' (Betz, *2 Cor. 8 & 9*, pp. 45-46). Verse 4 is again technical language that suggests that the Macedonians 'earnestly requested' that they be allowed to participate in the offering (BAGD, *s.v.*). They request the 'favor' of contributing to the Jerusalem offering. The 'favor' or benefaction (BAGD, *s.v.*) they seek is 'partnership' in the offering. They want to participate in 'the ministry meant for the saints'. In their 'ministry' they want to bind themselves to God and God's envoy in one simple act.

Paul is so buoyant that his thoughts bubble hyperbolically over the confines of syntax. He had hardly expected any substantial financial contribution from the Macedonians. Their performance exceeded any rational expectations. Paul's explanation for this miraculous *tour de force* uses the topos of self-sacrifice. The Macedonians gave themselves first to

God as living sacrifices (v. 5). Their self-sacrifice anticipates the supreme self-sacrifice of Christ in v. 9. A backward glance to 6.10, 'poor, yet making many rich' discloses a cross-reference associating Paul with Christ in self-sacrifice.

The Macedonians responded to grace with self-sacrifice and benevolence for the saints at Jerusalem. They gave themselves 'first' (i.e 'first' refers to importance, not to time) to God and then gave themselves to Paul. That this fundraising letter is parodic is seen when Paul says he is 'testing' the Corinthians whether they are as loyal to him as 'others' [the Macedonians]. The Macedonians gave themselves to Paul 'through the will of God', a formula associated with Paul's call to apostleship (e.g. 2 Cor. 1.1). This formula indicates they gave themselves to Paul as God's representative.

This encomiastic exemplum (a praiseworthy example) functions as an implied comparison that is a challenge to the Corinthians' honor. Poverty-stricken Macedonians have given 'beyond their means'. On the other hand, the Corinthians, who have 'wealth', have been recalcitrant. This is a cause for shame and the Corinthians should wish to protect their honor. Paul hopes the Corinthians will emulate the Macedonians, not only in the collection, but also in giving themselves to God and their apostle. His choice of the Macedonians is not accidental because he must have known of the ethnic and political rivalry between them and the Corinthians. There is no hesitation about stimulating competition between rivals by means of comparison. That Paul allows the Macedonians to be his partners serves to stimulate the Corinthians to complete the task they began 'more than a year ago' (v. 10).

2. An Appeal to Corinth (8.6-15)

That Paul wants the Corinthians to give to the Jerusalem offering is not in question. What makes this appeal parodic is Paul's purpose. This passage appears as a fundraising appeal in a deliberative argument but the ultimate purpose is to test 'the genuineness of your love against the earnestness of others' [the Macedonians for Paul] (8.8). Comparing the Corinthians with the Macedonians is a shaming technique intended to test their loyalty to him.

'In response to' (cf. BDF §402.2) the extraordinary example of the Macedonians, Paul 'requests' that Titus help the Corinthians complete what they had begun 'last year' with the offering. His relationship to Titus as 'partner in apostleship' (8.23) makes it unnecessary for him to do more than 'request' or 'urge' Titus to go to Corinth (contra Betz, *2 Cor. 8 & 9*, p. 54). Naming Titus flows unaffectedly from the discussion in 7.4-16, especially vv. 6, 7, 13b-15. In v. 6b, 'in order that' gives the purpose of Titus' assignment to help the Corinthians complete what they had begun 'last year'.

The verb 'to complete' echoes 7.1 and evokes the image of a benefactor who fulfills an obligation (Danker, 'II Cor.', p. 122). Titus had been in Corinth 'last year' and had helped the Corinthians start gathering the collection. At the time of writing this letter, the project was incomplete, to the disgrace of the Corinthians when compared with the Macedonians. Paul wants them to complete the 'gift' (*charis*). The 'act of grace' is the 'gift' for the saints at Jerusalem.

Along with accolades for the Corinthians (v. 7), Paul introduces the theme of escalated benevolence. Syntax is problematic in v. 7 because vv. 6 and 7 end with a purpose clause. Between the two purpose clauses, Paul sprinkles his praises that serve as the basis expressed in the second purpose clause. Thus, v. 7 is an amplification of the purpose clause of v. 6 and completes the thought in v. 6. The 'but' in v. 7 is not adversative but emphatic (BAGD, *s.v.*) and marks the introduction of a new section in this argument.

No one in Corinth disagrees with Paul when he declares, 'You excel in everything' (v. 7). Allusion to the affluence of gifts at Corinth recalls the applause offered in 1 Cor. 1.5-7 and is reminiscent of the gifts recited in 1 Cor. 12.7-11, 28-30. The apostle links the first four terms (all in the dative case) chiastically (i.e. chiasmus is inverted parallelism) so that the related terms 'faith' and 'diligence' create a frame around 'speech' and 'knowledge'.

Faith	Speech
Knowledge	Diligence

Two of these terms, 'speech' and 'knowledge', appear in 1 Cor. 1.5 where Paul praises the Corinthians for being wealthy in every way, especially the intellectual gifts of 'eloquent speech' and 'knowledge'. At 1 Cor. 12.9 'faith' is one of the charismatic gifts. 'Faith' may refer, in a broader sense, to 'faithfulness' (cf. BAGD, *s.v.*).

If this list of gifts is conventional, and not specifically Pauline, the broader meaning would be consonant with other terms in this list and corresponds to the Corinthians' self-understanding (contra. P.E. Hughes, p. 296; Furnish, p. 403). Since 'faithfulness' is relevant to contractual agreements, Paul properly uses it to initiate exhortations on the offering. Closely associated with 'faithfulness' is 'diligence' (eagerness or earnestness), which indicates the aggressiveness and efficiency needed to get things done (Louw *et al.*, §68.63; also §§ 68.64; 68.65, 79; 25.74). The inclusion of 'diligence', which is not one of the charismatic gifts, favors this being a list of virtues that are neither uniquely Pauline nor Christian.

'Love' is the crowning virtue (8.7b; cf. 1 Cor. 13). In the Nestle-Aland Greek text of the New Testament, Paul qualifies this virtue with the phrase 'which comes from us and dwells in you'. With the qualifying phrase, Paul reminds the Corinthians that the love in which they excel is not their own but his love for them. The Corinthians have restricted their devotion for Paul, while Paul has enlarged his heart toward them (6.11-12). Although the offering itself is important, the supreme test for the Corinthians is to prove their loyalty to Paul. A purpose clause and the subjunctive mood gives imperatival force to the phrase 'see that you excel in this gracious work (*charis*) also'. Turner thinks that more than imperatival force is intended and renders it 'see that ye abound in this grace also' (p. 47; cf. BDF, §§387(3); 388). Wordplay (i.e. punning or paronomasia) with 'grace' is a dramatic touch. The position of 'this' makes what Paul says emphatic: 'Excel in this gift'.

'Faithfulness' and 'diligence' frame the first four virtues in the chiasm, indicating their importance in the list. In the context of a discussion about an offering the Corinthians had begun a year ago and the prodding necessary to get them moving again, this is comical. Even the Corinthians could not have missed the parody. As if that were not enough, Paul's clincher is that 'you excel in my love for you'. In a list of virtues, one might expect 'your love' or 'your love for me', but not 'my love for you'. Seeming to correct the imperatival language of v. 7, Paul assures his addresses that he is not giving an order, but then comes the punch line: 'but I am testing the genuineness of your love [for me] against the earnestness of others [Macedonians]'.

Despite disclaimers that he does not give 'orders', Paul clearly engages in vigorous rhetorical arm-twisting. As he explains, the reason for the exemplum at 8.1-5 is to incite the Corinthians to similar acts of generosity. Appealing to the competitive spirit between Macedonia and Corinth, he informs them that aid to Jerusalem will prove their capability for altruistic love. In a project begun a year ago, they certainly have not been faithful and diligent. Paul transmutes the virtue of love to a test of Corinthian love. They can verify their love by taking an offering. Several words in chs. 8 and 9 reflect abundance and wealth; 8.14 explicitly calls for a 'balance between your present abundance and their need'. Corinthians have reneged on their promise, not because of lack of funds, but because at least some (perhaps a wealthy minority, led by the offender of 2.4) were not loyal to Paul. The offering becomes the way of testing their loyalty.

Although the Corinthians have an 'abundance' (8.14), Paul does not ask them to give beyond their means but only to effect a balance (8.12). It is clear that the Macedonians had gone 'beyond their means' (10.3), but the amount of the offering was not so important as that they verify their love for him. Removing himself further from the role of giving 'commands' (v. 8), Paul says that in this matter he is giving 'advice' (v. 10, NRSV). Note, however, that Ramsaran (pp. 531-41) argues that the Greek *gnomē* is a Greco-Roman rhetorical maxim and not simply advice or opinion. Here the *gnomē* is in v. 12 (Heinrici, p. 283): 'For if the eagerness is there, the gift is acceptable according to what one has, not according to what one does not have'.

If the love-in-action of the Macedonians is an exemplum (8.1-5), Christ is the Supreme Exemplum of love in action (8.9). There is a difference in Paul's use of the two exempla. Out of Macedonian poverty came a wealth of generosity (8.2); Christ was rich but became poor so that by his poverty the Corinthians could become rich (8.9b). One can hardly miss the connection of 8.9 and Paul's self-description 'as poor, yet making many rich' (6.10). Surely, Paul's purpose is for the Corinthians to associate him with Christ as the ambassador of Christ. Thus, the Macedonians and Christ are exempla and Paul is an implied exemplum. In each of the exempla their enrichment of others begins with poverty. Whether one interprets 'poverty' and 'riches' literally or figuratively, the principle is the same.

At 8.9 Paul's doctrinal statement is a concise formulation of his Christological and soteriological concepts of grace, one of the presuppositions of the entire letter. Paul and the Macedonians have become imitators of Christ. Now, the apostle challenges the Corinthians' honor and urges them to become self-sacrificing imitators of Christ. 'You know' (v. 9) signals that Paul assumes they know the doctrine. Thus, his exemplum of Christ functions as a reminder, making it an unquestioned example of a superlative order (Lausberg, pp. 415-18).

Whether ad hoc or a credal vestige, one may safely infer that 8.9 elicits a summary variation of Phil. 2.6-11. As the pre-eminent exemplum, Christ is the Benefactor of benefactors. Quite naturally, in a discussion of 'rich' and 'poor', Paul translates the theology of the cross into the language of benevolence. Verse 9 is a chiasmus that frames poverty with riches:

A Christ was rich
    B Christ became poor
    B' Corinthians were poor
A' Corinthians became rich

Paul and the Macedonians begin with poverty but enrich others. Christ begins with riches but becomes poor to enrich the Corinthians. Between the statement of his intention not to give a 'command' and saying he is giving 'advice' or a 'maxim' (v. 10), Paul interjects his doctrinal exemplum of Christ. Quintilian (*Inst. Orat.* 8.5.3) calls the Greek *gnomē*, a sententia or aphorism. It is an argument based on expediency (cf. discussion, Betz, *2 Cor. 8 & 9*, pp. 291-93). The basic common-sense presupposition is that it is better to finish what one has begun than to leave it unfinished. It would be an 'advantage' for the Corinthians (8.10). The Corinthians had desired and begun gathering a collection for Jerusalem. Now, it is time to make good on the pledge. They began 'more than a year ago' but have not completed it. Initial enthusiasm is praiseworthy but goes to waste unless one pursues the goal.

In v. 11 Paul has a tautological phrase, 'the willingness to be willing' (BDF, §400.2), but the idiom has been in use since Plato (*Laws* 3.697d; cf. BAGD, *s.v.*). In the ancient Greco-Roman world it was important for words to be consonant with one's deeds. An idle claim to benevolence is like talking out of an empty purse. Paul urges the Corinthians to align their cash with their words, or more colloquially, 'Put your money where your mouth is!' Paul's slogan is not 'Give until it hurts', but 'give according to your means' (v. 11b). Essentially Paul says, 'Give according to what you have'. Aristotle (*Nicomachean Ethics* 4.1.19) reminds his readers that 'Liberality is not determined by amounts given but on the basis of the donor's disposition'.

If there is the willingness and one gives according to their ability, the gift is acceptable. It is the disposition of the benefactor and not the size of the gift that makes it acceptable. In the context of Jewish almsgiving, Tob. 4.8 states the principle: 'If you have many possessions, make your gift from them in proportion; if few, do not be afraid to give according to the little you have'. For other parallels, see Betz, (*2 Cor. 8 & 9*, p. 66 n. 215) and Danker ('II Cor.', p. 128). Betz observes that the term translated 'acceptable' points to sacrificial gifts and their acceptability to the deity. Note that in v. 5, the Macedonians gave themselves to God and then to Paul.

Paul clearly endorses the time-honored principle of equality and assures the Corinthians he is not seeking to burden them to relieve other people of their responsibilities (8.13). Given the wealth in Corinth and the poverty in Jerusalem, equality requires that the Corinthians give much more than the Macedonians proportionately. This principle of equality (v. 13b) is not specifically Christian but Corinthians understand it. Equality is reciprocal and Paul reminds the Corinthians that 'at the present time' their surplus is for relieving poverty. Should the conditions be reversed in the future, Jerusalem should give to the Corinthians. When saints at Jerusalem have a need and the Corinthians have more than they need, the Corinthians should give 'according to their means'.

A quotation formula, 'As it is written' introduces LXX Exod. 16.18 to illustrate mutual reciprocity of resources: 'The one who had much did not have too much, and the one who had little did not have too little'. Use of the quotation without explanation suggests that the Corinthians were familiar with the passage. Taken from the story of gathering manna, this quotation functions to praise reciprocity and condemn avarice. Giving to the offering is praiseworthy but failing to give out of their abundance is greed. This strategy appeals to honor as Paul attempts to shame them into participation in the offering.

3. A Letter of Commendation (8.16-24)

Turning from exhortation, Paul returns to the arrangements he had begun in v. 6, especially the role of Titus who had proven to be an enthusiastic volunteer. There is a shift in form and content. Paul commends his delegation by stating their qualifications and mission. Titus is eager to return to Corinth (8.16-17). One brother is well known in the churches that have chosen him for this task (8.18-21). A second brother has served Paul well and is eager to go to Corinth. Paul summarizes the commendation (v.23) and concludes with an appeal in v. 24. He had to confront suspicions on two fronts: (1) Remaining doubts about his integrity regarding money (vv. 20-21; cf. 7.2; 11.20; 12.15-18); and (2) he must pave the way for a smooth transference of the collection to Jerusalem (Rom. 15.30-31; Hainz, p. 148).

This section is replete with terms and ideas that accentuate the trustworthiness of the harbingers to Corinth and Paul's desire to distance himself from the collection. His overly bountiful praise of the delegation, their eagerness to go to Corinth and their confidence in the Corinthians is striking. Surely Titus, who has been in Corinth (7.7-16) needs no grandiloquent commendation. A famous preacher chosen by the churches in a vote by a show of hands (vv. 18-19) should not require commendation from Paul. We know nothing of the brother whom Paul has tested (8.22) except that he has 'great confidence' in the Corinthians, suggesting that they know him.

Why, then, does Paul find it necessary to send letters of commendation? He admonishes them to accept this delegation, with a none-too-subtle hint that in doing so, they will verify the sincerity of their allegiance to their apostle. That he must indicate his extreme care that he be blameless before God and the Corinthians insinuates a suspicious environment. Since Paul shows his disdain for letters of commendation at 3.1-3, his excessive praise of the delegation, mixed with suspicions about his integrity regarding money, suggests that the paragraph is a caricature.

Always conscious of the Supreme Benefactor, who makes possible all human beneficence, Paul begins the commendations with 'Thanks be [*charis*] to God' (8.16). The expression is a verbless ejaculation that recalls 2.14 and returns to the mention of Titus at 8.6. The zeal attributed to Titus is the most important qualification of an administrator and the elaborate description is extraordinary. God gave 'zeal' to Titus; it is divine and miraculous, not simply natural ability. Titus has accepted Paul's 'request' to complete the offering (cf. 8.6). He welcomed the assignment 'most eagerly'. It is not simply an assignment from Paul, but eager elation motivates his voluntary action. The voluntary nature of the mission suggests Titus is going to Corinth at his own expense (Danker, 'II Cor.', p. 129). His actions correspond to his enthusiasm, something Paul could not say for the Corinthians.

Along with Titus, Paul is sending two 'brothers' (8.18-22). 'Brother' in the New Testament usually means 'fellow Christian', but it is sometimes a form of address a king uses when addressing persons of high rank (BAGD, *s.v.*, 5). Their commendation is separate from that of Titus and v. 23 suggests they are of lower rank than Titus. Envoys had the reputation of being persons of blameless fidelity in financial matters (Danker, 'II Cor.', pp. 92-93). One of the brothers is held in high repute throughout all the churches because of his preaching. Paul does not specify the role of the other 'brother' in the gospel. Georgi (*Opponents*, pp. 73-74) makes much of this brother being a preacher and theologian. Lacking any clear evidence that 'preaching' is in Paul's plans, it is preferable to render the phrase more generally (cf. NEB, NIV, NASB).

Digressing from the recommendation of the brothers and separating the 'famous brother' from the 'earnest brother', Paul explains the mission of the delegation (8.20). It is precautionary so Paul may escape a blotch on his reputation. One may construe 'avoiding' (v. 20; BAGD, *s.v.*) with 'we are sending' (8.18; Windisch, *Korintherbrief*, p. 264) or 'to accompany us' (8.19; BDF §468.1). It is probably better to construe it with 'sending' in v. 18. Paul is sending envoys so that he may avoid censure or disgrace at Corinth about 'this generous gift' (8.20). Taken at face value, apparently Paul hopes for a munificent gift out of their 'surplus' (8.14). However, in the context it is probably Paul's way of goading them in his parodical approach.

At 8.21, the phrase translated 'we intend' in NRSV means to think of something beforehand. This term and its cognates often occur in official letters describing forethought as a quality of an able official (*Danker*, 'II Cor.', pp. 359-60). Tertullus praises Felix for his 'forethought' (Acts 24.2). Having envoys and keeping his distance is Paul's way of demonstrating forethought in financial matters. Paul's concern is to protect his honor 'not only in the Lord's sight but also in the sight of others' (8.21; cf. Rom. 12.17).

Behind the word that the NRSV translates 'right' is an adjective used in honorary documents as a referent to performance that merits high marks for contributions to the public welfare (Danker, *Benefactor*, p. 63). This term has a wide range of meanings, including beautiful, good, fitting, honorable, morally good, blameless, excellence. There must be irony, perhaps even sarcasm, that Paul must take such pains to insure his integrity. Certainly, it makes it clear that he does not believe the Corinthians are loyal to him. It is Paul's way of parodying such desired commendations of his integrity.

After digressing to explain his precautions (8.20-21), Paul returns to practical matters about his delegation (v. 22). Besides Titus and the 'renowned brother', he has also dispatched an 'earnest brother'. In contrast to 'the brother' (v. 18), the third member of the trio is 'my brother' (v. 22). Paul has tested his brother and verified his 'earnestness' in a variety of ways at various times. Previously Paul has commented on the earnestness of the Corinthians (8.7; 7.11-12), of the Macedonians (8.8), and of Titus (8.16, 17). The 'earnest brother', however, is 'much more earnest' because of his 'great confidence' in the Corinthians. If Paul is testing their loyalty to him (8.8), how does it help his defense to assure the Corinthians of his integrity and a 'brother' who has passed the test? Moreover, how can Paul's envoy have 'great confidence' in a congregation that is not loyal to Paul? It becomes almost laughable, to the point of seeming farcical.

If anyone at Corinth has suspicions about the envoys, Paul makes it clear that they go with his blessings and authorization. Titus holds superior rank to the two brothers. In vv. 16 and 23 Paul names Titus first. Titus is Paul's 'partner' and 'co-worker' with the Corinthians. The envoys are 'messengers of the churches' and 'the glory of Christ' (v. 23). Coordinate conjunctions in the Greek create a distinction between Titus and the brothers. '*As for* Titus, he is my partner and co-worker in your service; *as for* the others, they are messengers of the churches' (v. 23). As Paul is the 'aroma of Christ', so his envoys are 'the glory of Christ'.

Paul's ambassadors have unimpeachable credentials. It seems reasonable that Paul should expect the Corinthians to demonstrate their love for the trio and the quality of his boast about the Corinthians. By means of a *figura etymologica* ('demonstrating…the demonstration'),

Paul makes an emphatic appeal in v. 24. It results in an emphatic imperative: 'Give proof of your love and my reason for boasting about you'. This admonition is not an appeal to love the envoys (contra R.P. Martin, p. 279), nor is it a general admonition to love (cf. 1 Cor. 16.14). It is not even an exhortation to love Paul (contra Danker, 'II Cor.', p. 134). It is a renewal of testing the authenticity of their love (8.8) and the way they can verify their love is to make the offering they started more than a year ago.

Love must embody action; the appeal is to make a public expression of their love. Giving of their surplus for Jerusalem's needs will prove their love 'in the presence of the churches'. The expression 'in the presence of the churches' may relate to the legal concept of *persona* (BAGD, *s.v.*). What the Corinthians do to the 'apostles of the churches' (v. 23), the legal and political persona of the churches, they will be doing to the sending churches. Paul throws down the gauntlet with the challenge to prove their loyalty to him.

At 8.16-24 parody functions much like epideictic. If the Corinthians do not accept Paul's credentials, why would they accept the credentials of men he commends to them? Through parody he hopes to evoke such a sense of shame that the Corinthians will fulfill their promise to raise funds for the needs of the Jerusalem saints. In effect he is saying, if you do not accept the integrity of my credentials, accept the credentials of my envoys. That strategy caricatures the letter of recommendation (cf. 3.1-3). It is a risky strategy but Paul is so desperate that he resorts to precarious tactics to test Corinth's loyalty.

4. A Challenge to Honor (9.1-5)

Betz (*2 Cor. 8 & 9*, pp. 36-38) thinks chs. 8 and 9 are separate fragments of administrative letters from which editors excised the epistolary prescripts but amazingly, both begin with an exordium and end with a peroratio (i.e. the beginning and end of a speech)! Bultmann (*2 Corinthians*, p. 256) states categorically that '2 Corinthians 9 cannot possibly follow chapter 8'. Nonetheless, the 'for' links 9.1 to 8.24 and Paul's boast about the Corinthians. That tie explains why it is 'superfluous' to write to the Corinthians about the collection. It is both an expression of confidence and a stratagem designed to facilitate elaboration of the theme of 'shame' that is tacit in his reference to boasting in 8.24.

The 'for' is resumptive (Bruce, *1 & 2 Cor.*, p. 225) and the correlative, 'on the one hand' anticipates the 'but on the other hand' in v. 3. 'Now on the one hand it is superfluous to write this to you...but, on the other hand, I am sending the brothers...' Demosthenes (*On the Crown* 50) uses a similar grammatical construction. Again Paul uses the phrase 'for the saints' (cf. 8.4) as an almost technical term for the poverty-stricken saints at Jerusalem.

'Because' ties 9.2 to 9.1 and begins to explain why it is superfluous to write about the offering: 'their goodwill'. Paul has already mentioned their goodwill at 8.11, 12, 19, another indication that ch. 9 belongs with ch. 8. 'Goodwill' is virtually synonymous with 'eagerness'. Both terms belong to the semantic field of benefaction and appear in chs. 8 and 9 (Danker, *Benefactor*, p. 321). Their 'goodwill' is the subject of his boasting to the Macedonians that they have 'been ready since last year'. The mention of this boast reminds the Corinthians that the apostle's honor is at stake. Surely the accolade is sarcastic because in chapter 8 he has attacked them for not having finished what they started 'more than a year ago'. Competition is also in view because Paul's boast about Corinth had created enthusiasm for the offering in Macedonia. The boast is parodic and intends to evoke feelings of shame.

'Zeal' is another word that belongs to the word-family repeatedly used in honorary documents about exceptional generosity. At 7.7-11 Paul used this term as a descriptor of the Corinthians. In chapter 8 Paul cites the exemplary eagerness of the Macedonians to provoke the Corinthians to action. Now in chapter 9 he redoubles his entreaty by affirming the Corinthians as paragons of zeal for the Macedonians. Apparently the ploy worked in Macedonia (8.1-5) and Paul hopes it will have the same effect in Corinth. At 9.2 Paul includes a *captatio benevolentiae*, a complimentary statement designed to secure the goodwill of the readers (Lausberg, pp. 273-79; G.A. Kennedy, *Classical Rhetoric*, p. 186). Paul appears to praise the Corinthians without reserve, but the statement functions also as parodic praise to insinuate blame as well.

Paul has incited philanthropic rivalry by setting each against the other (8.1-7; 9.1-5). Although he says he has confidence in the Corinthians and that it is superfluous to write, there is some reason why he feels compelled to send envoys. His explanation is that he wants to preserve his honor and that of the Corinthians. To make his reference to boasting emphatic, Paul repeats the article so it literally reads 'the boasting we do, the [boasting] about you' (BDF, §269.2). Wishing to avoid embarrassment, he is sending the brothers so that the Corinthians may be prepared 'just as I said' (9.3c). He does not want his boast to be 'deprived of [its] justification' (BAGD, *s.v.*). He limits his concern to 'in this particular point', that is, what he said in v. 2.

Honor and shame are major issues in this passage. Paul resorts to a thinly veiled threat of embarrassment to the Corinthians (9.4). The conditional clause in v. 4, with an aorist subjunctive, refers to a real possibility of what is expected to occur (BAGD, *s.v.*). 'If you are not ready, I would be embarrassed—to say nothing of you!' Unless Paul could actually appear in Corinth with a Macedonian entourage, his threat would be empty. In this complicated verse, Paul uses a technique that makes him not seem to say what he has actually said. The noun translated as 'confidence' in most English translations (RSV, NAB, 'trust'; NASB, NIV); the NRSV correctly translates 'undertaking'. Here Paul's concern is not personal disgrace because of unjustified boasting, as in 7.14, but the abortion of collection—and the Corinthians would face disgrace.

It is not 'necessary' to write, but it is 'necessary' to ask representatives to precede him to Corinth (cf. Phil. 2.25; 2 Macc. 9.21 and BAGD, *s.v.* for more parallels). Paul asks the Corinthians to prepare the way for his arrival in Corinth. 'To go in advance' is the operative word in Paul's plan. With the alliterative use of three verbs in this verse with the prefix *pro*, Paul literally 'rubs it in' that their pledge is long overdue. The messenger will 'go in advance' to 'organize in advance' for an offering the Corinthians promised 'in advance'. Fulfillment of a promise was a primary responsibility in the Hellenic world. Paul reminds the Corinthians they had 'promised' the gift. Time has come to pay the IOU. The apostle uses the word 'blessing' as a referent to the gift; it is another euphemism for money. With another not-too-subtle insinuation of a threat, he says he still wants it to be a 'blessing', not an 'extortion'.

Alliterative and anaphoric use of the prefix *pro* embellishes Paul's style and reminds the Corinthians of a threat to their honor. Paul also uses antithesis: 'necessary' and 'unnecessary', 'blessing' and 'greed'. Hughes (1980, p. 328) cites Herveius who observes that 'giving is called avarice when it is done with a grasping and niggardly and sad heart, but a blessing when it is done with a generous and eager heart'. Paul knows as well as Cicero (*De officiis* 2.21.75) that 'the main thing in all public administration and public service is to avoid even the slightest suspicion of avarice'. The apostle wants a blessing, not an extortion.

5. A Theology of Benevolence (9.6-15)

As Paul uses the form of a defense to criticize the Corinthian criteria, so here he uses the form of theology to continue his invective against the church. He is not so much interested in teaching theology as in shaming the Corinthians for failing to fulfill their promise to raise an offering. In an ostensible appeal to raise funds, Paul uses theological language of benevolence in order to test the loyalty of the Corinthians to their apostle.

Throughout his discussion of the offering, Paul shuns all use of the word 'money'. He uses terms with distinctly religious connotations. With terms the Greco-Roman world would understand he frames his 'task theology' as beneficence. When the apostle designated the offering 'a gift of blessing' (9.5bc), he hints the direction he will take. With a genius for bridging cultures, Paul dresses the 'grace-gratitude' nexus of biblical religion in the garments of sowing and reaping. Generosity does not foster destitution because to give is to sow and to sow is to reap a harvest. The world enriches itself by 'greed' but Christians enrich themselves through 'blessing'. Giving to others enriches the giver.

Greco-Romans cherished axiomatic advice because axioms taught a balanced view of life and nurtured judicious reasoning. With didactic loci he justifies the notion 'gift of blessing' in order to heap shame on the Corinthians. He draws his arguments from 'definition' (Quintilian, *Inst. Orat.* 5.10.55). There are two classes of definitions, one defines things that exist and the other, things apprehended by the mind (Cicero, *Topics* 5.26-28). Paul's argument from definition belongs to the latter and in 9.6-15, it is the definition of 'gift of blessing'.

'Now this' (NRSV has 'The point is this') is an elliptical expression. The phrase may correspond to a formula Paul sometimes uses to introduce doctrinal instruction (cf. 1 Cor. 5.5; 7.29; Gal. 3.17; 1 Thess. 4.5). 'This' introduces what follows and forms a link with what preceded: 'The point is this: the one who sows sparingly will also reap sparingly and the one who sows bountifully will also reap bountifully' (BDF, §481). Ellipsis presumes certain knowledge and sometimes mimics colloquial speech. The idea of commensurate sowing and reaping is widespread in Jewish wisdom tradition (LXX Prov. 11.21, 24, 26, 30; 22.28; Job 4.8; Sir. 7.3; 3 *Apoc. Bar.* 15.2-3; Gal. 6.7-9). Proverbs 11.24 may be in Paul's mind when he creates this proverb.

In Paul's proverb, lines 1 and 2 are antithetical but each forms a chiastic structure:

A The Sower	A The Sower
B Sparingly	B Bountifully
B' Sparingly	B' Bountifully
A' The Reaper	A' The Reaper

By employing antithetical parallelism, Paul transforms his proverb into a maxim. He advances his argument on the basis of consequences. The language of reciprocity was well known to the Corinthians. Paul's point is easily decipherable: Corinthians who give sparingly in the offering will reap sparingly in the blessings, but the one who gives generously will reap bountiful blessings. The term 'sparingly' in v. 6 corresponds to 'greed' in v. 5 and 'gifts of blessings' in v. 6 corresponds to 'gift of blessing' in v. 5. The proverb (maxim) in v. 6 expands on the idea already enunciated in v. 5bc. Paul proceeds to give 'principles of benevolence'.

First, one should give 'from the heart' (9.7). 'Let each one give just as they have decided in their heart, not grudgingly or under compulsion; for God loves a cheerful giver' (v. 7). Heart-decided giving is not painful or reluctant (*BAGD*, *s.v.*). Paul's slogan is not 'Give until it hurts, but give until it is hilarious (cheerful)'. Heart-decided giving of a generous person is a pleasure and not a pain. Virtuous behavior is a source of pleasure. Heart-decided giving is inconsistent with giving under compulsion. Each person must decide in their heart what to give. 'God loves a cheerful giver' is a proverb that alludes to LXX Prov. 22.8a. The proverb explains why 'each person gives as the heart decides'.

'Heart-decided' giving is at home in many cultural contexts. Giving to the poor is especially virtuous: 'Give to him [the poor person] and lend them as much as they lack, according to their need; you shall not be grudging in your heart as you are giving to them, because on account of this the Lord your God will bless you in all your works...' (LXX Deut. 15.10). In LXX Prov. 19.17, the same theme advises: 'The one who is merciful to the poor lends to God and according to the gift [God] will repay that one in full'.

Seneca (*On Benefits* 2.2.2) uses the same topic: 'One who acts thus [giving to the poor] readily leaves no doubt that he acts willingly; and so he acts gladly, and his face is clothed with the joy he feels'. In Sir. 35.11, the admonition is 'With every gift show a cheerful face, and dedicate your tithe with gladness' (LXX 35.8,). *Leviticus Rabbah* 34.9 (131b) advises: 'When a man gives alms he should do it with a joyful heart'. Philo (*Spec. Leg.* 4.74) says, 'So then let not the rich man collect great store of gold and silver... but bring it out for general use that he may soften the hard lot of the needy with the unction of his cheerfully given liberality', and adds that one should 'honor equality' (cf. 2 Cor. 8.13-15).

'God loves a cheerful giver' explains why the giver should give as 'the heart has decided'. Bultmann ('Hilaros', p. 299) remarks that 'Judaism and the Gentile world, as well as Christianity, believe that cheerfulness belongs to the inner freedom of generosity'. Paul had rich sources from which to draw when he wrote his proverb. Its function is to encourage generosity at Corinth. The verb, 'to love', probably means nothing more than 'approves' (Barrett, p. 236; BAGD, *s.v.*). Certainly Paul is not suggesting that God loves 'cheerful givers' more than 'grumpy tightwads'. The cheerful giver is the generous giver who voluntarily offers 'a gift of blessing' (contra Nickle, p. 99). It is the generosity that God approves. In this context 'cheerful' means generous, kind and gracious (BAGD, *s.v.*).

At v. 8, Paul states a second theological affirmation: God is the source of all beneficence. Verse 8 confirms the interpretation in v. 7: the cheerful (generous) giver's bountiful harvest is a benefit of grace. As a benefit, grace is a gift, not payment for services rendered. The benefit leads to more generous giving. God is able to supply an abundance of 'grace' (i.e. 'gifts of material blessings') so the Corinthians can always be magnanimous with needy people. In Greco-Roman culture, it was almost a cliché that God is the source of every 'blessing' (i.e. 'grace') that humans enjoy. Xenophon (4.3.3) recalls that Socrates once asked Euthydemos, 'Have you ever reflected how carefully the deities supply human being with everything they need?' No one is innately generous; it is only God's grace that makes one generous. One becomes a benefactor by the grace of God. Grace is the efficient cause of all human generosity; all human generosity is a response to God's grace.

Paul's Greek in v. 8 is almost impossible to reproduce in English. Alliteration, wordplay and anaphora abound. In an attempt to preserve the literary and rhetorical figures, one may paraphrase to read, 'God has the power to make all benefits abound to you in order that in all ways, at all times, you may have all sufficiency and more for all kinds of good works'. 'God' is the expressed subject and mention of human beneficence comes only at the end of the sentence. God acts so that human action is possible. God acts by expressing divine power to cause all grace to abound so that it is possible for humans to abound in 'every good work' for others. Correct Greek grammar requires that 'grace' be a plural noun, but Paul writes the singular. There is only one divine grace, no matter how varied it may appear in its visible results. Likewise, Paul avoids speaking of 'good works' because he thinks 'good work' is a continuing action. Every specific instance of beneficence is part of a larger whole demonstrating the grace of God (Kümmel, *Korinther*, p. 207). Grace continues to produce good work.

Windisch (*Korintherbrief*, p. 277) thinks Paul is 'turning back from the love of God to the reward gained through love', that is to say, to verse 6b. However, he insists that it is not a question of material returns but of spiritual powers granted in exchange. Paul's use of 'grace', rather 'gift of blessing', argues against Windisch. When Paul promises the Corinthians they will have 'some to spare', he borrows a term favored by Cynics and Stoics as a referent to 'self-sufficiency'. Paul does not give the word its full technical sense but in a more restricted use of having enough resources to be independent of other people and to be able to help the poor, thus affirming one's community by expressing 'grace' to them (cf. Georgi, *Remembering*, pp. 97-98).

At Phil. 4.11, Paul's only other use of the term *autarkēs,* he uses it in the context of vv 11-13 and transforms its meaning into 'Christ-sufficient'. Likewise, in v. 8, he makes it mean 'God-sufficient'. A 'good work' in Greco-Roman parlance refers to a philanthropic enterprise. Structurally, 9.8 is like 1.3-4 (God comforts us so we can comfort others) and here God provides benefits so the beneficiary can benefit other persons in need. Paul significantly modifies the Hellenistic ideal of 'self-sufficiency'. He believes philanthropy has its origin in the benefits God bestows; it is a gift from God, not self-discipline. Also he thinks of the Cynic-Stoic *autarkeia* (self-sufficiency) as God's grace in Christians enabling them to grace the needy people.

Paul's third theological affirmation encompasses vv. 9-11: There is an indissoluble link between righteousness and beneficence. In the ancient world it was a commonplace to bond righteousness and philanthropy. Righteousness requires mercy for the poor and the oppressed (Dan. 4.27). 'Righteousness' becomes synonymous with 'generosity' in early Judaism. In late Hebrew, *ṣadaqah* (righteousness) came to mean generosity and later rabbinic interpretation of Ps. 112.9, quoted in 9.9, adopts this meaning (Cf. Lev. 19.9-10; Deut. 15.7-11).

At v. 9 Paul resumes the metaphor of 'sowing' that began in v. 6. He synthesizes the affirmations of vv. 6, 7b and 8 in support of his appeal in v. 7a. Liberal sowing brings a bumper crop (v. 6) and God applauds the generous giver (v. 7b). In view of God's generous provisions, God's people can afford to overflow in 'every good work' (v. 8) and beneficence is part and parcel of the righteousness of God (v. 9). Plummer (p. 261) and Betz (*2 Cor 8 & 9*, p. 111) make 'God' the subject in v. 9 but Georgi (*Remembering*, p. 99) correctly sees that Paul understood the quotation from LXX Ps. 111.9 as did the psalmist. The sower is the righteous person.

A quotation formula, 'as it is written', designates v. 9 as a scriptural citation. In this context, the one who 'scatters' seed and 'gives to the poor' obviously conforms to the apostle's appeal in vv. 6-7. The Corinthians can 'prove' their righteousness by giving to the poor saints at Jerusalem. If they give to the poor, their righteousness will 'endure forever' (v. 9b). For Paul, as for the Hebrew Bible, righteousness is more than moral purity; it is also 'justice' and beneficence is righteousness. Words must clothe themselves with deeds. Chrysostom (XII.369) defines 'righteousness' in 2 Cor. 9.9 as 'philanthropy'.

Everything accented in vv. 6-9 comes to clearest expression in v. 10. Verse 10 is not an allegorical interpretation of v. 9 (against Betz, *2 Cor. 8 & 9*, p. 111), but a biblical foundation for the generosity of the righteous person in v. 9. Excerpting 'seed to the sower and bread for food' from

LXX Isa. 55.10, Paul shapes it into a portrayal of God. God is the Chief Benefactor who (1) supplies seed to the sower; (2) supplies and multiplies the seed; and (3) increases the harvest of the righteous. These provisions imply (1) seed for this year's sowing; (2) seed for next year; and (3) bread for present consumption (Betz, *2 Cor. 8 & 9*, p. 112). God's provision takes the form of multiplication of seed that produces the necessary surplus. Several times in chs. 8 and 9 Paul has alluded to the surplus of the Corinthians. He continues to challenge them to release the purse strings with the knowledge that God will supply all their needs.

Hearing Paul for the first time, they could not miss the implied invective in the promise. The Corinthians' 'seed' is their money. God's grace provides 'seed' and makes it possible for the Corinthians to be generous. If they 'sow' generously in the collection, they will have enough for 'seed' next year as well as 'bread for consumption' now. With a possible allusion to LXX Hos. 10.12, Paul adds that God will 'increase the yield of your righteousness'. In Paul's theology righteousness marries beneficence and the two become one. Chrysostom declares: 'For it is not possible that lust of wealth and righteousness should dwell together'. Paul insinuates that unless the Corinthians give for the collection, their righteousness is in doubt. There is no question that the apostle thinks the Corinthians have been stingy regarding the offering. The Corinthians are on trial and they have not acquitted themselves well.

Verse 11 appeals to a common topic for benefaction: advantage. The 'advantage' takes a peculiar form here. Where one expects a future tense, Paul uses the present tense: 'You are enriched' and subsequently he continues that thought. The NRSV incorrectly treats the participial verb as a future tense. Although the Corinthians have not yet made any substantial contribution to the offering, Paul treats it as a *fait accompli*. They are being enriched 'for the greatest generosity'. It is possible that Paul is writing proleptically, but it is more probable in this parodic context that he is adding pressure to invective. Although he talks about giving voluntarily, he is tightening the screws on the Corinthians. He has already boasted to the Macedonians about the generosity of the Corinthian church (9.2).

The Corinthians have not yet been generous but God has enriched them so they can be generous. Hermas (*Parable* 1.9) writes: 'This is why God made you rich, that you may perform these services for him'. Paul is giving the same message to the Corinthians. He is their benefactor, but with a master stroke, Paul offers them the opportunity, like the Macedonians, to be benefactors with Paul. Their generosity will accrue as a 'benefit' to God-thanksgiving. This 'benefit' is hardly what the Corinthians had expected! By parodying the patron-client system, Paul tells the Corinthians the greatest benefit of their gift will be that in Jerusalem the saints will thank God for the gift.

Paul's fourth theological affirmation is 'Beneficence evokes the worship of thanksgiving to God'. Especially striking here is that Paul does not say the Jerusalem saints will thank the Corinthians. Instead, they will thank God. Corinthian beneficence would heighten the honor and glory of God as the Great Benefactor. A gift to Jerusalem would be a gift to God. Religious and theological language permeates the discussion of the collection. Paul uses 'grace' when he appeals for a generous contribution. Now he uses a cognate of grace, 'thanksgiving' when he talks about the receipt for the offering. Héring (p. 75) says v. 12 is a 'an idea already expressed in v. 11'. The subordinating causal conjunction 'because' shows that v. 12 is an explanation of v. 11b (BDF, p. 456).

Paul's use of 'ministry' and 'service' affirms two results for the conveyance of the collection to Jerusalem: (1) it will supply the needs of poor saints; (2) it will overflow with many thanksgivings to God (cf. 1.11; 4.15). Clearly Paul makes 'ministry' a synonym for 'collection'. 'Service' here is a service to God (BAGD, *s.v.)*. There can be little doubt in this discussion that the religious connotation of these terms is paramount (contra Betz, *2 Cor. 8 & 9*, p. 117, Danker, 'II Cor.', p. 144). Paul is talking neither about voluntary service nor enforced public service. Conveyance of the offering becomes a priestly service. The offering is a benefaction to God and its conveyance is a priestly service, intimating a sacrifice to God.

'Not only' in v. 12 is not a negation of the function of supplying the needs of the saints. Rather, Paul is affirming the usual function of such 'services' (liturgies?). A periphrastic phrase translated 'supplies' (NRSV) is difficult to adequately understand. It means 'to fill up by adding to' something. In adding to the collection, the Corinthians will add something to the offering that will bring it up to a state of fullness. *Periphrasis* renders the verb emphatic and expresses linear action (BDF, §353). While 'not only' does not nullify the significance of the offering, it does demonstrate that 'many thanksgivings to God' is more important (BDF, §448.1). It is not an antithetical construction and the first element is not entirely negated but only toned down (Smyth, §2764). Boobyer (pp. 79-82) observes that thanksgivings are the return of grace received from God to God; the more deeds of grace, the more thanksgivings to God. It is difficult to imagine that this 'benefit' would create much enthusiasm in Corinth!

Paul's fifth theological affirmation is 'Beneficence produces honor to God'. Continuing to speak of the collection as a *fait accompli*, Paul presents yet another 'test' for the Corinthians. The grammatical construction in v. 13 renders it 'because of the proof' (BAGD, *s.v.*) of the Corinthians having taking an offering, thanksgivings will 'overflow'. Their participation will provide unimpeachable 'evidence' of their Christian credentials. Receiving the offering is a test and when they collect the funds, it will prove that they are Christians. This 'test' is remarkably similar to the one in 13.5.

In Jerusalem, the saints will 'glorify [give honor] to God' because of (1) the collection for poor saints; and (2) the Corinthians' obedience to their confession of the gospel of Christ. Significantly, in v. 12 there will be 'thanksgivings' to God, and not to the Corinthians. In v. 13 Jesus people at Jerusalem will 'honor God', not the Corinthians. The test of obedience (2.8) and the test of love (loyalty, 8.8) is now a test of their being Christian at all. Paul's appeal is still pastoral but it is also parodic. At their conversion, the Corinthians 'contracted' for participation in the Gospel of Christ (Danker, 'II Cor.', p. 145). Their participation in the collection can verify they have made good on their contractual obligations.

Only after giving thanks for the 'grace of God' will the Jerusalem saints express gratitude to God for the collection. They will 'glorify God' for the generosity of Corinth, demonstrated by sharing with them 'and all people'. The referent for ***koinonia*** (fellowship, partnership) is the offering but to translate 'contribution' (cf. NASB) weakens the force of Paul's words. He speaks of the 'simple goodness' (Georgi, *Remembering*, pp. 105, 204 n. 43) of participation with the Jerusalem Christians. The offering will demonstrate that the Corinthians have entered into a 'partnership' (fellowship) with Jesus people at Jerusalem and throughout the world. Parallelism in v. 13 reveals three bases for honor to God in Jerusalem: (1) submission to the gospel; (2) generosity toward Jerusalem saints; (3) generosity toward all people. Corinthians are inextricably related to Jesus people throughout the world. They cannot have a solo performance that allows them to steal the center of the stage. In addition to the Jerusalem offering, they must allow their 'simple goodness' to result in generosity repeatedly when other people are in need.

In Jerusalem the saints long for and pray for the Corinthians 'because of the surpassing grace' God has bestowed on the Corinthians. The collection becomes evidence of the surpassing grace of God on the Corinthians. God's 'inexpressible gift' of beneficence is so bountiful that no recital of acclamations could do it justice. All attempts to sing the grace of God are destined to failure in the final analysis. God's grace surpasses all human efforts to describe or understand it. Paul creates a 'circle of grace' by beginning with God's grace (8.1), describing operative grace in Macedonia (8.1-5), giving Corinth the opportunity to participate in this grace (8.7), portraying Christ as the supreme exemplum of grace

(8.9), making the offering grace (8.7), saying Jerusalem will honor God because of the grace bestowed on the Corinthians (9.14) and concluding with a doxology: 'Thanks be ('grace') to God for this inexpressible gift' (9.15) of grace from the Corinthian church. 'Grace' at 8.1 and 9.15 forms an inclusio. It is grace all the way home.

There is little in 2 Corinthians 8–9 that is unique. Paul's genius lies in his ability to adopt the ideas and language of Jewish, Christian and even pagan sources, only to make something entirely new of them. Paul can use topics found in Greco-Roman rhetorical handbooks and present Jewish-Christian ideas in Hellenistic dress. He uses the language of benefaction, known in Hebrew Scripture and in Greco-Roman literature, to develop a theological understanding of Christian beneficence. Indeed, 2 Corinthians 8–9 is not so much about the collection as it is about Paul's theological understanding of grace and apostolic criteria.

Ostensibly Paul writes to enlist the Corinthians in a collection for the poor Jerusalem saints. There is no reason to believe Paul was not interested in the collection. However, the offering is his opportunity to 'test the genuineness of your love [for me] against the earnestness of others' [the Macedonians] (8.8). To accomplish his purpose, Paul exploits the language of benefaction. However, throughout he parodies benefaction. With invective he appeals to a competitive spirit by describing Macedonian generosity to shame the Corinthians into participating in the offering. He repeatedly says the offering is voluntary, but he makes it a test and challenges their Christian credentials (9.13). He parodies letters of recommendation (8.16-24).

Paul offers them the privilege of becoming benefactors with him. Benefactors usually receive glory and honor for their beneficence. However, Paul inverts the system when he speaks of the 'benefits' that will accrue to them. The Jerusalem saints will honor God, not the Corinthians. They will thank God, not the Corinthians. Paul calls into question the zealous desires of the Corinthians to be the apostle's patron and make him their client. If they participate in the collection, they can prove their loyalty to Paul and their Christian credentials by their 'obedience to the confession of the gospel of Christ'. Saints at Jerusalem will long for and pray for the Corinthians because of the 'surpassing grace of God' upon them.

Human beneficence begins and ends with God. God is the Supreme Benefactor from whom all beneficence originates. Anaphorically, Paul reminds the Corinthians that all beneficence is a form of grace. As a benefactor to the Corinthians, Paul is a servant of Christ (2.14), of God (6.4), and of the Corinthians (4.5). The benefaction of grace is antithetical to the Greco-Roman patronage system. Their gift to Jerusalem becomes

God's gift and with Paul the saints cry 'Thanks be to God'. If the Corinthians will prove their loyalty to Paul and accept the beneficence of grace, they can validate their claim to be Christian. For Paul, apostleship, gospel and salvation are inseparably bonded. Paul's concerns are pastoral and he believes the salvation of the Corinthians depends on their acceptance of his apostleship and the gospel of Christ as Paul articulates it.

A Parodic Defense of Authority (2 Corinthians 10–13)

Scholars have made much ado about the sharp turn at 2 Cor. 10.1, following 9.15. If the argument advanced thus far is correct, the break may not be as great as commentators have thought. Paul is 'testing' their obedience in chapters 1–7. Parody in chapters 1–7 concludes with a subversion of expectation as Paul becomes prosecutor and the Corinthians are on trial, albeit with a provisional acquittal. There are hints in chapter 7 that Paul has not restored paradise in the church.

A parody of beneficence (chs. 8–9), closes with a subversion of expectation as Paul upends all the expectations of the patronage system. He has extended the promise that the Corinthians might become benefactors. In the grand finale, the Jesus people in Jerusalem are glorifying and honoring God, not the Corinthians. They give thanks to God with the jubilant, 'Thanks be to God for God's indescribable gift!' God, not the Corinthians, is the Benefactor. The Corinthians will not receive a 'Thank You' card; they will not even get credit for the gift. Paul is 'testing' their love [loyalty] and they can verify their loyalty to the apostle and their Christian credentials by contributing to the collection.

At 2.1-3; 12.21; 13.1 and possibly at 8.4 Paul indicates plans for another visit to Corinth. He suggests the possibility of a visit at 9.4. Later (12.14; 13.1) Paul solidifies his plans and he definitely intends to visit Corinth. Everything in chapters 10–13 anticipates that visit (13.10), including the comprehensive appeal of 10.1-6. Paul supports his appeal, first, by his insistence that he will not fail to deal with trouble-makers (10.2-6) and then, more extensively by remarks about apostolic authority (10.7-11) and his jurisdiction in Corinth (10.12-18). In chs. 10–13, as in chapters 1–9, parody is the literary form Paul chooses to use.

A number of clues throughout 2 Corinthians points to the unity of 2 Corinthians. At 1.17 and 10.10 Paul responds to the perception that he is fickle. The apostle is not a 'peddler of God's word' (2.17); he does not 'adulterate God's word' (4.4) and he will not accept money from the Corinthians now (11.7-12). Paul refuses to practice 'deceit' (4.2), takes precautions in financial matters (8.20) but believes the Corinthians suspect him of chicanery (12.16-18). Throughout, Paul affirms love for the Corinthians (2.4; 8.7; 11.11; cf. 6.11; 7.3). At 2.9 Paul 'tests' their obedience, at 8.7 he tests their love and loyalty and at 13.5 he admonishes them to 'test' themselves because he has passed the 'test' (13.5-6).

Tribulation catalogs appear at 4.8-9, 6.4-10, 11.23-29 and 12.10. Fitzgerald (*Cracks*, p. 187) argues that the hardship list at 6.4-10 presupposes 4.8-9 and prepares for 11.23-29 and 12.10. Constantly Paul refers to benefits he hopes the Corinthians will receive from his ministry (1.5, 7, 24; 3.2-3; 4.5, 12; 7.3; 8.16; 10.8; 12.19; 13.10). In chs. 1-9 there are nine occurrences of the term 'boast' and its cognates; there is one occurrence in chs. 8–9 and 19 in chs. 10–13. Commendation language appears at 3.1-3; 4.2; 5.12; 6.4; 7.3; 8.16-20; 10.8; 12.19; 13.10. In chapters 1–7 Paul parodies a defense of apostolic behavior, in chs. 8–9 he parodies beneficence and in chs. 10–13 he parodies a defense of apostolic authority. Moreover, there is no textual evidence for any partition hypothesis in 2 Corinthians.

Bjerkelund (pp. 149-55) observes that Paul's thanksgivings or doxologies customarily precede a 'beseeching' period, as in Rom 12.1; a 'beseeching' period at 1 Thess. 4.1 follows a thanksgiving in 3.11-13. Thus, there is no more reason to sever 2 Corinthians 10–13 from 2 Corinthians 1–9 than Romans 12 from Romans 1–11 or 1 Thessalonians 4–5 from 1 Thessalonians 1–3. Indeed, the tone changes more sharply between 10.18 and 11.1 than between 9.15 and 10.1. At 2 Cor. 10.1 and Gal. 5.2 Paul reverts to first person singular. In both 2 Corinthians 10–13 and Galatians 5–6 the syntax is more abrupt and the style more violent than in the main body of the letters (Bates, pp. 56-59). In 2 Corinthians 10–13 and Galatians 5–6 there is more frequent use of the first person singular. Galatians 5–6 add nothing of substance to chs. 1–4 and 2 Corinthians 10–13 is a recapitulation of chs. 1–9 (Bates, p. 67).

After a speaker states the facts, the next step 'is to make the audience feel the right emotions—pity, indignation, anger, hatred, envy, emulation, antagonism or whatever the case requires' (Aristotle, *Rhetoric* 3.19.1419b). Fitzgerald ('2 Cor. 10–13', pp. 190-200). maintains that these chapters are Paul's final attempt to persuade the Corinthians and avoid the use of discipline. Demosthenes (*De Corona* 278) used this technique to justify his closing histrionics by asking, 'But under what circumstances ought the politician and orator to be vehement? Of course, when the city is in any way imperiled and when the public is faced by adversaries. Such is the obligation of a noble and patriotic citizen'. Paul believes his converts are in danger and it is his duty to do whatever it takes to persuade them. When Paul 'defends' his apostolate, he believes he is defending the gospel; to reject his apostleship is to reject the gospel he preaches.

1. 'Defense' of Apostolic Authority (10.1-18)

a. 'When Present ... When Present' (10.1-11)

'When present' at v. 2 and 'When present' at v. 11 forms an inclusio and delimits a unit. Paul continues a parodic defense on five fronts: (1) Humility and boldness (v. 1b); (2) Living 'according to the flesh' (v. 2b); (3) Belonging to Christ (v. 7b); (4) Boasting too much (v. 8a); (5) Weighty letters, weak presence (v. 10). Without 'mirror reading', we cannot say Paul is responding to 'charges' at Corinth. There is no doubt that problems exist and Paul perceives that these issues require attention. At v. 2b, Paul says 'the ones who think'; at v. 7b he delivers a direct challenge; at v. 10b, 'they say'; at v. 11a 'Let such people'. Paul's style, not outside 'opponents', may be responsible for the 'charges'. Apuleius of Madura's *Apology* against magic provides evidence that stating charges and responding to them was a standard literary technique in ancient literature.

This 'defense' *in absentia* begins with a request formula (10.1-2). The phrase 'I myself, Paul' is emphatic and expresses authority, as well as more personal involvement (cf. 2 Cor. 12.13; Rom. 7.25; 9.3; 15.4). Coupled with a formula for authority, it is surprising to hear 'appeal to you', suggesting a request, not a command. Paul dons the mantle of apostolic authority but moderates it with an 'appeal'. His approach is one of confidence blended with humility. This combination is not a problem (so Bjerklund, p. 190) and Paul can speak to the congregations, knowing they will acknowledge his apostleship. However, authority is problematic in this context. Paul parodies a life and death struggle for his apostleship but the struggle is really for the salvation of the Corinthian church (12.19).

Paul makes his appeal 'through the meekness and gentleness of Christ' (10.1a). When Paul delivers an appeal, the verb of entreaty precedes a prepositional phrase. Bjerklund (pp. 164-67) has shown that this combination functions as an oath formula. Ancient texts often pair meekness and gentleness (e.g. Philo, *Op. Mund.* 103; Plutarch, *Pericles* 39.1; Lucian, *The Dream* X). The two terms overlap in meaning, forming a hendiadys describing a gentle, humble and modest attitude (Leivestad, pp. 159-60). The term translated 'gentleness' also means 'graciousness' and tends to connote 'forbearance as contrasted with vindictiveness' (BAGD, *s.v.*). Aristotle (*Nicomachean Ethics* 4.5.1-12) translates the term, 'slowness to anger'.

This description probably reveals no knowledge Paul has of the character of the earthly Jesus (against Kümmel, *Introduction*, p. 273; Plummer, p. 273) and probably is not an echo of Mt. 11.29. More likely, Paul refers to the pre-existent Lord, who, through condescension to incarnation became lowly, weak and poor (Leivestad, p. 172). This view is consonant with the kenotic theology of 8.9 and Rom. 15.3. At 8.9 there is a clear cross reference to 6.10, making Paul a 'second Christ'. Often he associates himself with the kenotic ('self-emptying', cf. Phil. 2.5-11) Christ.

Humility and boldness is Paul's first issue. With self-inflicted irony Paul parodically describes himself as 'humble when face to face with you, but bold toward you when I am away!' (10.1). This fallacy recalls 1.17; in both cases, Paul perceives that they believe he vacillates. Interestingly, at 8.10-11, Paul suggests the same weakness in the Corinthians. Paul's statement is a variation on a common charge against politicians: all words and no performance (cf. Marshall, *Enmity*, pp. 118, 499). Hellenistic writers often employed the topic of 'humility' to denigrate flatterers. With demeaning language, Paul ironically characterizes himself as humble at home, bold when he writes. The term translated 'humility' means being stripped of one's dignity and sense of worth. It may connote 'nothingness', reduced to such an elemental state as seems not to exist (Philo, *Rer. Div. Her.* 29). It describes a person who is uncultured, lowly and of no account (BAGD, *s.v.*).

A pusillanimous, groveling apostle when present, Paul becomes bold when he is away. Humility and boldness are antithetical. Here, in contrast to humility, boldness connotes haughtiness, arrogance, even insolence or impudence. This antithetical parallelism forms a chiasmus.

face to face	humble
bold	being away

The chiasmus reveals two contradictory attitudes, servility and arrogance. Verse 11 completes the inclusio and the antitheses create another chiasmus:

What we say	When absent
When present	We will do

Suggestions that this is a 'new crisis' in chapters 10–13 are not necessary. Apparently Paul had not acted authoritatively on his 'painful visit' as he had threatened to do (1 Cor. 4.18-21). He had promised to visit Corinth but had broken the promise. While he was 'away', he wrote a painful letter (2.4; 7.8) that made him appear inconsistent (1.17). Reflecting on this misapprehension, Paul describes himself as sniveling when present, but when absent as 'a craven dog that barks loudly at a safe distance' (P.E. Hughes, *Second Corinthians*, p. 346). He had to deal with the painful letter in chapters 1–2; now he must speak to the misperception that his 'letters are weighty and strong, but his bodily presence is weak, and his speech contemptible' (10.10). Perhaps the crisis is not so 'new' after all (contra Barrett, *Commentary*, p. 244).

Witherington (p. 437) thinks Paul is answering his opponents but addressing the Corinthians because he cares about them and does not want them to be swayed by such slander. Witherington thinks the function is to build the self-esteem of the Corinthians! This view harmonizes poorly with Paul's appeal that he prefers not to demonstrate apostolic boldness in Corinth (10.2). The 'majority' supported Paul against an offender (2.6) but apparently a minority [wealthy?] did not. At 10.2 Paul does not wish to be bold with 'some' at Corinth. The apostle wants to 'build up' the Corinthians (10.8; 13.10). So, where are the alleged 'opponents?' More probably, he again wants the church to act on his behalf against the [same?] slanderers as at 2.6.

Paul begs 'Please do not make it necessary for me to be bold when I am present' (10.2; Talbert, p. 112). The appeal in v. 2 resumes the one in v. 1 and, here, as at 5.20, he is 'entreating' the Corinthians. Against Bultmann (*2 Corinthians*, p. 183) the 'but' in v. 2 is probably resumptive, not emphatic. This apparent Corinthian misunderstanding assumes Paul can be 'bold' only at a distance. What Paul lacks in boldness, he would prefer not to produce and one should be cautious about provoking the apostle. His humility can change to boldness without notice because he has apostolic 'confidence' (1.9, 15; 2.3; 3.4). He takes second place to no one (10.7). On the basis of his confidence Paul has decided now to be 'bold' against Corinthian muckrakers—to venture on an attack, almost to challenge them (10.12; 11.21). 'Boldness' may imply to be so bold as to challenge a possible danger, to dare (Louw *et al.*, §25.161). Still he does not want to be 'audacious' and pleads with the majority to help him avoid a showdown.

Anaphoric use of 'to decide' (twice at 10.2; once at 10.7, 11; 11.5; 12.6; cf. 3.5) signifies its importance. It may be an allusion to a slogan of the Corinthian minority with a presumption to judge Paul and whose 'decision' he repudiates in v. 4 by 'overthrowing arguments', so that 'to decide' connotes 'to fancy oneself' (Bultmann, *2 Corinthians*, p 184). Accordingly, 'I fancy myself' is ironic and properly belongs within quotation marks. The sneering opinion that Paul lives 'according to the flesh' supports an ironic interpretation. Paul does not think highly of such an 'opinion' and believes that by the power of God he can overthrow their arguments (v. 4).

A second battleground for Paul is that he lives 'according to the flesh' (v. 3). At v. 3 Paul's anger has reached the point of war (*strateuesthai*). He lives 'in the flesh', but not 'according to the flesh', forming an antithesis at 10.3. He denies waging war according to worldly standards (cf. 5.16a). To live 'according to the flesh' is to be unreliable and insincere (cf. 1 Cor. 3.3). Antithetically, Paul says his weapons of warfare are not 'fleshly', but his weapons of war are 'according to the power of God'. With divine weapons he can destroy 'arguments and every proud obstacle raised up against the knowledge of God' (10.4b-5).

Paul's pleonastic use of military metaphors is remarkable: making war, weapons, warfare, strongholds, high things, taking captive, state of readiness. Although he does not want war, he is in a state of readiness for war and will not fight 'according to the flesh'. With weapons of divine power, he will bring down bulwarks, false reasoning and every rampart that opposes the knowledge of God. The knowledge of God is the gospel he proclaims everywhere (cf. 2.14; 4.6). His formulation, 'the knowledge of God' may be an allusion to the 'knowledge' of which the Corinthians boast (1 Cor. 8.11-13) but deny to Paul (11.6).

At v. 6 Paul reveals that the purpose of his appeal is to gain the obedience of the Corinthians, a purpose already implicit in v. 2. Soon Paul will visit Corinth and he wants to avoid a bold confrontation. He does not want to exercise apostolic authority to punish them (13.10; cf. 12.21; 13.2; 1 Cor. 4.21). Apostolic authority is 'for building you up and not for tearing you down' (10.8). Paul thinks of himself as a 'parent' (11.2; 12.14) to the Corinthians who combines gentle appeal with the threat of severe action if they do not heed the entreaty.

If his plea should prove unpersuasive, Paul will resort to power and force (cf. 1 Cor. 4.16-21). He is going to Corinth (1 Cor. 4.19; 2 Cor. 2.4; 12.21; 13.1); his demeanor depends on their response (1 Cor. 4.21; 2 Cor. 12.20; 13.10). Paul may go in meekness or with a rod (1 Cor. 4.20-21), as a storm trooper (10.3-6) or in the weakness he displayed at Corinth (1 Cor. 2.3). The decision is theirs and they will come to the right decision only if they realize that Paul is God's approved apostle (10.18) and that Christ speaks in him (13.3). At 13.6 Paul informs them that he has passed the 'test'. The one who is not 'counterfeit' is obviously 'genuine' and has the commendation of God (10.18). Paul believes that once the Corinthians recognize his credentials, their esteem for him will increase (10.15). He closes his appeal by reiterating what he said at 10.8, 'I write these things while I am away from you, so that when I come, I may not have to be severe in using the authority that Lord has given me for building up and not for tearing down' (13.10).

'In readiness' denotes a present state, not a continual state. He is ready to 'punish all disobedience'. The term 'punish' is forensic and indicates the intention to render justice to the disobedient Corinthians. Paul's style is awkward because his concern is with two groups: (1) 'When your obedience is complete' indicates one group; and (2) 'Punish all disobedience' is a threat to the minority troublemakers. We have no information about what is lacking in the first group. As in v. 5, Paul is probably thinking of obedience to Christ, but he also wants them to be obedient to him. Obedience to Christ would be obedience to the apostle (contra Furnish, p. 459). In 2 Corinthians, there is an inseparable bond between Christ, the apostle and the gospel.

'Belonging to Christ' is a third combat zone for Paul (v. 7b). Significantly, Paul does not deny that the Corinthians belong to Christ, but only asserts that he also belongs to Christ. However, at 11.13-15, he seems to have doubts about their commitment to Christ. Scholars differ on the mood of the verb 'see'. Robinson (p. 26) thinks it is indicative and ironic: 'You see only the end of your nose'. J.H. Kennedy (p. 184) reads it as an interrogative. Furnish (p. 465) and others think it is imperative. The form Paul uses here is usually imperative in his letters (1 Cor. 8.9; 10.18; 16.10; Gal. 5.15; Phil. 3.2; Eph. 5.15; Col. 2.8; 4.17). He is saying 'Look out for...'

At v. 7 Paul throws down the gauntlet to the Corinthians (but see Bultmann, *2 Corinthians*, p. 187). With confrontational language, Paul challenges: 'Look at what is right in front of you!' At 10.7, as at 10.1, 'according to face' means 'face to face'. Paul's challenge is 'If anyone thinks they belong to Christ, look at me because I also belong to Christ'. This challenge is similar to the one at 13.5-6, 'Examine yourselves...I have passed the test'.

Data does not permit a precise definition of 'belonging to Christ', but the theological imperative, 'Look...Christ' leaves no doubt about who is in charge. Paul refuses to let anyone draw a circle that excludes him. 'Belonging to Christ' taken with 11.23 and the context of chapters 10–13 probably means Paul uses the phrase in a forensic sense. At 11.23, Paul, like one who is insane, claims to be a superior servant of Christ. Paul's plea of insanity is, of course, ironic. There was at Corinth, as Betz demonstrates (*Der Apostel*, pp. 132-37) a problem of evidence. If the Corinthians will open their eyes, the evidence is staring them in the face.

Boasting too much about his authority is a fourth issue requiring attention. Verses 8-10 seem to restate the 'present...absent' problem in v. 1. Verse 9 indicates an allusion to a 'boast' in his letters. The object of his boast is his apostolic authority, as in 13.10. His letters are replete with boasts and authoritative language but face to face, Paul behaves like a milksop. When present, Paul does not demonstrate 'power' appropriate to the office of an apostle of Christ. Paul responds that his 'authority' is a gift from God 'for building you up and not for tearing you down' (v. 8a). Defiantly, he declares, 'I will not be ashamed of it' (v. 8b). One-upmanship or winning a debate has no interest to one who wants to 'build up' the Corinthians. Paul's authority is from the Lord and verifies that he belongs to Christ (v.7). Verse 8 provides the basis for v. 7 and anyone who denies that Paul 'belongs to Christ' and contests his authority will get a taste of his authority as one who 'belongs to Christ'.

'Now even if' (not simply 'if', BDF, §443.3) is not a concession that Paul boasts too much (contra Bultmann, *2 Corinthians*, p. 188). The syntax and the subjunctive aorist of 'boast' show clearly that the statement is hypothetical, although at 11.1–12.18 he will 'play the fool' as he boasts. Verse 8 addresses the Corinthians ('you'), not outside, hostile intruders. Paul is not talking about 'boasting too much' so much as making a comparative statement (Barrett, *Commentary*, pp. 258-59). He has boasted about belonging to Christ. Now, if he should boast about his authority, no one will discredit him. Here we have the first of many instances of boasting in chs. 10–13 (10.8, 13, 15, 16, 17; 11.12, 16, 18, 30; 12.1, 5, 6, 9; the noun at 11.10, 17).

The exact link between vv. 8 and 9 remains uncertain. A resolution hinges on the force of 'that I might not seem'. The NEB regards the 'in order that' as imperatival and opening a new sentence, 'So you must not think of me...'. The NRSV starts a new sentence but regards it as indicative. Barrett (*Second Corinthians*, pp. 258-59) thinks Paul is saying, 'But I will say no more about this authority'. The NRSV rendition, 'I do not want to seem as though I am trying to frighten you' obscures the point. Through a colloquial turn of speech Paul is saying, 'as though all I can do is scare people through letters'. Verse 10 supports this interpretation of v. 9. Paul knows how to exercise authority 'face to face' as well as 'through letters'.

'To frighten' is an intensive compound verb: to terrify, intimidate or frighten to distraction. Paul has no intention of scaring the Corinthians out of their wits. The real question is whether Paul can exercise, 'face to face', the authority he assumes in letters. Verse 10 indicates that 'through letters' refers to previous letters and not to the present letter. Indeed, Paul must still confront the topic of 'weighty letters' and 'weak presence and contemptible speech' (10.10).

Verse 10 is the clue for interpreting 10.1-11. Most translations render the verb *phēsin as* 'they say' in v. 10. The verb is singular and more accurately translates 'he/she says'. Paul's use here is typical of the ancient diatribe form (Kustas, p. 11; BDF, §130.3) and means 'one says', but is indefinite and nonspecific. Pauline rhetoric, not calumniators in Corinth, is responsible for 'charges' in this paragraph. Perhaps 'one says' indicates that the criticism originated with one individual (Barrett, *Second Corinthians*, p. 260; Talbert, *Commentary*, p. 112); it may be the offender of 2.4 who leads a [wealthy?] minority at Corinth. Bruce (*Paul*, p. 73) paraphrases v. 10 rather humorously:

> He will not say 'Boo' to a goose when he is here himself...but when he is away he pretends to be bold and fearless and writes strong letters; if he were sure of his authority, he would show some of his letter-writing severity when he is dealing with us face to face.

Insincerity seems to be one of, if not the, most pressing issue for Paul. Paul begins this letter with the assertion that he has 'behaved in the world with frankness and godly sincerity' (1.12). Apparently, failure to make a promised visit evoked suspicions of insincerity (1.13–2.4) at Corinth. Interestingly, Paul's letters were as problematic for the Corinthian reader as for the modern reader. At 2.17 he affirms his sincerity and develops the theme at 4.2-6 and 4.13–5.10. The lachrymose (tearful) letter takes center stage in ch. 7 where there are hints of remaining problems at Corinth, as confirmed by 8.20-22. Even his precautions did not resolve the matter (12.14-18). Chapter 13 provides evidence that inconsistency in face-to-face encounters and communications in his letters are still a problem. Paul concludes 'So I write these things while I am away from you, so that when I come, I may not have to be severe in using the authority that the Lord has given me for building you up and not for tearing you down' (13.10). This theme persists throughout the letter.

When he is away, Paul's letters are 'weighty and strong' but the apostle cuts a sorry figure when he appears—'his bodily presence is weak'. Epictetus (3.22.86-88) testifies to the importance of physical appearance for the communicator. Aeschines (*Against Timarchus* 26), four centuries later, ridiculed Timarchus for appearing in public with his 'body so shamefully debilitated by drink and debauchery'. At the beginning of the Socratic Apology, Socrates alludes to this problem regarding himself. Paul's weak bodily appearance denotes his demeanour, not an illness.

Contemptible speech and weak appearance are parallel, not consecutive, attributions. Paul uses the same parallel with 'contemptible' and 'weak' at 1 Cor. 1.27-28. Bultmann (*2 Corinthians*, p. 218) thinks everything in 11.23-29 is under the viewpoint of weakness in ironic reference to 10.1, 10. Bultmann (*2 Corinthians*, p. 190) also believes that 11.6 is an ironic reference to contemptible speech in 10.10. Here, as in 10.1, Paul states the antithesis chiastically.

Letters when away	Bodily weakness when present
Weakness and contemptible speech	Heavy and weighty

Throughout 10.1-11 inconsistency is an issue. Apparently the perception is that he has no pneumatic power and is thus a charlatan. In a firm rebuttal, Paul seeks to put the matter to rest: 'Let such people understand that what we say in word by letters when absent, we will also do in deed when present' (v. 11). The chiastic structure shows Paul is still working with the 'present...absent' motif he used in v. 1.

In word	Being absent
Being present	In deed

In an almost threatening tone, Paul warns that anyone who thinks he inconsistent in presence and by letters will soon learn that Paul does what he says.

Throughout 2 Corinthians Paul presents himself as a benefactor to the Corinthians and uses the word-pair 'word and deed' ironically. He wants to be the kind of person who is recognized as a benefactor who 'builds up' (v. 8). Instead, he faces the possibility that some destruction may be necessary to protect his congregation. The stage is set for the irony and satire in the rest of the letter. Persons familiar with modes of expressions among Cynic philosophers (e.g. Epictetus 3.22.81-82) would recognize that beneath the vehemence there breathed the spirit of a loving parent, or perhaps a loving pastor.

b. Self-Commendation (10.12-18)

An inclusio or ring composition ('commend', v. 12; 'commends', v. 18) holds this section together. Verse 12 is the introduction, followed by two corresponding segments (vv. 13-14 and vv. 15-18). In his introductory statement the apostle rejects any comparison of himself with other people whose self-commendation presupposes comparing themselves with one another. The dilemma is that Paul must state that he does not and will not boast as others do, and at the same time, he must show that he is superior to them in apostolic authority and power. If boasting is a necessity, Paul will offer a parodic commendation.

The anemic translation 'Now that we venture' (v. 12, RSV) blunts the satirical double-edged jab of Paul's Greek. Sarcasm sharpens the parody as Paul announces 'I do not dare to classify or compare myself with persons who commend themselves' (v. 12; cf. 11.21). The verb is 'to be so bold as to challenge or defy possible danger or opposition' (Louw *et al.*, §25.161). Sarcasm persists with the indictment of self-commenders, 'they do not show good sense' (v. 12b). Paul will not go beyond the realm of propriety by comparing himself with 'fools' (cf. 11.21). Parody enables him to criticize persons who commend themselves.

The introductory 'for' in v. 12 is ironical (Bultmann, *2 Corinthians*, p. 192). In vv. 2-6 Paul makes it clear that he can be bold when necessary; that is the point of v. 11. Against Windisch (*Korintherbrief*, p. 308), there is no evidence of a hiatus between vv. 11 and 12 due to 'a pause in dictation'. 'I do not dare' is ironic, as though Paul's refusal to be daring is a 'weakness' when he is denoting his 'superiority'. Here Paul no longer speaks with 'meekness and gentleness' (v. 1), but with superior pride. He refuses to lower himself to the level of self-commenders. With wordplay Paul is saying something like 'I will not pair...or... compare...' (Plummer, p. 286; BAGD, *s.v.*). He will not make himself an 'equal' with such people. Piquant sarcasm suggests that the self-aggrandizers 'measure themselves by themselves' (v. 12).

Taut structure in v. 12 reveals Paul's skill as he balances 'For I do have the audacity' with 'They have no understanding'. He balances 'to class or compare myself' with 'compare themselves with one another'. It is a scathing indictment against persons who commend themselves and compare themselves with one another. He parodies 'self-commendation' because he would not want to be their 'equal'. At v. 12 Paul begins a demonstration of his ingenious expertise with words and leaves to the imagination the proportional weights of the deeds promised in v. 11. The tactic of comparing one person with another of acknowledged superiority is a form of mock-praise (Betz, *Der Apostel*, pp. 119-21; Forbes, pp. 1-30).

Paul disavows 'self-praise' (v. 12) but seems unable to avoid it. Plutarch, in his discussion of 'self-praise', observes that 'not many, even of those who condemn such conduct, avoid the odium of it' (*Moralia*, 539A-b). It is a no-win situation because Paul does not believe he is inferior to the 'super apostles' or 'false brothers' (11.5) even when he adds 'I am nothing' (13.5). Although done 'in foolishness', Paul boldly compares himself with these people. Demosthenes (*De Corona* 3-4) similarly claims to have been in a no-win situation in which to praise himself would lead to public disapproval but to fail to defend his reputation would suggest he was incapable of doing so.

After satirizing the self-commenders, Paul contrasts it with his 'measured' approach to self-praise. The 'we' in v. 13 is in emphatic contrast with 'they' in v. 12. Paul does not 'boast beyond limits' but he 'keeps within the field God has assigned' to him (v. 13). To boast 'within limits' explains v. 12 and is the theme of vv. 13-16. As an apostle, he will not boast excessively or beyond the limits of propriety. In v. 15, Paul repeats the phrase, suggesting he is also thinking of the proper limits regarding areas where he has planted the gospel. He will not boast beyond 'a sphere of action, influence or province' (BAGD, *s.v.*) or beyond 'the measure of jurisdiction' (Furnish, p. 471) God has assigned to him.

In this context, 'to boast' refers to apostolic authority (v. 8), including Corinth (vv. 13-15) and beyond (v. 16; see Barrett, *Second Corinthians*, pp. 264-65). Paul writes 'measured' instead of 'gave', suggesting the share due to one in a distribution. The criterion of boasting is the one God set. When Paul boasts, he will 'boast in the Lord' (v. 17). Paul still maintains his claim on the Corinthians with the phrase 'and to reach out as far as you' (v. 13). The emphatic 'and' gives the force of 'yes, surely, precisely you, too fall within my jurisdiction' (Bultmann, *2 Corinthians*, p. 194). His mission to Corinth did not overreach God's assignment.

Verses 14-16 form one sentence and state that Paul has jurisdiction according to God's assignment. 'Not overstretching myself' (v. 14) replaces 'not boasting beyond measure' in v. 13. He was not overstretching God's boundaries when he went to Corinth. He is saying, 'In coming to you, I did not exceed the limits of God's boundaries for me'. Moreover, he can justly claim 'I was the first to come all the way to you with the gospel of Christ' (v. 14). Thus, he supports his claim that God assigned Corinth to him. However, unless one resorts to 'mirror reading', it does not prove the presence of rival missionaries in Corinth (Fridrichsen, p. 21). Paul formulates the so-called 'charges' in 2 Corinthians. The conundrum of identifying opponents in any Pauline letter arises from the transparent fact that our only source of information is Paul's unmistakably one-sided, probably overstated, even distorted portrayals of them (Barrett, *Second Corinthians*, pp. 35-38). Detached objectivity would have served poorly Paul's purpose (cf. Mussner, pp. 24-27). He wants to establish apostolic authority and jurisdiction over the Corinthians.

Verse 15 repeats vv. 12-13, but with the addition 'in the labors of others', Paul gives 'beyond measure' concrete meaning as poaching on another's missionary territory. The term translated 'labors' often refers to missionary labors. Here the labors are specifically taking the gospel to places that no one has evangelized. Paul would agree with a proverb that Plutarch quotes: 'One who sets foot in someone else's chorus is a meddler and a laughingstock' ('On Inoffensive Praise', *Moralia* 540b). Paul has not set foot in another person's chorus; he planted the gospel in Corinth and has the right to boast (v. 14). Paul became their 'father', a claim no one else can make (1 Cor. 4.15) and he is their 'parent' (12.14).

Always the eternal optimist, Paul still hopes all will end well in Corinth (cf. 1.7, 10, 13; 5.11; 7.6-16; 10.15c-16; 13.6). The basis of his hope is that as 'your faith increases' it will enlarge the sphere of action among the Corinthians and beyond (v. 16). 'Faith' may refer to their faith in Paul's gospel or faithfulness to his mission which will act as a support for his future ministry. Here, Paul includes both meanings of the term. 'Hope' in the New Testament is always a 'good hope' which anticipates and articulates the Christian's confidence in God. Paul wants to avoid any misconception that maintenance of 'limits' restricts him to Corinth or his present achievements. His motive is not modesty, but 'having hope' expresses his proud superiority over persons who poach on another missionary's territory.

Paul's hope lies in the phrase 'to be magnified among you...to excess' (Bultmann, *2 Corinthians*, p. 196). He is saying, 'as your faith grows I will be magnified to excess among you' or 'I will be exalted to the loftiest heights among you'. Paul hopes to achieve greatness among the Corinthians. Of course, he qualifies such high esteem with the delimiting phrase 'within our sphere'. This phrase supports the interpretation of 'faith' as faithfulness or loyalty to Paul's apostolate and his gospel. The result of their increased loyalty will be the recognition that Corinth is part of Paul's bailiwick. The infinitive 'to preach', like 'to magnify', goes with 'our hope is' (v. 15). He hopes to preach 'in lands that lie beyond you' (v. 16; BDF §205). Paul may be thinking of places to the West, perhaps Spain (Rom. 15.24, 28). He will not boast in the labors of any other person.

In vv. 15b-16 Paul underscores his determination to preach only in virgin territory. Everything in these verses relates to the phrase 'but having hope'.

> But having hope
>   as your faith increases
>   I may be exalted among you
>   I may preach the gospel in areas beyond you
>   I may not boast in the work of another

Paul has a hope that their faithfulness will increase and that their intensified loyalty will increase his status among them. He hopes their validation of his apostleship will launch him into virgin mission fields and that he will not boast in work already done by other missionaries. The exaltation for which Paul hopes will empower him for yet greater tasks, reaching for 'the cosmic range of the mission' (Käsemann, 'Die Legitimät', p. 306). Paul will never be content with past accomplishments; success for him is a moving target (cf. Phil. 3.13-14).

Deflecting attention from himself to 'the Lord', Paul enunciates a fundamental principle for boasting: 'Let the one who boasts, boast in the Lord' (v. 17). His appeal to Scripture (LXX Jer. 9.24) gives authority to the admonition and reflects knowledge of the conventions of self-praise. Ancient orators know that audiences find self-praise offensive. Plutarch ('On Praising Oneself Inoffensively', *Moralia* 539-547F) offers the most extensive ancient discussion of self-praise. He thinks of it in terms of any autobiographical remark. While Plutarch distinguishes justified self-praise and empty flattery (539C), he believes self-praise easily becomes self-deification. One may boast if one attributes part of the success to God (Plutarch, 'How to Tell a Flatterer From a Friend', *Moralia* 48E-49A). Perhaps unwittingly, Paul conforms to the convention by boasting 'in the Lord'.

Boasting in the Lord is a Pauline principle and means one's acceptance of the righteousness that God bestows in Christ as a gift of grace (Rom. 3.24-26; 1 Cor. 4.7). At 1 Cor. 1.31 Paul quotes LXX Jer. 9.24, relating it to grace, and he writes of boasting 'in Christ Jesus' (Phil. 3.3, 9) and 'in the cross of our Lord Jesus Christ' (Gal. 6.14). Paul's inclusio for this passage is the verb 'to commend' at vv. 12, 18 and its impact could not have been lost on the audience. Paul explains that the meaning of boasting in the Lord is that 'it is not those who commend themselves that are approved, but those whom the Lord commends' (v. 18). The hookword is 'commend' and the issue is one's sphere that God assigns. What matters most to Paul is the commendation of God (1 Cor. 4.1-5). True praise comes from God, not from oneself or other people.

The apostle condemns all self-commendation (3.1-3; 5.12) and he wants only God's commendation. Apparently the Corinthians want some 'proof of authenticity' from Paul (12.12; 13.3); they want to know whether he is 'unapproved' (13.5). Insofar as Paul responds with any self-commendation, he does so hesitantly and with important qualifications, as in 4.2 and 6.4. Since the Corinthians came to Christ through his ministry, the Lord has commended his ministry (1 Cor. 2.1-5). Therefore, any defense of his credentials must be parodic. God has given him jurisdiction at Corinth and the Corinthians have no jurisdiction over his apostleship.

2. The Foolishness of Boasting (11.1–12.18)

After a brief discussion of the proper limits of boasting, Paul turns to a lengthy exercise in foolish boasting (11.1–12.18). An inclusio, 'not inferior to these super apostles' (11.5) and 'not inferior to these super apostles' (12.11) binds this unit of discourse. Anaphoric use of key words 'fool' (11.16, 17, 19, 21; 12.6), 'foolish' (11.16) and 'foolishness' (11.1) gives cohesion to the 'Foolish Discourse'. After stating the theologically and socially acceptable perspective, both Jewish and Hellenistic, on self-praise, Paul sets the stage for a superb demonstration of one-upmanship in parodic boasting. At 10.12-18, Paul criticized people who commend themselves. His criticism becomes more caustic and sarcastic in the 'Fool's Speech' (11.1–12.18). This tactic is dangerous because Paul has quoted Scripture against this sort of boasting (10.17-18).

Paul certainly boasts, but his boast is parodic. Moreover, he observes the conventions of self-praise. 'Whenever Paul writes autobiographically in apparent self-praise, he always does so inoffensively' (Lyons, p. 71). Paul claims to base his practice, not on current Hellenistic convention, but on the Hebrew Bible (Jer. 9.24; cf. 1 Cor. 1.31; 2 Cor. 10.17). He alludes to Jer. 9.24 at Phil. 3.3-4, 10. Following Rudolf Bultmann and William Beardslee, Betz (*Plutarch's*, p. 379) suggests that the application of this rule is the basis for all Pauline theology.

With a literary device called prodiorthosis, that is, advance justification (BDF §495.3), Paul begs in advance for the indulgence of the Corinthians (11.1) because he prognosticates that the braggadocio performance that will follow may antagonize some of his readers. The advance notice here is an expansive introduction to the 'Fool's Speech', which begins in earnest only with v. 21b. This 'rhetorical salve' could have been reduced to 'Let no one think I am a fool; but if you do, then accept me as a fool so that I may boast a little' (11.16b).

The extended justification of his approach may indicate Paul's anxiety about the tactic he is using. 'Only an imbecile would boast in the manner in which I am about to boast'. With that self-excoriation he hauls with him, to the heights of folly, anyone who takes pride in worldly standards of appraising success. With poignant irony, he makes use of the stock motifs of Greco-Roman adulation in amplifying his office and his beneficence for the well-being of the Corinthians, all with a view to demolishing the benefits of such indulgence. By playing the fool, he discloses what dunderheads the Corinthians are for questioning his credentials and sphere of action.

Paul assumes the role of a 'fool'—a foolish or ignorant person (BAGD, *s.v.*) which he accomplishes with the literary form, the Foolish Discourse. Betz (*Plutarch's*, p. 75) traces it to the Greek Mimus and the Platonic Socrates. Taking the role of a 'fool', Paul dons the mask of the Greek *eirōn* ('fool'). The Greeks gave the name *eirōn* to that person who slyly pretended to be less than one really was (Sedgewick, p. 7).

Because the 'fool' engages in 'foolish discourse', two literary forms, irony and parody, become prominent. Thus, the entire Foolish Discourse becomes a parody of self-praise or boasting, which inevitably uses irony. Paul must become a 'fool' because the Corinthians force him to boast, but his boast is ironic and parodic because he boasts only in his weaknesses (11.30). When an audience is reluctant to hear a speaker's message, the speaker resorts to indirect discourse and the queen of indirectness is irony 'which looks down, as it were, on plain and ordinary discourse' (Kierkegaard, *Irony*, p. 265). Quintilian (*Inst. Orat.* 9.2.46) says it was playing the role of a 'fool' that brought Socrates into disrepute. Socrates came to typify and later to dignify the term *eirōn*.

Paul's prodiorthosis (i.e. 'rhetorical ointment') opens with an unattainable 'wish' (*ophelon*, BDF §359) that the Corinthians bear with a little of his 'foolishness' and then ironically says they are already 'bearing with him'. That 'bear with me' is ironic in v. 1b is indicated by the use of 'I wish that' as well as 11.20 where he uses the same verb and irony becomes sarcasm. Fully cognizant that his boasting is not like the Lord, Paul clarifies that he is speaking 'as in foolishness' (11.17). Scathing sarcasm castigates the Corinthians as 'wise people' who bear gladly with 'fools' (v. 19). Sarcasm intensifies as the beleaguered apostle concedes, 'To my shame I must say, I was too weak for that!' (11.21). Even when he compares his 'boldness' with that of others, he acknowledges it is 'foolishness' (11.21b) and with this reference to 'foolishness', Paul begins the body of the 'Fool's Speech' (11.21b–12.10). In his *eugeneia* (pedigree, noble birth, 'bragging rights') Paul asserts that he is equal to any Israelite ('and I', 11.23), but he quickly disengages parenthetically to admit that his 'foolishness' has now reached the point of 'insanity' (11.23b).

Foolishness becomes absurdity in the paradox: 'If I must boast, I will boast in my weaknesses' (11.30). It is a no-win situation, similar to one in which Demosthenes claims to have found himself. Paul's paradoxical boast controls all boasting in this parodic defense. Corinthians force the necessity of boasting but 'it is useless' (12.1) and thus, foolish. As if momentarily departing from his role as a 'fool', Paul warrants that he could boast straightforwardly without becoming a fool (12.6a) but forfeits that right. Having completed the 'Fool's Speech', Paul begins the literary 'rhetorical salve' passage with the lamentation: 'I have become a fool!' (12.11). Consequently, the role of the 'fool', which Paul plays with exquisite skill, places 11.1–12.18 in the theater of parody (Duke, pp. 1-62; Spencer (pp. 349-60). 'Boasting in weakness' is a parody of boasting and is ironical'. (Forbes, pp. 1-30).

a. Caution: The Following May Be Offensive (11.1-21a)

1. A 'Defense' of Folly (11.1-6)

The entire prodiorthosis (advance rhetorical ointment) concentrates on the 'indulgence' idea. An inclusio, 'bear with' (vv. 1 and 20) confines this section. Significantly, this same verb appears in a Pauline catalog of surrendering (1 Cor. 4.12), but nowhere else apart from this passage, in which it is conspicuous (twice, v. 1; vv. 4, 19, 20). In his speech (*De Corona* 60), Demosthenes asks the Athenians to 'bear with' him as he regales them with his heroic exploits for Athens. The speech discusses the orator's patriotic concern for Athens. The practice of asking an audience to 'bear with' the speaker became safely ensconced in Greco-Roman rhetorical tradition. Chrysostom (*Discourse* 25.35.10) observes that his sophisticated audience refused to 'put up with' any but the most skilled orators.

Although he knows he will not get it, Paul asks the Corinthians to 'bear with' him. The mood of the Greek, 'I wish', expresses an unattainable wish. Under the guise of a 'fool', he asks that they 'endure' a bit of foolishness. 'Foolishness' is a major theme in chs. 11–12, the fact of which Paul constantly reminds his readers (11.1, 16, 19, 21; 12.6, 11). Eight of the 12 occurrences of terms in this word group in the New Testament appear here. 'Foolishness' is antithetical to 'moderation' or 'reasonableness'. Ironically, he teases them with a taunt, 'But, indeed, you do put up with me!' If the Corinthians are, in fact, indulging Paul, the request, and especially the prodiorthosis, is superfluous. If Paul assumes they will grant his wish the 'foolishness' of v. 1 does not materialize. Against Furnish (p. 485), the verb 'endure' can hardly be imperative because Paul is scarcely in a position to give orders for indulgence.

Twice Paul makes his plea that the Corinthians bear with his foolishness (11.1, 16). Verses 2-6 provide a triple motivation for the request: (1) Paul's 'divine jealousy' in view of dangers to the community (vv. 2-3); (2) the community's willingness to 'indulge' scoundrels (v. 4); (3) refusal to concede inferiority to the 'super apostles' (vv. 5-6). A brief digression (vv. 2-15) explains the reason for foolish boasting. Paul cares for the Corinthians with a 'divine jealousy', the first basis for engaging in foolish boasting. Using a nuptial metaphor, Paul explains that it is the jealousy of a father of a bride who has arranged a betrothal and is responsible for her conduct until there is a wedding; that is, the parousia. R.P. Martin (p. 332) mistakenly sees Paul as the 'friend of the bridegroom'.

Jewish custom delegates to the father of the bride the responsibility to safeguard her virginity until the groom accepts her into his house (Deut. 22.13-21). Violation of a betrothed virgin was no less serious that if the couple had consummated the marriage (Philo, *Spec. Leg.* 1.107; 3.72). The metaphor of God's betrothal to Israel is common in the Hebrew Bible (cf. Isa. 50; 54.5-6; 62.5; Ezek. 16; Hos. 2.19-20). Paul has betrothed the Corinthians to Christ (on bridal imagery, see Chavasse; Batey). Traditional Jewish social practice, known to the Corinthians through the Septuagint, bore legal overtones that assist Paul in making a strong appeal for exclusive allegiance to Christ. Greeks and Romans, as well as Jews, agreed on the importance of monogamous marriage. Paul draws his metaphor of marriage from the character of God as Israel's sole husband.

As 'father' and 'parent' (11.2; 12.14), Paul has affianced his 'daughter' to Christ. Paul's deepest desire is that, at the parousia, he might present his 'daughter' to her husband as a pure virgin (11.2). 'Present' here places the marriage metaphor in an eschatological setting. By placing 'to Christ' at the end of the sentence, Paul makes it emphatic. He gives equal weight to 'one husband' and 'pure virgin'. If Paul has betrothed Corinth to Christ, Corinthians commit adultery when they give allegiance to persons who preach 'another Jesus', 'a different spirit', or 'a different gospel' (11.4). A chiastic structure clarifies the relationship:

Marriage betrothal	To one man
To Christ	A pure virgin

Abandonment of Paul is apostasy from the true gospel for 'another Jesus'. Defectors from Paul run the risk of 'spiritual adultery'. The Corinthians think they can reject Paul and his gospel and keep Paul's Jesus. Paul says that constitutes spiritual adultery.

Their spiritual father fears the 'serpent' will deceive Corinth as it did Eve (v. 3). The apprehension qualifies Paul's desire to preserve the church's virginal dignity. In addition to Genesis 3, he may have had in mind the rabbinic legend of the serpent's sexual seduction of Eve (*Apoc. Abr*. 23; *2 Enoch* 31.6). The term 'chaste virgin' also appears at *4 Macc.* 18.6-8 and may be Paul's source for the same phrase. Such interpretations persisted in the first century CE (*1 Enoch* 69.6; *Apoc. Abr.* 23, perhaps, 1 Macc. 18.7-8). Jewish literature (Wis. 2.24; *Apoc. Mos.* 16) identifies the serpent of Genesis 3 with 'the devil' or 'Satan' (cf. Winston, pp. 121-22). Verse 14 may suggest that Paul identifies the serpent as 'Satan'.

A reference to Eve's deception alludes to Gen. 3.13 where Eve says 'The serpent deceived me and I ate'. Paul's intensive compound form of the verb renders it 'completely deceived' (P.E. Hughes, p. 375 n. 33). This rendition accentuates the totality of Eve's deception and the possible deception of the Corinthians. The serpent is 'ready to do anything' and will adopt any device of trickery for the achievement of its ends. 'Deception' here is the same word Paul uses when he affirms that he does not practice 'craftiness' (4.2), and later when he ironically calls himself a 'crafty fellow' (12.16). Satan is the consummate 'deceiver' and anyone who lures the Corinthians away from a sincere and pure devotion to Christ is satanic (11.13-15). Betz thinks Paul's use of the term goes back to anti-sophistic polemics. Paul denies being a 'deceiver' or 'charlatan' and anyone who prostitutes Christ's bride is a 'minister of Satan' (11.15).

Paul's second motivation for foolish boasting is the Corinthians' readiness to 'indulge' the 'deceivers' at Corinth (v. 4), which shows clearly that 'bear with me' (v. 1) is ironic. Verse 4 is the key for understanding the troublemakers at Corinth (Käsemann, 'Die Legitimät', p. 14; Furnish, p. 488; cf. BDF, §372) treats the 'bear with' in v. 4 as an indicative of reality that expresses 'a real condition, not just a hypothetical possibility'. Undoubtedly Paul is dealing with a real danger at Corinth (vv. 19-20), but against both Käsemann and Furnish, that fact does not prove the presence of 'outside opponents' in Corinth. At v. 3 Paul's 'fear' is hypothetical as the subjunctive verb surely confirms. Verse 4 then means that Paul fears the Corinthians 'may be led astray' or perhaps as the NRSV translates 'will be led astray'.

Context is important in the determination of a contingent element in a sentence (Dana and Mantey, p. 169). At 2 Cor. 11.4, the context is the prodiorthosis (advance justification) of a 'Fool's Discourse'. Paul is giving reasons for foolish boasting. Irony sets the tone throughout the 'Fool's Speech'. The apostle expresses an unattainable wish for 'indulgence' and now observes their readiness to 'indulge' any Machiavellian charlatan, which is almost certainly ironic. Immediately before v. 4 Paul has expressed fear (v. 3) that the Corinthians 'might be seduced away from a sincere and pure devotion to Christ' (11.4b); he does not say they have already been led astray!

In this context, Paul offers no specific reference to a person(s) and makes no allusion to any specifically heretical teaching. Therefore v. 4 expresses a possibility that reveals the source of the apostle's distress (Munck, p. 177). 'The one who comes' does not verify the presence of 'outside missionaries'. It refers to anyone who preaches a gospel unlike Paul's. In v. 4 Paul is speaking to and about Corinthians. To argue otherwise requires the presuppositions of the 'mirror reading' technique. Paul's hypothetical language keeps the focus on the Corinthians. If there were outsider agitators in Corinth, Paul deflects attention from them to the Corinthian congregation.

Nowhere else in Paul's letters are Jesus, the Spirit and the gospel united as they are in v. 4. Against Schmithals (*Gnosticism*, pp. 128-29), the adjective 'other' used with Jesus and 'different' with gospel and spirit can be used interchangeably (BAGD, *s.v.*; BDF §304.4). Any effort to use this formula to identify 'outside opponents' at Corinth is a blind alley. Debate over circumcision does not surface in 2 Corinthians. Paul's concern is not so much that someone may offer 'another gospel', as that the

Corinthians do not accept his cruciform vision of ministry. Paul's debate with Corinth was theological, but it was theology with a practical purpose. The fundamental hazard that Paul fears is rejection of his apostolic authority (10.7-18; 11.12-15), which means rejection of the gospel and of salvation from his standpoint.

A third motivation for 'foolish boasting' is that Paul claims he is in no way inferior to the 'super apostles' (vv. 5-6). Paul begins with a Greek accounting term, *logizomai*, usually translated 'I consider' or 'I think' (11.5; cf. 10:2, 7; Louw *et al.*, §57.227). When Paul reviews debits and credits and 'adds it all up', he considers that he is in absolutely no way inferior to the 'super apostles'. The 'super apostles' in v. 5 correspond to 'the one who comes' in v. 4, and perhaps to the 'pseudo apostles' (v. 13) and 'pseudo-brothers' (v. 26). In each case they are probably leaders at Corinth who have managed to secure positions of influence in the Corinthian assembly. It is possible that it is a wealthy minority led by the offender at 2.4.

Nothing in the text aids the search for the origin or identity of the 'super apostles'. Unless one resorts to 'mirror reading', they cannot discern any false teachings at Corinth. 'It is not possible to simply conclude from the words of the defense that there must have been a corresponding accusation' (Betz, 'Paul's Apology', p. 3). Interestingly, Betz and many other scholars continue to reveal the 'charges' made at Corinth. What one may safely say is that Paul's 'defense' is parodic and ironic. According to Quintilian (*Inst. Orat.* 9.1.29), irony is 'the most effective of all means of stealing into people's mind'. Paul seems to view his entire cruciform ministry through the lens of irony.

The Greek term translated 'super' emphasizes an excessive degree and Paul's use is hyperbolic and parodic (cf. Thrall and Hibbard, pp. 248-49). In no way is Paul inferior to 'those super apostles'. To clarify the irony, one might translate 'I do not think I am the least bit inferior to those very special so-called "apostles" of yours' (TEV). Compound verbs with the preposition *hyper* (i.e. 'super') are particularly frequent in 2 Corinthians; 15 of the 34 occurrences of such words in the seven indisputably Pauline letters occur in 2 Corinthians (seven times in chs. 1–9 and eight times in chs. 10–13). This heavy concentration of words beginning with *hyper* suggests a saturation of hyperbolic, ironic and parodic language in chs. 10–13.

Ancient orators thought irony was appropriate in invective (Forbes, p. 12). Irony is the use of words or phrases to mean the opposite of their usual meaning and the *eirōn* ('fool') becomes pre-eminently the self-depreciator. Paul's reference to 'super apostles' is more than mildly ironic and derogatory and expresses a strongly reproachful tone. He engages in a little foolishness and, for the sake of argument, concedes that comparison between him and the super apostles is not possible. Corinth has no superstars with whom Paul would compare himself.

Now Paul reminds the Corinthians, with exquisite *asteismos* (a form of irony in which one urbanely displays one's skill by affecting the lack of it) that although he lacks rhetorical skills, he is not deficient in knowledge (v. 6). Likewise, Chrysostom can say: 'I am quite ordinary and prosaic in my public speaking, though not ordinary in my theme' (*Discourses* 32.39). In the same breath Chrysostom emits a golden stream of brilliant oratory. Paul, like Chrysostom, says he is 'unskilled' (the Greek *idiōtēs tōi logō* in both authors) in oratory and then, like Chrysostom again, he displays masterful control of oratorical skills. Any concession that he is an amateur orator is purely ironic (against G.A. Kennedy, *NT Interpretation*, p. 95). In a parodic 'Fool's Speech', he concedes he is 'oratorically disadvantaged', but implies that the Corinthian lack of faithfulness does not even have the excuse of ignorance. Before one makes Paul an 'unskilled' orator, they must remember this is a 'Fool's Speech'.

A 'mirror reading' of 11.6 concludes that Paul's 'opponents' categorized him as 'an unskilled orator'. Judge argues that Paul's statement is *asteismos*, a form of irony ('Paul's Boasting', p. 37). Betz (*Der Apostel*, p. 66) thinks Paul's concession of a lack of oratorical euphony conforms to the way philosophers in the Socratic tradition denounced the pomposity of the Sophists. When Paul concedes that he is an amateur orator, he does so with a figure that is highly reproachful of the Corinthians. Paul preaches 'Christ crucified', and he knows that 'The foolishness of God is wiser than human wisdom' (1 Cor. 1.25).

2. A Free Gospel (11.7-15)

A rhetorical question that anticipates a negative response opens this section. Paul's irony here is brutal and bitter (cf. Barrett, *Second Corinthians*, p. 281). Emphasis in the sentence falls on the juxtaposed words, 'the gospel of God' offered 'free of charge' (v. 7). Ironically Paul has 'humbled' himself to 'exalt' the Corinthians and he has preached the gospel to them without charge. He 'robbed' other churches of their 'wages' to avoid 'burdening' (lit. to anesthetize) the Corinthians. Here Paul employs military terms. The verb 'to rob' is a military metaphor for taking booty from the war. Moreover, the term for 'wages' refers to a soldier's pay. With almost inexplicable irony, Paul's refusal to be a burden to the Corinthians has made him a burden to other churches but Paul seems to sense no tension or paradox created by his metaphors.

Furthermore, he will not change his policy; he has no intention of taking money from them (vv. 9, 12). With another rhetorical question, he inquires, 'Did I commit a sin by humbling myself so that you might be exalted, because I proclaimed the gospel of God to you free of charge?' (11.7). Paul could have argued he had a right to expect financial support (1 Cor. 9.4-6). Theissen (pp. 40-44) thinks that in 1 Cor. 9.4ff. Paul faces the charge of evading 'charismatic poverty' and in 2 Corinthians, the charge is that working displayed a lack of trust in God's provision. More to the point, Paul refuses to be a client of the Corinthian church.

Everyone in the Greco-Roman world knew that the mark of a benefactor was to bestow beneficence 'without cost'. Sophists justified taking money for teaching on the basis that if teaching were free it was worth nothing (Xenophon, *Memorabilia* 1.6.10, 12) and Antiphon disparaged the practice, saying to Socrates, 'Your knowledge is not worth anything'. However, Plato and Aristotle objected to selling wisdom for money. Aristotle (*Nicomachean Ethics* 9.1.7) says the Sophists demand advance payment 'since nobody would pay money for the knowledge which they possess'. Greek philosophers, however, would criticize Paul for doing manual labor.

Paul refused support at Corinth and instead worked with his hands. Manual labor was a deliberate choice to step down the social ladder. He did not suffer from the 'self-made-person-escapes-humble-origins syndrome'. For the apostle to be brought low and his converts exalted is the pattern of his gospel (4.12) and nothing could make it clearer than his behavior. Paul lives in physical poverty so the Corinthians may become spiritually rich (6.10; 8.9; 9.11; 1 Cor. 1.5). There is no respect in which Paul could be more like his Lord (8.9). His behavior exhibits the true nature of apostolic life and message to clarify the true meaning of apostolicity. Paul does not 'hawk the word of God' (2.17) and he does not adulterate the word of God (4.2) for personal gain. He preaches the gospel 'free of charge'.

Two military metaphors ('robbed' and 'wages') explain how it was possible for Paul to preach the gospel without charge at Corinth. He devoted the spoils of his earlier victims for Christ in Macedonia to a new campaign at Corinth. P.E. Hughes (p. 385) explains, 'The salary or ration-money which was his due as an apostle he had obtained by pillaging or despoiling other places which, in the course of his missionary campaign he had already conquered for the gospel'.

Furnish argues that patrons are benefactors who have a right to expect expressions of gratitude from their clients. The Corinthians are patrons, but Paul, the client, failed to honor the relationships and violated social conventions (pp. 507-508). The basic error in Furnish's assessment is the assumption that Paul is the client. Contrarily, Paul designates himself a benefactor to the Corinthians and he has 'enriched many' (6.3-10). The Corinthians are Paul's clients and have not reciprocated with gratitude, which is at least a faux pas in the Greco-Roman world. Perhaps it was a battle about who would be the benefactor. There is no documentation that the Corinthians entreated Paul for the privilege of providing financial support for him while he was in Corinth. Paul took booty from the other churches, not for his personal benefit but 'to serve you' (v. 8).

At 1 Corinthians 9 Paul declares (1) the right of the apostle to expect support from the congregation (9.3-12a, 13-14); and (2) his right to refuse support because it might impede his work (9.16-18). Paul received aid from elsewhere while he was at Corinth (2 Cor. 11.8-9a). At Thessalonica, Paul received at least two contributions from the Philippians (1 Thess. 2.9) and the Philippians continued their support after he left Macedonia (Phil. 4.15). The gift he received from Macedonia while he was at Corinth was probably from the Philippian congregation.

If Paul's acceptance of 'gifts' from the impoverished Macedonians (cf. 8.2) is problematic, Paul has an answer. He refers to the financial aid from the Macedonians as 'plunder' or 'booty', the exact opposite of benefaction. Thereby, he clarifies the relationship with the Macedonians: He is the benefactor and they are the clients. He is an 'ambassador of Christ' (5.20) and in the Greco-Roman world an envoy ought not to be a burden in the locality he visits (Danker, *Benefactor*, pp. 77-78). Only God can be Paul's Benefactor and he will gladly be a servant of God.

Obviously, Paul's fiscal policies at Corinth caused some misunder standing, but we cannot determine what, if any 'charges' the Corinthians lodged. After all, 2 Corinthians is a monologue, not a dialogue. Twice in v. 9, Paul declares he has not been a burden to the Corinthian church. Elsewhere the verb 'to burden' appears only as a medical term, 'to anesthetize' (Bultmann, *2 Corinthians*, p. 206). In light of the satirical vein of most of ch.11, Danker, ('II Cor.', p. 169) thinks that here it means 'to knock out', or 'shake down'. In other words, Paul has not take the Corinthians to the cleaners. He is not a 'sponger' and has not been a 'dead weight'.

To his first claim, Paul adds, 'I refrained and will continue to refrain from burdening you in any way' (11.9; 12.16). This statement begins an explanation and clarifies v. 8. He replaces his medical metaphor with an adjective that means 'weightless' (Thayer, *s.v.*). Figuratively, it means 'not a burden'. Strelan (pp. 266-76) argues that the root of this word means 'burden' and refers to imposing a financial charge. In a context where Paul mentions his 'need' and the Macedonians 'supplied' the necessities, 'burden' here almost certainly has financial burden for its referent. Fiscally, Paul was and will be 'weightless' to the Corinthians.

Verse 9 is a shaming device for Paul (Danker, 'II Cor.', p. 170; Bultmann, *2 Corinthians*, p. 206). It compares Paul's gratitude and the lack of gratitude at Corinth. Paul is saying, 'I have not been a burden to you because others have borne your burden'. With a military metaphor of 'booty' and shaming language concerning the 'burden', Paul is serving them a double whammy. At the same time, Paul defiantly says he will not change his policy of financial independence at Corinth. The language in 11.7-11 is not what one finds in the philosophers. The apostle 'describes his manual labor as a demonstration of his self-giving love for his converts' (Malherbe, p. 70).

It is the apostle's 'boast' that he proclaims the gospel free of charge (v. 10). With an oath formula, 'as the truth of Christ is in me' (v. 10; Bultmann, *2 Corinthians*, p. 206), he indignantly explodes with 'This boasting of mine will not be silenced in the regions of Achaia' (10.10). The verb here translated 'to silence' literally means 'to obstruct'. Used with the noun 'mouth', it means 'to block the mouth'. Although Paul exhibits uneasiness with boasting (10.8, 13, 15; 11.16, 18, 30; 12.1, 5, 6), he unabashedly declares that it is his 'boast' that he proclaims the gospel gratis. No one will block his mouth and he will boast about it 'throughout Achaia'. This boasting is another way for Paul to shame the Corinthians.

From defiant boasting, Paul quickly turns to sensitive pastoral care. Employing an anti-sophist topos (BAGD, *s.v.*), he asks, 'Why? Because I do not love you?' (11.11). With great protestation of concern for the welfare of the Corinthians, he again uses an oath formula: 'God knows I do!' The oath emphasizes Paul's veracity. Spicq (p. 32) identifies Paul's question 'Because I do not love you?' as *litotes* (a literary form of understatement). A common literary device in ironic expression, liotes makes Paul's interrogative statement indicative and a positive affirmation of his love for the Corinthians. Paul does not offer arguments to the contrary (cf. 11.2; 12.14-15; also 6.11-13; 7.2-3), but invokes God as his witness that his behavior is an expression of his love.

He wants to (1) exalt the Corinthians; and (2) refrain from becoming a burden to them. Far from despising them, he believes that as their spiritual father, he is responsible for them (11.2; 12.14-15). Because Paul wants to imitate Christ (8.9), self-humiliation is not a sign of inferior status but of the authenticity of his apostleship. Paul is sending them a double message: (1) He is imitating Christ, which is subversive in a society that values status; (2) He is not a 'profit for hire' apostle and because he is a servant of Christ, the Corinthians cannot buy him. In the context of the bridal metaphor, Paul is expressing pastoral concern in both points: (1) One cannot marry Christ and social status at the same time; (2) If they cannot buy Paul, neither can they buy the gospel, in terms of grace and sovereignty. The gospel is free and it is a gift one cannot manipulate. Paul is their servant, but by refusing pay, he shows them that they are not his master.

With an ancient maneuver of comparison slanted in favor of the speaker, Paul turns up the volume in v. 12b. His most astute and sarcastic statements on rank and status reach their zenith in this passage. Earlier Paul says he is equal to anyone (10.7b; 11.5) and he will do so again (11.21b–12.10; 12.11-18). Here he ironically depicts the troublemakers as the ones on the defensive and seeking to be his equal (v. 12). That is impossible from Paul's standpoint because the verb 'to do' in v. 12 belongs to the behavior designated in v. 7 and v. 9b. The allusion is to Paul's refusal to accept fiscal aid from the Corinthians.

The aim of Paul's insistence on the gospel gratis is that he might 'cut off' the chance for persons seeking to be his compeers. Polemic becomes more cacophonous and the assault becomes more brutal on persons in disagreement with Paul concerning the free gospel. However, the pastoral tone of v. 11 shows that polemic derives from his profound affection for his 'children'. Analogously Demosthenes, who made an amulet of civism, deprives his opponents of all éclat. After rehearsing his far-reaching contributions as a patron to Athens, he belittles Aeschines by reciting his pathetic attempts at public service (*De Corona* 259-60). Paul is escalating toward a Vesuvian eruption of volcanic eloquence that denies probity to persons who criticize his salary-free ministry and contaminate his integrity.

The RSV's rendition of the second phrase of v. 12 obscures the idiomatic tone and the banter in Paul's statement. Danker's interpretive paraphrase preserves both: 'My aim is to cut off the ' "assets" of those who like to have "assets" so they can boast about their activities and win credit for being what we claim to be, namely, your benefactors'. A word usually translated 'opportunity' occurs twice in v. 12 and provides the basis for wordplay. Literally, it means 'the starting point' or the base of operations for an expedition, then generally the resources needed to carry through such an undertaking' (BAGD, *s.v.*). Louw *et al* (§89.22) translate our phrase 'in order that I may remove the excuse for those who wish an excuse'. Paul wants to cut off the 'assets' of anyone opposing his policy.

'To cut off' is an arboricultural term for pruning (cf. Rom. 11.23, 24; Mt. 3.10; 7.19). It is also a medical term for 'amputate' (Stählin, pp. 857-60). At Gal. 5.12 Paul uses another term in this semantic domain that means 'to castrate'. The two terms are synonymous, and reveal how violent Paul's language is. The language is emotional because Paul envisages radical action consonant with his earlier threats (10.6-8). For persons desiring 'assets' that can permit them 'to be found' with a boast that they are equal to the apostle, Paul wants to 'cut off' their 'assets'. Wearing his 'fool's' mask, Paul's 'boast' is that he refuses all Corinthian support. In establishing this negative comparison, Paul turns their criticism on its head. He makes his behavior the criterion of their actions, rather than attempting to establish their behavior as the criterion for his practice (cf. Hafemann, p. 163). Not an opportunist (12.16-18), Paul's policy provides concrete evidence that he is not duplicitous and authenticates his apostleship.

Having 'cut off' the 'assets' of such people, Paul has opened the door for the invective in vv. 13-15 and the remainder of the 'Fool's Speech'. 'Such persons' in v. 13 refers to boasters desirous of equality with Paul in v. 12. 'Pseudo-apostles' is a term that appears only here in the New Testament, perhaps on the model of 'pseudo-prophets', but Paul may have minted the term. Clearly the term is ironic since, in this context there is an adjectival contradiction and the term is oxymoronic. To be a 'false apostle' is to be no apostle. Rather such a person is a 'con artist' posing as an apostle. In a 'Fool's Speech' Paul says what is pointedly foolish and brings together contradictory terms that make it more emphatic. Abusive language further describes the 'false apostles' as 'deceitful workers'. There is satirical bite in the term since 'workers' elsewhere applies to Christ's envoys (Mt. 9.37, 38; Lk. 10.2). In the early church 'worker' is a technical term for 'missionary'.

'False apostles' are 'deceitful workers' who are con artists disguising themselves as 'apostles of Christ'. The verb 'to transform' means 'disguise' in the middle voice, as it is here; it means to masquerade as someone else. They are the ones who preach another Jesus, spirit and gospel (11.4). They pretend to be 'ministers of righteousness' (11.15) or 'ministers of Christ' (11.23a), but they are 'ministers of Satan' (11.15). Satan disguises himself as 'an angel of light' (11.14). Bultmann (*2 Corinthians*, p. 208) opines that the motives of the 'ministers of Satan' are not in question, but the denigrating descriptors Paul uses implies it is precisely their motives that disqualify them. Paul asks, 'Are they ministers of Christ?' and responds explosively to his question 'I am talking like an insane person' (v. 23). His ballistic response suggests how preposterously insane it is to even ask the question.

'Disguising themselves' is no cause for amazement (11.14). Paul pours scorn on pretenders posing as 'apostles of Christ' when they are 'ministers of Satan'. 'And no wonder!' is a diatribe formula (Windisch, *Korintherbrief*, p. 341-42) filled with irony and is exceptionally striking; its staccato style corresponds to 'no great surprise' in v. 15. 'And it is no wonder' is an exclamation meaning that the ability to 'disguise themselves' is not astonishing (on omission of the verb to be, cf. BDF, §127.4). It is not startling because 'Satan does it all the time' (v. 14b). Danker ('II Cor.', p. 174) paraphrases colorfully, 'It's no big trick, then, if his assistants are disguised as upright assistants'. The invective concludes with a verdict: 'Their end will match their deeds'. God will judge them and they will get what they deserve (cf. Phil. 3.19; 1 Thess. 2.16; Rom. 2.6; 3.8; Gal. 5.10). 'You reap whatever you sow' (Gal. 6.7) is the Pauline summation.

'The serpent' (11.3) becomes 'the Satan' (11.14). At 2.11, 'the Satan' is capable of fraudulent intent; here, he is the arch-deceiver. 'The serpent' in v. 3 anticipates 'the Satan' in v. 14. Since Genesis 3 makes no reference to 'Satan' or an 'angel of light', Paul is most likely alluding to extracanonical sources (e.g., *Apoc. Mos.* 16; *LAE* 9.1). More important than his allusions to the Satan myth is Paul's perception that some people at Corinth are satanic.

3. A 'Fool's' Welcome (11.16-21a)

After exposing the false apostles, Paul readjusts his fool's mask: 'Again I say' (11.16). Most commentators (Bultmann, Barrett, Furnish, Danker, *et al.*) interpret the phrase to be a resumption of Paul's plea for 'indulgence' in v. 1 but R.P. Martin (p. 360) thinks Paul is saying something different here. Although the words following 'I repeat' do not appear in this or any other extant letter to Corinth, the 'welcome me' (v. 16) corresponds to 'Bear with me' in v. 1. Zmijewski (p. 194) is probably correct that 'welcome me' goes beyond 'bear with me'. Paul wishes the Corinthians would not consider him a fool. The phrase 'do not think of me' is ingressive: 'Do not let it come to mind' and corresponds with v. 1 with the concessive 'but if you do' in v. 1 (BDF, §439.1). If it is all he can get, Paul will accept a 'fool's welcome' (11.16). In v. 1 Paul begs his readers to put up with his 'foolishness', but here he warns against taking him for a 'fool' (v. 16). However, the apparent contradiction (cf. BDF, §§18, 374) is in appearance only. Clearly the 'foolishness' in v. 1 is an assumed disguise and in v. 16 Paul warns against misconstruing that role. Even at the risk of being misunderstood, Paul will wear his 'fool's mask' so he can 'boast a little' (v. 16).

Although he pleads for indulgence in his boasting, Paul knows 'boasting' is uncouth. Greek philosophers repudiate boasting and self-praise as an insult to nobility that vitiates self-respect and breeds sycophantic reliance on others. Paul is averse to boasting because it takes away praise that belongs to God (10.17) and forgets that everyone depends on God's grace (12.9; 4.7; 1 Cor. 15.10). Paul believes Corinthian rivals have forced boasting on him and he wants to minimize boasting. When forced to engage in self-praise, he is always inoffensive according to cultural conventions. It is abundantly clear that the apostle is uncomfortable with his role (11.1). His boasting is 'not according to the Lord, but as a fool' (11.17) and he speaks as a 'fool' (11.21), sometimes reaching the point of 'insanity' (11.23). Paradoxically he boasts only in his 'weaknesses' (11.30) and he knows it is not 'profitable' (12.1). He has been a 'fool' but the Corinthians forced him into that role (12.11). Paul provides a parody of boasting.

Engagement in self-praise is a hazardous game Paul wishes to avoid but others have forced him to become a 'fool' (11.30; 12.1, 11). The term 'fool' occurs twice in v. 16, and again in v. 19; 12.1, 6, 11. Neither here, nor elsewhere, does Paul concede that he is a fool but he knows he has 'played the fool' (12.11). When he disavows engrossment in bragging, Paul's audience is cognizant of current reaction against such hubris. Pindar (*Olympian* 9.38) declares that 'untimely boasting is in tune with madness' (cf. 11.23, 'I am talking like a mad person'.).

Folly continues as does Paul's embarrassment with the folly of boasting (11.17). Paul is uneasy in this situation (11.17c). The phrase 'in this matter of boasting' comes at the end of the Greek sentence for emphasis and to qualify 'as in foolishness' (v. 17b). Many commentators translate 'in confidence of boasting' (e.g. NRSV, NASB, NIV, NAB; Allo, Barrett). It is much better to render the noun as 'matter', 'situation', 'plan', or 'undertaking' (BAGD, *s.v.*). Paul's boasting is not 'according to the Lord', but 'as in foolishness' (v. 18). In his idiomatic prose, Paul is saying, 'When it comes to this business of boasting, what I am saying is not from the Lord's perspective but from the perspective of a fool'. Since 'the many' are boasting 'according to the flesh', Paul will also boast 'according to the flesh' (v. 18).

Here, as at 2.17, 'the many' is equivalent to 'the general public' or 'the masses'. Epictetus (1.3.4) contrasts 'the many' with 'the few' and with 'the philosophers'. Philo (*Rer. Div. Her.* 42) compares 'the many' with 'the praiseworthy'. It is a contemptuous term without any specific referent. In antithesis to boasting 'according to the Lord' (v. 17), boasting 'according to the flesh' means 'boasting in a fleshly manner', corresponding to the intention of the flesh (cf. 10.3). In this context, it attaches to 'boasting on the basis of fleshly advantage' such as he enumerates in vv. 22-29 (cf. 5.12; Phil. 3.3-4). Boasting 'according to the flesh' is opportunistic (cf. 1.17; 5.16; 10.2, 3). 'Since many are boasting according to the flesh, I will join in the contest; I also will boast according to the flesh, but be forewarned that I know such boasting is not of the Lord'.

After his parenthetical explanation of foolish boasting, Paul resumes his plea in v. 16 (also see v. 1). The introductory 'for' joins v. 19 to v. 16, and clarifies vv. 17-18. Verse 19 ('For you gladly endure fools, being wise yourselves!') gives an ironic twist to 'Welcome me' in v. 16, corresponding to 'you endure it beautifully' at v. 4. Pauline syntax heightens the irony: the word 'gladly' or 'sweetly' (Thayer, *s.v.*) stands first in the sentence. The terms 'fools' and 'wise people' stand side by side. In this contiguous juxtaposition, even the verb is ironic: 'Gladly you indulge the fools, wise people that you are'.

This collation ('fools', 'wise people') is emphatic, as well as being oxymoronic and sarcastic. Danker ('II Cor.', p. 177) seizes satirical wordplay with a colloquial paraphrase: 'You brainy people are delighted to put up with the brainless'. Designating the Corinthians as 'brainy people' is poignantly sarcastic. The phrase 'being wise people' is probably an allusion to the Corinthian boast of wisdom (1 Cor 3.18-20; 4.10; 6.5; 8.1-7; 13.2). Irony inverts Paul's praise and exposes the Corinthians as consummate fools.

Amplifying v. 19, Paul repeats the word 'endure' (v. 20) as the invective continues and 'endure' is ironic as it is at vv. 4 and 19. The anaphoric 'if anyone' intensifies the passion. Like a series of hammer blows, the repetition connects and reinforces the successive thought (Kennedy, *NT Interpretation*, p. 27).

If anyone enslaves you
If anyone devours you
If anyone takes advantage of you
If anyone exalts themselves
If anyone slaps you in the face
You endure it!

This strategy keeps the focus on the Corinthians, not outside 'opponents'.

Aural anaphora is more effective than written anaphora. Obviously the emphasis is on 'If anyone' or 'Whoever' and in the Greek, the effect is devastating: 'You people put up with anything and everything' (BAGD,

§VII). Paul's style has many arresting features, such as *enumeratio*, listing five verbs in rapid fire succession in a climactic way, following the 'law of increasing numbers' (Zmijewski, p. 207). Each verb amplifies Paul's exposé of the Corinthians 'putting up with' abusive leadership. The concatenation of verbs, with two words that appear only here in Paul letters, amplifies the anaphoric fivefold reiteration of 'If anyone' and the epiphoric (Soulen, p. 54) euphony (repetition or words or sounds at the end of at least two sentences) of the resonant ending in Greek *-oi, -ei, -ei, -ai, -ei*.

In Greek, 'if' here is a conditional particle, 'a marker of a condition, real or hypothetical, actual or contrary to fact' (Louw *et al*, §89.65). The indefinite pronoun 'anyone at all' is not susceptible of a singular interpretation. The combination of a conditional particle that is hypothetical with an indefinite pronoun makes any attempt to identify a particular person(s) highly suspect (cf. Furnish, p. 497). The anaphoric 'if anyone' and the intensely sarcastic tone argue against specificity in the identification of opponents. Certainly, it overweighs the evidence to identify the abuser(s) as 'intruders' at Corinth. Paul is engaging in the game of invective and it is ill-advised to find a precise referent in the community's experience for each verb.

Paul's intention in the 'catalog of abuse' (Fitzgerald, *Cracks*, pp. 206-207) is clear, but whether one construes the verbs literally (Allo, *Seconde*, p. 290), metaphorically (Bultmann, *2 Corinthians*, p. 213) or rhetorically (Betz, *Der Apostel*, pp. 116, 117) is debatable. In a sarcastic parody, Paul says the Corinthians 'put up with' anyone who reduces them to 'absolute servitude'. They will endure anyone who 'exploits' them, 'takes advantage' of them, 'puts on airs' (i.e. assumes superiority over them, BAGD, *s.v.*). Bulldozing parody *ad absurdum*, the Corinthians put up with anyone who 'beats you in the face'.

This pleonastic description of abuse is ironic and parodic, making the 'wise' Corinthians appear conspicuously stupid. As in 1 Corinthians 4, Paul ironically calls the Corinthians 'wise people'. Here, the 'catalog of abuse' serves the dual function of castigating possible exploiter(s) by describing their abusive acts and shames the Corinthians with mock praise. Winter (pp. 243-46) thinks the behaviors in this 'catalog of abuse' are characteristic of Sophistic rhetors during and after Paul's time. The description of leadership in v. 20 contrasts sharply with Paul's concept of pastoral leadership. Paul does not 'lord it over' their faith (1.24). Rather, 'for Jesus' sake' he has become their slave (4.5). Using a different metaphor, Paul is also their 'father' (11.3) and 'parent' (12.14b-15).

Acidic sarcasm drips from Paul's lips with 'To my shame, I must say I was too weak for that!' (v. 21a). The flesh-tearing sarcasm intensifies with 'I was too weak for that'. His concession to 'weakness' is sarcastic when he speaks of being too weak to behave abusively. He is still wearing the 'fool's' mask. With this final statement in the prodiorthosis, Paul caricatures himself as a weakling and his ministry as one of weakness. This self-caricature is a grotesque parody of Paul as a servant of Christ (Zmijewski, p. 230). Ironic weakness here anticipates the weakness of which he boasts in the catalog of suffering (11.23-29). With a fresh start in v. 30, he declares 'If I must boast, I will boast of the things that show my weaknesses'.

Polemic in vv. 16-21a is eminently effective. It is an oblique assault on the abuser(s) through a recital of Corinthian sufferance of exploitation and Paul's sarcastic self-derogation as a nonbenefactor. Ironically Paul is saying that anyone who exploits and abuses them is a benefactor in Corinth. If that be the case, Paul cannot be a benefactor, because he refuses to exploit and abuse people under his care. The passkey to his satire is 'I was too weak for that', conceivably an indirect reference to 10.10, but here he gives it a new twist. This satirical self-denigration is akin to a jab delivered by Demosthenes (*De Corona* 230) against Aeschines: 'I confess it. I am weak, but all the more loyal than you to my fellow citizens'. Dio Chysostom (12.13), speaking to a crowd gathered for the Olympic games in 97 CE, said: 'I lack the courage to lie and deceive when I promise something'. Paul is too weak to abuse the Corinthians!

If the prodiorthosis is advance justification for what might be offensive, Paul's prodiorthosis is parodic, and functions as invective from start to finish. The language is filled with irony and sarcasm. Nothing that follows the prodiorthosis could be more offensive. When Paul completes his application of 'rhetorical ointment', any sensitive listener at Corinth would know he made them appear to be incredibly stupid. In a 'Fool's Speech', one might expect parody and Paul does not fail. He transmutes a literary device intended to soften the blows of offensive elements so it becomes a means of heaping more invective on the heads of the Corinthians.

b. Outboasting the Boasters (11.21b-29)

After an exceedingly extensive 'advance justification' (BDF, §495.3), Paul finally embarks on the 'foolish discourse', from which he has been disinclined. As he begins, his apprehension is evident: 'I am speaking foolishly' (v. 21b) and 'I am talking like an insane person' (11.23a). It is as if Paul pulls himself from his 'weakness' to explode: 'Whatever anyone else summons the courage to boast of [I am talking like an insane person] I shall also dare to boast of that' (11.21b). The apostle can outboast the best of the braggarts! Paul still wears his 'fool's' mask. His boldness here is not the same Greek term as in 10.2, 12, but a boldness that is audacious and can only appear as strength in the eyes of the Corinthians. This boldness requires boasting and so Paul notes parenthetically that he speaks like an insane person. He has described abuser(s) in terms usually reserved for arrogant sophists and now he will parody their boasting. Note that we have no evidence of actual abusers fitting Paul's description in Corinth. It is more properly understood as another way to shame the Corinthians.

1. Establishing 'Bragging Rights' (11.22-23)

Pedigree or 'good breeding' is a standard *topos* in Hellenistic oratory. Theon (*Preliminary Exercises*) advises that in a comparison of persons, one first juxtaposes their status, education, offspring, positions held, prestige and physique. Verse 21b publicizes Paul's intention to boast. By Hellenistic standards, what becomes evident is his dishonor. It is Paul's doctrine of 'boasting' and knowledge of rhetorical skills that enable him to deal with his weakness in a positive manner. For him, all boasting is foolish and thus, he will boast parodically.

A threefold anaphoric 'and I' in v. 22 continues the 'and I' in v. 21. It belongs to the repertoire of popular philosophers to ridicule the *topos* of pedigree because it is the genre of self-praise. In the Cynic tradition, it is the other side of the philosophical commonplace that the 'true' pedigree is that of the wise person only. If Paul admits his dishonor, he is complimenting himself. Three rhetorical questions in v. 22 reveal the three titles of honor for Palestinian Jews and describe the nation as a natural community as well as the people of salvation history with its promises. The absence of particles or conjunctions in a condensed expression marks the three rhetorical questions as the literary form *asyndeton* (BDF, §494; Soulen, *s.v.*; Thrall and Hibbard, *s.v.*). The emphatic force of asyndeton is obvious, as the chart below demonstrates.

Are they Hebrews?	And I
Are they Israelites?	And I
Are they the seed of Abraham?	And I

Paul achieves balance and variety in parallelism. The terms Hebrews, Israelites and seed of Abraham are synonyms balanced by 'And I' (Spencer, p. 353). Synonymous parallelism allows Paul to amplify his punch by saying three times, 'Are they Jews? And so am I'. There may be slight nuances to each term, but caution counsels against making absolute distinctions. In the entire verse, Paul says little more than 'Are they Jews? And so am I'. He amplifies that statement by reiterating it with various emphases and nuances, clarifying that there is no conceivable Jewish qualification he does not share on equal terms with any other Jew. Parodically, he argues that in pedigree he is equal to the abusers although in the previous verse he excluded himself from equality saying, 'I am too weak for that'. Now he is saying he can trump anyone's genetic card. He enumerates them in foolishness because Paul regards these privileges as worthless.

2. Superiority in Successful Suffering (11.23-29)

By attaching 'servants of Christ' in v. 23 with the titles of honor in v. 22, R.P. Martin (p. 372) finds four titles. Against Martin, the three titles in v. 22 are distinctively Jewish but 'servants of Christ' is not. The retort to questions in v. 22 is 'And I', but with v. 23, the retort is 'And I more'. In v. 22, Paul speaks in 'foolishness', while in v. 23, he speaks in 'insanity'. With the fourth question, Paul begins parodic boasting with the *topos* of tribulation. In the extant Corinthian correspondence, Paul compiles five catalogs of suffering (1 Cor. 4.9-13; 2 Cor. 4.9-10; 6.3-10; 11.23-29; 12.10). In chapter 11 the catalog is parodic for it is anything but what the Corinthians expected from Paul.

Paul's indebtedness to the *topos* of tribulation seems obvious. The commonest links in style and theme are (1) the preposition 'in' denotes negative circumstances; (2) rhetorical questions; (3) triumph over liabilities; (4) christological interpretation of suffering. Throughout the catalog, Paul continues to speak as a 'fool' and is describing himself as a minister of Christ. He asks three rhetorical questions at v. 22, and to introduce his catalog, he asks another rhetorical question. His eruption, 'I am speaking like an insane person', is parenthetical and heightens the foolishness and madness of v. 21. The Greek term, translated 'more so', functions adverbially here (BDF, §230) and means 'to a higher degree', or 'better'. Abandoning his claim to equality (v. 22), Paul now claims superiority (v. 23) and rehearses 30 instances of suffering to substantiate the boast that he is a superior minister of Christ.

In the first group of tribulations (v. 23) the preposition 'in' precedes each of the four items. Paul asks a rhetorical question, makes a parenthetical aside, and answers 'I more!' He has the adverb in items 1 and 2, creating assonance of nouns and adverbs.

1. Tribulations Governed By 'In'

Are they ministers of Christ?
[I speak as an insane person.]
I more!

in	labors	far greater
in	imprisonments	far more
in	floggings	countless
in	deaths	often near

The pattern reveals Paul's meticulous care in constructing four elliptical phrases. Complete sentences would read, 'I am a better servant of Christ than they are' (cf. Spencer, p. 353). Although Paul does not repeat 'I more', its force continues throughout vv. 23-29 in a parodic comparison of Paul as 'more a servant of Christ' than detractors who would challenge his credentials.

This pattern includes parallelism, rhythm and cadence. Climactic development, from labors to deaths, amplifies Paul's recital of sufferings. The substantives are in ascending order of the severity of the sufferings. The term 'labors' describes the wear and tear of missionary work (vv. 27-28). 'Imprisonments' designate many incarcerations but Acts records only one (Acts 17.23-40). 'Floggings' alludes to blows endured under various circumstances (vv. 24-25; Acts 16.23). 'Deaths' suggest more than mortal dangers, but particular experiences that brought him near death. The plural form is well-established in Hellenistic usage (Danker, 'II Cor.', p. 181).

Paul refers to himself as 'a servant of a new covenant' (3.6) and as 'a servant of God' (6.4). Here he is a superior 'servant of Christ' and vv. 23-29 narrate his extensive record of performance beyond the call of duty to document his claim. Paul wants to be the benefactor of the Corinthians. In keeping with Greco-Roman recitals of distinguished performance, Paul's peristatic (suffering) recital portrays him as an endangered benefactor who survives perilous tribulations. The account is within the canons of good taste because instead of praising himself, Paul recites hardships he has endured. In the end, this classical maneuver allows Paul to stand securely as an exceptional benefactor who has endured much for the sake of the gospel. At the same time, he appeals to what his service to Christ has cost him, and thus the *topos* is a form of self-praise.

The four items that head the list of hardships in v. 23b are not specific instances of adversity. Three of the four also appear at 6.4c-5 and by repetition of items from a previous catalog and the introduction of new ones, an author not only reminds his readers of the previous catalog but suggests that what follows is a supplement to the previous list. This list typifies the kinds of adversities Paul intends to discuss.

In the second set of adversities, Paul illustrates the fourth item in the first set, 'in many deaths', that is, often at the point of death. The first two items in the second list point to a 'catalog of punishments'. Numerical specification amplifies the tribulations: five, three, one, three, night and day. Paul's use of *enumeratio* is typical of other ancient lists of the exploits of notable persons (Judge, 'The Conflict', p. 44 nn. 113, 114). In vv. 24-25, Paul amplifies two items he has already mentioned in v. 23b.

***2.** Tribulations Governed by Enumeratio*

Five times	I received	forty lashes less one
Three times	I was beaten	with rods
Once	I received	a stoning
Three times	I was	shipwrecked
A night and day	I was	adrift at sea

Reference to the potential 'death blow' by the Jews (v. 23) sounds a note of pathos after a three-fold affirmation of his ethnicity in v. 22. According to Paul, five times he received '40 lashes less one' from Jews. Deuteronomy 25.1-3 allows flogging for one convicted in court, the number of blows to be proportionate to the seriousness of the offense, but in no case could it exceed 40 lashes. Josephus (*Ant.* 4.8.21) describes these thrashings as a 'most disgraceful penalty'. Because the administrator of the lashes was liable if he gave more than 40 lashes, he stopped at 39 to avoid a miscount (*t. Mak.* 3.10-14). In Acts there is no account of the Jews flogging Paul, and Paul does not indict Jews generally for he writes 'by Jews', not 'by the Jews' (Danker, 'II Cor.', p. 181). If Paul suffered synagogue floggings five times, it reminds the readers of the tenacity with which he held to his Jewish heritage.

The three beatings with rods (11.25a) insinuate punishment by Roman lictors ('rod bearers') who carried wooden rods with which they inflicted the blows (Acts 16.22). According to Acts, Paul was a Roman citizen. A law enacted under M. Porcius Cato, probably in 198 BCE, prohibited scourging of Roman citizens (Livy 10.9.4-5), but some officials ignored it. Josephus (*War* 2.14.9) refers to Florus, who scourged and even crucified Jews of Roman equestrian rank. At 1 Thess. 2.2 Paul recalls 'having previously suffered and been shamefully treated at Philippi' (cf. Sherwin-White, pp. 48-119).

Presumably the stoning (11.25b) refers to the incident when mobs from Antioch and Iconium stoned Paul at Lystra (Acts 14.5, 19). There is in 1 Clem. 5.6 a report of a stoning of Paul. Stoning was a Jewish penalty

(Deut. 17.5-7), the consequence of which was usually death. Since judicial stoning would result in death, the stoning at Lystra was likely fomented by mob action, not judicial process. Outside of Paul's statement, we know nothing of his account of three shipwrecks. To his tribulation list he adds that 'a day and a night I have spent in the deep'. The copulative compound literally means 'night-day', and denotes one day and one night or 24 hours (BDF, §121). It marks the climax of this set of 'tribulations'.

'On frequent journeys' (v. 26) provides the generalizing rubric and heading for a third group of hardships. All the datives are instrumental and the 'servant of Christ' is always visible. Paul details the dangers anaphorically; the plural noun, 'in dangers' appears eight times. The preposition 'out of' appears twice and the preposition 'in' four times. The genitive in the first two items identifies the source of Paul's dangers; in items three and four, the 'out of' identifies the source of danger (BDF, §166). In items 5-8, the 'in' with a dative indicates the location of lurking danger (BAGD, *s.v.*). It is unnecessary to suggest particular events to which Paul might allude in this pleonastic list of dangers with the anaphoric 'in dangers'.

3. *Tribulations Governed by Anaphoric 'in Dangers'*

In dangers	from	rivers
In dangers	from	bandits
In dangers	from	my own people
In dangers	from	Gentiles
In dangers	in	the city
In dangers	in	the wilderness
In dangers	in	the sea
In dangers	in (among)	false brothers

The purpose of this list is not to provide information but to evoke strong emotions. Only as a 'servant of Christ' did Paul survive these catastrophes, not as a private citizen or tourist. Dangers from rivers remind the reader that rivers could overflow from rains and could be hazardous for other reasons. 'Bandits' are a surprise because Epictetus (3.13.9) says there was no brigandage on a large scale. However, Seneca (*On Benefits* 4.17.4) suggests that defenseless travelers did experience dangers from bandits (cf. MacMullen, pp. 255-68). Acts (9.20-29; 13.44-45; 14.1-6, 19-20; 17.5-9; 18.5-17) support his claim to have suffered at the hands of his 'own people'. Acts 18.5-17 mentions Jewish hostility toward Paul at Corinth. Threats from Gentiles (Acts 16.20; 19.23) appear to be less brutal.

The phrases 'in the city', 'in the desert' and 'in the sea' together include the whole world (Plummer, p. 326-27), wherever he went. The final and climactic item in the third list is 'dangers from false brothers and sisters'. The only other instance of Pauline use of this term is Gal. 2.4, where Judaizers are in view. Since nothing in 2 Corinthians suggests Judaizers, here he may be referring to Christians Paul regards as unfaithful to his gospel. Paul could cope with other dangers, but insincerity among 'brothers and sisters' wounded him deeply. With this pleonastic peristatic catalog, Paul is saying that in no place and under no circumstances was he free from danger and his most formidable peril as 'false sisters and brothers'.

All the adversities in the fourth set of tribulations (v. 27) come under the heading of labor and toil. The nouns are paired by association and the adverb 'many times' links the parts and provide functional power to amplify the gravity of Paul's recital. Bujard (p. 187) notes the parallelism in this arrangement. Paul constructs the list forming a pattern A-B-A-B-A.

4. Tribulations Governed by Deprivations

Form	First Term	Conjunction	Second Term	Pattern Break	Adverb
Synonym (A)	toil	and	hardship		
(B)				sleepless nights	many times
Antonym (A)	famine	and	thirst		
(B)				fasting	many times
Metonym (A)	cold	and	naked		

This sentence is a generalizing summary and concentrates on the deprivations the apostle endured as a direct consequence of his missionary service. Here, as throughout the catalog of tribulations, the hardships substantiate Paul's claim in v. 23 that he is a 'superior servant of Christ'.

In the first phrase, 'labors and hardships', Paul uses synonymous terms. The end-rhyme of the Greek adds expression to the pathos. We cannot determine if the reference is to tentmaking or intense absorption in evangelism. Furnish (p. 518) thinks Paul surely refers to tentmaking. While it is possible, as 1 Thess. 2.9 and 2 Thess. 3.8 illustrate, in this context where Paul is speaking of himself as a superior servant of Christ, it probably refers to his missionary labors. With the phrase 'through sleepless nights many times', Paul uses 'sleepless nights' just as he did in 6.5 and in both cases 'sleepless nights' follows mention of his labors. He gives no reason for the sleepless nights but the context places it under the rubric of extraordinary service for Christ.

The second pair of hardships, 'hungry and thirsty', is antonymous. This couplet certainly speaks of enforced, not voluntary hardships (contra Barrett, *Commentary*, p. 300). 'In many fastings' is not religious fasting but a lack of food and Paul still wants to persuade the Corinthians of his superior status as a 'servant of Christ'. Paul was 'often without food' (6.5). With the last pair, 'cold and naked', he uses a figure of speech called metonymy: a word is substituted for the thing it intends to suggest. 'Cold and naked' correspond as marks of extreme loss, indicating a loss of dignity and self-esteem (cf. 1 Cor. 4.11; Rom. 8.35; Rev. 3.18; Gen. 2.25; Ezek. 16.8; Neh. 3.5; Mic 1.11 on the shame of nakedness). Ancient letters sometimes include requests for garments (2 Tim. 4.13; Epictetus 3.22.45).

The formal inventory of tribulations concludes with the fourth set of adversities. However, it is certain from what follows that Paul could extend the list *ad infinitum*. Instead of making a direct statement, he finds himself adding yet another sort of problem that burdens him (vv. 28-29). The expression 'Apart from such external things' is in Greek an example of *paralipsis*; that is, Paul indicates that he will omit something but he proceeds to include it (R.P. Martin, p. 381). The phrase means 'not to mention other things' (BAGD, *s.v.*; LSJ, *s.v.*). Although the apostle says he will not mention other things, he proceeds to designate 'pressure' as another instance of tribulation.

The noun 'pressure' is amenable to various translations. Scholars have proposed many interpretations of this expression. P.E. Hughes (pp. 415-16 n. 79) surveys the various interpretations. A majority of commentators prefer to read the phrase as 'I am under daily pressure'. The sense of 'pressure' for the Greek noun is 'an outstanding possibility' (BAGD, *s.v.*). The following phrase, 'my anxiety for all the churches', is exepigetical in apposition to 'pressure'. Paul's daily pressure is his anxiety or worry about all the churches. Paul is probably thinking of the congregations he 'fathered' (7.2-4; 12.14) and for which he feels responsible. If there were no other evidence, the Corinthian correspondence provides ample evidence of the anxiety-producing situations that kept the pressures on Paul's pastoral heart. This statement of pastoral concern stands at the highest point of Paul's 'list of hardships'.

Two rhetorical questions in v. 29 reiterate and amplify the 'anxiety' at v. 28. Both questions appeal to the emotions and illustrate Paul's pastoral compassion. These questions emphasize how the constant 'pressure' and persistent 'worry' are for Paul yet another kind of 'tribulation'. The questions are parallel and have an 'and' occurring in the middle that functions as a *consecutivum*; that is, the 'and' means 'and so' (BDF, §442.2). The accent falls, not on the question itself, but on what comes as the second-member reply in the composite sentence. With apparent emotion, Paul asks, 'Who is weak and I am not weak?' (v. 29). The sense of Paul's interrogative statement, then, is 'Who is weak? And so, I am obviously weak'.

The 'and I am not weak' is not an accommodation to the standpoint of the 'weak', but rather a shared pastoral concern. 'To be weak' is a key word in the Fool's Speech (11.21a, 30; 12.5, 9, 10) and has a wide range of meanings. Paul includes references to his weakness in other hardship lists (12.10a; 1 Cor. 4.10b). Whatever the nature of this weakness is, it is clear that Paul plans to boast about it. Paul's identification with weakness v. 29 anticipates the Pauline principle of boasting in weakness (v. 30). The second rhetorical question (v. 29b) is parallel to the first: 'Who is made to fall and I do not burn with indignation?' Paul does not allude to identification with people 'who are made to stumble', but to his indignation toward the person(s) who caused the stumbling. He is still presenting himself as a superior servant of Christ, as he has since v. 23.

c. Upending Corinthian Apostolic Criteria (11.30–12.10)

Pauline boasting finds its locus classicus at 2 Corinthians 10–13 (10.8, 13, 15, twice in v. 17; 11.10, 12, 16, 17, twice in v. 18; twice in v. 30; 12.1, twice in v. 5, 6, 9). When Paul boasts, in apparent self-praise, he always does so inoffensively and consonant with conventions later enunciated by Plutarch (c. 120 CE). This fact and the subtleties of Paul's writing hardly support the position that his finesse may have been 'a complete coincidence–what any gifted natural orator would do' (Dillon, p. 29).

Although they remain unsystematized, Paul articulates his 'principles' for boasting. (1) Apologetic boasting is always inappropriate; (2) boasting is not 'according to the Lord', but 'according to the flesh' and thus he boasts 'in foolishness' (11.17); (3) one should not boast 'beyond measure' (10.13, 15); (4) Paul forbids comparisons (10.12), but engages the technique parodically; (5) boasting 'in the Lord' is appropriate (10.18); (6) one may boast in weaknesses (11.30; 12.5, 9, 10); (7) one may boast in the role of a 'fool' (11.1, 10, 16, 17, 21, 23; 12.11); (8) sometimes boasting is necessary (11.30; 12.1a). Paul finds the foundation for boasting 'in weakness', which is already boasting 'in the Lord', in his Christology and theology of the cross.

Paul's boasting is 'in foolishness' and is thus ironical, a parody of boasting (11.21). With bold foolishness he parodies the boast of pedigree, engages in the odious practice of comparison of himself with others (11.22-23) and declares himself a superior 'servant of Christ' (11.23-29) and is thus a parody of boasting in which he claims superiority. The 'fool' boasts 'in weakness' (11.30) and illustrates the weakness with parodies of (1) *corona muralis* at 11.32-33; (2) a heavenly rapture at 12.1-5; and

(3) a healing story at 12.7-10. The second and third are parodic aretalogies, that is, they are miracle stories.

An operative principle for Paul is 'If I must boast, I will boast of the things of my weakness' (11.30). Calvin (p. 148) sees in 11.30 a conclusion but his view does not account for the future, 'I will boast'. Bultmann (*2 Corinthians*, p. 217) correctly sees that 'everything in vv. 23-29 is under the viewpoint of weakness...this viewpoint is further developed in 12.1-5'. However, he incorrectly thinks Paul now drops the feature of 'foolishness' since the boast is no longer 'according to the flesh'. Then, quite inconsistently, Bultmann notes that Paul retains the role of the 'fool' in 12.11. Furnish (p. 521) comments that 'The future tense is used, not because Paul will only now begin to boast, but because his statement here is a summary of his reason for carrying on as he must in his "fool's speech" '. Paul has boasted 'according to the flesh' (11.18) and he will continue this boasting while wearing the mask of a fool.

1. Negating the 'Hero' Criterion (11.31-33)

Paul introduces this parody with a 'solemn oath formula' (Bultmann, *2 Corinthians*, p. 217; cf. 11.10; 13.3). Multiple divine predications, 'The God and Father-Mother of our Lord Jesus (blessed be God forever!) knows that I do not lie' (NRSV, Inclusive Version). It makes the entire sentence rich in construction by the addition of a Jewish eulogistic formula and a christological expansion: 'Blessed be God' and 'Jesus is Lord' as a confessional utterance in the early Christian movement (Rom. 10.9; 1 Cor. 12.3; Phil. 2.11). The verbal form, using a participle as a substantive has an individualizing effect: 'the one who is' (BDF, §413.1). The asseveration, 'I do not lie' is a *litotes*, for what one might more simply express with 'I am speaking the truth'. Paul invokes God as a witness to his veracity when he boasts only in weakness and reveals again the parodic nature of his boasting.

From his experiences of failure and rejection, Paul illustrates the *topos* on weakness by 'boasting in weakness'. His first illustration recalls an encounter at Damascus near the beginning of his ministry. The story (11.32-33) marks a change in style from listing hardships to narrating a hardship. This narrative is so surprising that Bultmann (*2 Corinthians*, p. 218) can find 'no reason for it'. On the other hand, Barrett (*2 Corinthians*, p. 303) thinks its deletion sharpens the problem, 'for who would have inserted it at this point?' The verses are a culminating elucidation of the weakness and humiliation of which Paul boasts.

There are at least three good reasons for its inclusion here. First, it mentions danger in a city which Paul mentions in v. 26. Second, after the outburst of vv. 23-29, the narrative functions as a brief respite for both author and readers. Third, Paul is following a convention Plutarch ('On Praising Oneself Inoffensively', 13) advocates: 'one should mix with self-praise some remarks about personal flaws to temper the eulogy'. Acts (9.23-25) relates a different, highly stylized version of the Damascus escape. The Acts narrative shows how God delivers God's servant; Paul makes it a parody to illustrate his humiliation. In Acts, the account is a story of divine providence; in the Fool's Speech, Paul is an example *par excellence* of humiliation and weakness.

Data related to Aretas and his ethnarch are complex. For our purpose, we greatly diminish the problems if we remember Paul's primary concern is persuasion, not historical accuracy. Scholars have not identified the ethnarch and we do not know the function of an ethnarch in Damascus. The king is Aretas IV, who reigned at Petra from 9 BCE to about 40 CE. This fact helps fix the time of Paul's presence in Damascus (Gal. 1.17) and he may have escaped from that city before the end of 40 CE.

E.A. Judge (p.45; cf. Travis, 'The Conflict', pp. 527-33) suggests that Paul's escape is a conscious parody of the criterion for the award of the *corona muralis*, the Roman decoration for the first soldier up the wall in a besieged city. Everyone in antiquity, including the Corinthians, knew the highest award for valor was the *corona muralis*. By inversion of the criterion for a hero, Paul rains contempt on boasting, as he does more directly at 12.11. Instead of scaling over the wall, Paul escapes by having some unnamed person(s) let him down the city wall through a window in the wall in a fish basket like a load of contraband merchandise. He was not victorious and was not a hero. He escaped ignominiously as a defeated apostle who never went 'over the wall'. He escaped from the city through a wall, rather than going over the wall into the city. Boasting in weakness inverts the Corinthian criterion for the legitimate apostle.

If Paul is responding to their criteria, the Corinthians wanted their apostle to be a hero. In the context, it appears Paul's rivals wanted an apostle who could heroically 'go over the wall'. He did not go over the wall; he did not even let himself down the wall. Unnamed persons smuggled him out of Damascus. By using this parody as the climactic moment in his recital, Paul demonstrates how absurd it is to engage in any bragging contest. He inverts the 'hero' criterion for apostleship and claims that although he failed the test of an 'over the wall' hero, he nonetheless remains an apostle of Jesus Christ.

2. Nullifying the 'Ecstatic' Criterion (12.1-5)

As distasteful as it is, necessity (12.1) requires Paul to continue boasting, but he will boast of 'weakness' with the mask of the 'fool' firmly in place. Paul offers a precautionary statement (12.1), a disclaimer, before he continues: 'It is necessary to boast; nothing is to be gained from it'. Danker ('II Cor.', p. 186) preserves the satirical thrust with a paraphrase: 'I can't escape boasting. It won't be helpful to you, but I will go on to visions and revelations of the Lord'. At v. 5. Paul says, 'On behalf of such a person, I will boast, but on my behalf, I will not boast, except in my weaknesses'. Having given his disclaimer, Paul is ready to 'go on to visions and revelations of the Lord' (12.1).

In vv. 2-4 Paul gives two parallel descriptions of the heavenly journey. The first description comes in v. 2 and the second in vv. 3-4.

Parallel Accounts of the Heavenly Rapture

The First Description (v. 2)	The Second Description (vv. 3-4)
(a) I know a person in Christ	(a) And I know such a person
(b) Fourteen years ago	(b)
(c) Whether in the body, I do not know	(c) Whether in the body, I do not know
(d) Whether out of the body, I do not know	(d) Whether out of the body, I do not know
(e) God knows	(e) God knows
(f) Was caught up to the third heaven	(f) Was caught up into paradise
(g)	(g) And I heard unutterable utterings which a mortal is not permitted to repeat.

Some commentators (e.g. Plummer, p. 344) find here accounts of two ecstatic experiences. It is more probable here that the 'and' is ascensive, not a simple conjunction and reads, 'Indeed, I know such a person'. Stylistically, the parallel structure is a Semitic device called synthetic parallelism. Repetition amplifies, saying the same thing in a slightly different way, while it makes what is said more emphatic. Reiteration here intensifies the satirical tone by adding a note of simulated suspense at the threshold of utmost disclosure. Since there is only one temporal point of reference (12.1) and only one enigmatic revelation, it appears the apostle intends to describe only one event (Lincoln, 'Paul the Visionary', p. 211).

Paul's parodic rapture story introduces an aretalogy (cf. Smith, pp. 174-99 on aretalogy). Still speaking as a fool in a fool's speech with a parodic defense in the context of parodic boasting in weakness, Paul tells about 'a person' who was 'caught up' to paradise or the third heaven. The 'Fool' in splendid irony complies with conventions of 'self-praise' by speaking in the third person: 'I know a person' (12.2). It is not until v. 7 that he identifies 'the person' in v. 2 as Paul. Although the 'Fool' promises 'visions and revelations' (v. 1), his 'person' has only one revelation.

There is no vision and v. 7 drops 'visions', as there is only one date in v. 2.

Third person narration indicates irony because 'distancing is central to the ironic perspective' (Duke, p. 69). Furthermore, it is consistent with Plutarch's convention ('Inoffensive Praise' 542C). When the 'fool' claims not to know whether the heavenly experience was somatic or nonsomatic, it provides more evidence of irony. Theologically Paul may intend the contrast between the repeated 'I do not know' and 'God knows' to indicate that revelations are within the provenance of God and do not legitimize an apostle. Paul's 'person' arrives in the 'third heaven' (v. 2) or 'paradise' (v. 4, cf. Lincoln, *Paradise Now*). In this ecstatic experience, the person hears only 'unutterable words' (v. 4), but cannot repeat what he heard because it is not lawful (v. 4). Some scholars (e.g. Danker, Bultmann, Furnish, Martin, Barrett *et al.*) seek parallels to Paul's oxymoronic 'unutterable utterings' (v. 4) in the literature of the mystery religions. The parallels are hardly parallels. The apostle begins by declaring the boast about the rapture will be worthless, signaling the ironic, parodic nature of the pericope.

P.E. Hughes (p. 439) opines that this extraordinary revelation 'must have exercised an incalculable influence on Paul's whole ministry and apostleship'. Such an assessment sounds more like a Corinthian reading than a Pauline reading of the text. Consider the difficulties of this view. If Hughes is correct, someone should explain: (1) why Paul waits 14 years (v. 2) to tell it; (2) this statement appears in a 'Fool's Speech' and a parodic aretalogy which signals irony; (3) Paul designates this story as an example of 'boasting in weakness' (12.5; 11.30); (4) twice the 'person' claims ignorance about the somatic or nonsomatic nature of the experience, another marker for irony; (5) 'unutterable utterings' is oxymoronic, combining two incompatible ideas; (6) if the words are 'unutterable', why is it necessary to declare it unlawful to repeat them? Again, the idea is oxymoronic; (7) if Paul hears 'unutterable utterings' that he cannot repeat, what is its value in a 'defense speech?'; (8) the indirectness of Paul's speech indicate irony. If Paul is using mystery religion language, he is parodying the language and lampooning a false criterion of apostleship. In this passage, irony works overtime!

Apparently the Corinthians are looking for 'the signs of the apostle' (12.12a). The crux of the issue is evidence. After Paul's rapturous experience, he still did not have the evidence to satisfy the Corinthians and Paul never thought it would. He returns from ecstasy with empty hands. Spittler's remarks are instructive:

> The thrust of his polemic is by no means an attempt to outdo his opponents by detailing a superior ecstatic experience. Rather, and still

> speaking 'as a fool', he inverts the very criterion of his opponents by saying in essence that ecstasy is no proper cause for boasting nor does it provide any adequate apostolic accreditation (p. 261) .

Paul never denies the right of the Corinthians to evaluate his apostolate but he satirizes their criteria *ad absurdum*. The *sine qua non* of an aretalogy is a hero (Smith, p. 196), but in his aretalogy, Paul returns from his rapture, unlike the Gnostics, with empty hands. By the parody of an aretalogy, Paul invalidates the Corinthian criterion. He is an 'apostle of weakness' who wants the Corinthians to critique his apostolate on the basis of what they 'see and hear' (12.6).

Distancing, the charade of talking about a person other than oneself (2.1-5) allows Paul to suggest facetiously that he avoids the odium of self-praise. He will boast only in his weaknesses. In irony, Paul expresses concern that the 'extraordinary quality' of his experiences (v. 7) should lead to an overestimation of him. Stylistic and text-critical considerations weigh in favor of v. 7a linking to v. 6 rather than v. 7b. Paul wants the Corinthians to judge him by what they 'see' and 'hear' from him. He will not try to impress them with advantages that might bribe them. They should see him as an humble and weak apostle. Only in this way can they perceive the character of the life the extraordinary power of God reveals (4.7-12).

3. Upending the 'Healer-Apostle' Criterion (12.7-10)

A transition from the parodic rapture story (12.1-5) to the parodic healing story is difficult because of text-critical problems and issues of versification in vv. 6-7 (cf. Barrett, *Commentary*, p. 305). Form-critically, 12.7-10 is a parodic aretalogy presented as a healing story (Betz, 'Christus-Aretalogie', pp. 297-303). Although the accounts of the heavenly rapture and healing story are formally and functionally distinct, and one need not fuse the stories, the 'in order that I might not exalt myself' (12.7a; repeated in v. 7c) insures a connection between the stories. Still speaking ironically as a 'fool', Paul declares the 'thorn in the flesh' to be a consequence of being 'caught up' to the third heaven (i.e. paradise).

Spencer's suggestive study of irony in Paul alerts us that 'I exalt myself' in v. 7 is ironic (p. 355). However, when she thinks Paul is indirectly saying that his opponents are 'puffed up with pride', she ignores her insight and appears to be unaware of Betz's form-critical analysis that 12.1-5 is a parody of a rapture. The irony is that anyone who has returned from a heavenly experience without the evidence should be so tempted to pride that God gives a 'thorn in the flesh' to insure humility! How can Paul speak straightforwardly of the 'extraordinary quality' of a revelation that produced no evidence? That the rapture results in a 'thorn' instead of evidence that Paul is an apostle is undeniably ironic. The rapture provides no evidence that Paul is a legitimate apostle.

To narrate the rapture story is 'useless' (12.1) and Paul further satirizes the Corinthian criterion of apostleship with ironical references to the 'extraordinary quality' of a revelation that produced nothing. He could not understand the 'unutterable utterings', but contradictorily he then says he cannot tell what he heard because 'it is not lawful for any human to repeat' it. Without the evidence from the ecstatic experience, humiliation is more appropriate than pride. Paul is inverting the Corinthian criterion with parody and irony. The Greek term that characterizes the revelation may be translated 'abundance' or 'extraordinary quality'. Paul promised 'visions and revelations' at 12.1 but he gives no account of visions and reports only one revelation. In a context in which irony pervades a parodic account of only one revelation, 'extraordinary quality' is certainly a more appropriate translation than 'abundance'.

More than a century ago, Søren Kierkegaard (*Edifying Discourses*, p. 164) opined that Paul's thorn in the flesh 'seems to have afforded an uncommonly favorable opportunity for everyone to become an interpreter of the Bible'. Deissmann (p. 60 n. 5) suggests that 'a small library could be assembled, all dealing with Paul's illness'. Notwithstanding, Lenski (*2 Cor.*, p. 442) thinks we have 'nothing but hypotheses'. Some interpreters (Barrett, *Commentary*, p. 248) say that certainty about the identification of Paul's thorn is unattainable, that no one knows exactly what it was (e.g. Keck, p. 106). However, a review of the literature might lead to the illusion that there is a consensus that the thorn was some form of physical debility (cf. Mullins, p. 299, for a review).

Throughout the history of New Testament interpretation, some scholars have dissented from the 'malady hypothesis'. Tertullian (*De Pudic* 13.6; *Against Marcion* 5.12) thought Paul's thorn was a pain in the apostle's head or ear. In *De Fuga in Persecutione* (9.2) he understands 'thorn' to be a stake. On the other hand, Chrysostom (*Homilies on II Corinthians*, Hom. 26) thought the thorn was Paul's opponents: Alexander the coppersmith (2 Tim. 4.14), the party of Hymenaeus and Philetus (2 Tim. 2.17) and all the adversaries of the Word. Lightfoot (p. 190) thinks Gal. 4.13-14 is a parallel to 2 Cor. 12.7 and points to some malady of the eyes. The context, rather than relating 2 Cor. 12.7 to Gal 4.13-14, provides clues for a more adequate identification of the 'thorn'.

The Greek term *skolops,* translated 'thorn', appears nowhere else in the New Testament. However, just as second-century Christian storytellers loved to 'fill in' the biographical blanks in the Gospels and Letters, so commentators have filled the literature of interpretation with long lists of assumptions. Creative interpretation may use the technique of equating 'thorn in the flesh' at 2 Cor. 12.7 with Gal. 4.13-14, but it hardly advances exegesis of either passage. Lightfoot justifies the harmonization of these texts by claiming the passages so closely resemble each other that is natural to suppose the allusion to be to the same in both. A comparison of the texts is quite revealing: (1) in Galatians it is 'weakness of my flesh'; in 2 Corinthians it is a 'thorn in the flesh'; (2) in Galatians, the construction has the preposition 'in' and the personal pronoun 'my'; 2 Corinthians has neither; (3) in Galatians Paul's condition is temporary while the present subjunctives in 2 Corinthians suggest a chronic condition; (4) in Galatians it paves the way for preaching, but in 2 Corinthians, it is a hindrance to ministry; (5) in 2 Corinthians, the 'thorn' is a consequence of a rapture, but Galatians has no such association; (6) the term 'flesh' appears in both texts but in different cases, dative in 2 Corinthians and genitive in Galatians. A simple chart makes the issues quite clear.

2 Cor. 12.7	Gal. 4.13-14
thorn [*in*] the flesh	*weakness* of the flesh
	in my flesh
Permanent	Temporary
Hinders ministry	Facilitates ministry
Rapture and thorn	

Since the similarity in the two texts rests only with the use of 'flesh', Mullins (p. 30) correctly rejects the hypothesis. Even if one proved the allusions in the texts to be identical, the argument for the 'physical malady' theory would be far from conclusive. However, an analysis of the texts has shown they are by no means identical. There is no a priori reason for assuming any physical ailment in the phrase 'thorn in the flesh'. Witherington (p. 462) thinks (against McCant, pp. 550-72) that the thorn was to keep Paul from being too elated. 'In other words, it brought him right back down to earth' (Witherington, p. 465). Witherington misses or ignores the irony although he concedes that 'Betz may be right' that at vv. 7-9 Paul gives a parody of a healing story' (Witherington, p. 461). He argues that although the parallels are not exact, that the term 'flesh' points to 'something physical'. It is a gross understatement for Witherington to concede the texts 'are not exact'! One term used with different cases and contexts does not make a case for any malady hypothesis.

Without any doubt, the majority of New Testament scholars have been partial to the 'sickness hypothesis'. However, as Barrett (*Second Corinthians*, p. 315) reminds us, 'The very variety of these suggestions shows that certainty is unattainable' with specific diagnoses. With biting sarcasm, Lenski (*2 Cor.*, p. 1303) complains that theologians who are laypersons in medicine diagnose Paul's disease and insist on the correctness of their diagnoses. He labels them 'quacks' and accuses anyone who accepts their diagnoses of condoning quackery. One might also add, the diagnoses are made posthumously without a patient! For a sobering experience, consider some of the many diagnoses: hypochondria, gallstones, gout, rheumatism, sciatica, gastritis, head lice, deafness, dental infection, neurasthenia, speech impediment, remorse for persecuting Christians, epilepsy, aphasia, malarial fever, headaches, earaches, acute opthalmia, hysteria, *ad infinitum, ad nauseam*.

Literally, Paul's word for 'thorn' means 'what is pointed' and is a cognate of the verb 'to hack'. Its first attestation is as 'a pointed stake' (Delling, p. 409; BAGD, *s.v.*). With the sense of a stake, a *skolops* ('thorn') was an instrument of execution. The first attestation as a 'splinter' or 'thorn' is in the Septuagint (Sir. 43.19; Hos. 2.8; Josh. 23.13). The closest parallel is LXX Num. 33.55 where it is 'thorn in your eyes'. Both LXX Num. 33.55 and Ezek. 28.24 use Paul's word (*skolops*) as a metaphor for persons. Ezekiel uses the singular 'thorn', as does Paul, but clearly refers to a group of persons. Mullins (p. 302) thinks any Jew in Paul's time would have recognized it as a literary idiom for an enemy. Strack and Billerbeck (p. 534) are more cautious but state that in Rabbinic usage, 'thorn' refers to what causes pain, but not especially to sickness. In Numbers, the Israelites are to destroy their 'thorns', whereas not even prayer removes Paul's thorn.

Since 'messenger of Satan' [or 'angel of Satan'] is an appositional explicative for 'thorn in the flesh', the most natural interpretation is that 'messenger' refers to a person or group of persons. The Hebrew Bible views angels as representatives of the heavenly world and, for the most part, this is taken over into the New Testament. Seldom does 'angel' or 'messenger' mean a human messenger in the New Testament, but see Jas. 2.25; Lk. 7.24; 9.52. Josephus uses the term for 'angel' and 'messenger'. Jewish Christian texts (1QS 3.21-24; *Herm. Man*. 6.2.1) call Satan an angel. However, Kittel (pp. 74-87) has found no other instance of 'angel of Satan'. Some texts refer to Satan's angels (*T. Asher* 6.4; Mt. 25.41; Rev. 12.7, 9; Barn. 18.1). Paul alludes to 'ministers of Satan' (2 Cor. 11.15). In its normal usage, the referent for 'angel' is a person, whether earthly or heavenly. Paul uses the term only to designate a person (R.P. Martin, p. 413; Mullins, p. 302). 'Thorn' and 'angel' refer to a person or group of persons.

Without any evidence, parallels or justification, Thayer (*s.v.*) interprets 'angel of Satan' as 'a grievous bodily ailment sent by Satan'. BAGD (*s.v.*) makes no advance with his explanation, 'that which causes pain'. Presuppositions rather than evidence determine these interpretations. For the apostle, this is a conflict between God and Satan. Paul is an 'ambassador for Christ' (5.20) and anyone who questions his apostolic authority becomes 'an angel of Satan' (12.7). The battle is no less intense when Satan masquerades as 'an angel of light' (11.14). In *Barn.* 18.1, the 'angels of God' oppose the 'angels of Satan'.

With the keen sense of humor that prompts comedians to make themselves the butts of their own jokes, Paul says that because of the extraordinary quality of his revelation that produced no evidence, God gave him a 'thorn' as an antidote for pride! Repetition of the phrase 'in order that I might not exalt myself' (v. 7ab) amplifies the satire of a 'thorn' as an antitoxin for his poisonous pride. Persisting in his folly, Paul caricatures the 'thorn' as a benefaction given to him. Grammatically, the logical donor is Satan; the donor is an 'angel of Satan'. However, scholars generally take 'was given' as a 'divine passive', making God the donor. Satan, who is God's arch rival, has a colossal ego and would gladly prance across the stage as a competitor who sends Paul an antidote to arrogant pride. Because God is ultimately responsible for giving the thorn, the ironic humor is doubly sharp and the parody is certain.

Ironically, the purpose of this antidotal thorn is to 'buffet me', as if Paul had not had enough buffeting already. Plummer (p. 352) notes that having 'angel' precede 'to buffet' saves us from mixed metaphors; a thorn cannot strike with a fist, but a messenger can. Plummer overlooks the fact that 'angel' is an elucidating appositive and 'thorn' is the main subject and it does not affect the interpretation. A relatively rare word in the Greek New Testament, 'to buffet' means 'to hit with a closed first' (K.L. Schmidt, p. 818). 'To hit with a closed first' is the usual meaning of the term (Mk. 14.65 = Mt. 26.67; 1 Cor. 4.11; 1 Pet. 2.20).

Given the consistent use of the verb, it is strange for BAGD to define 'buffet' figuratively only in 2 Cor. 12.7 as 'painful attacks of illness' (*s.v.*). Moreover, BAGD provides no evidence but is content to list various diagnoses suggested by non-medical scholars. A.T. Robertson (*Word Pictures*, V, p. 225; cf. Bultmann, *2 Corinthians*, p. 225), likewise defines 'thorn' and 'buffet' as 'some physical malady'. 'To buffet' is the distinct act of a person beating someone with a clenched fist. As with 'thorn' and 'angel', Paul retains his reference to a person with the verb 'to buffet' (Mullins, p. 301). The durative force of the present subjunctive makes the text read 'that he should continue to abuse me'. This interpretation ties the thorn to the 'hardship list' (11.23-29).

In the New Testament, the verb 'to remove' or 'depart' always refers to persons (R.P. Martin, p. 417). BAGD (*s.v.*) finds a reference to 'illness' in the first three terms but, surprisingly, finds no such figurative meaning with 'to remove'. Mullins (p. 301) notes that all four terms have personal referents. Consistent with his use of words referring to person, at v. 8, Paul uses the masculine 'this person', not the neuter 'it', although one should not press too far on this interpretation.

As a consequence of a locative interpretation of the dative 'in the flesh', malady hypotheses have proliferated. However, if Paul had intended a physical referent, he could have expressed it more precisely in the Greek, as he does at Gal. 4.14. The expression here is more probably a *dativus incommodi*, 'for the flesh' (BDF, §§188, 199). Taken with Paul's use of four metaphors, all of which have personal referents, and his likely allusion to Num. 33.55, it is highly probable that Paul refers to a group of persons when he discusses his 'thorn for the flesh'. The evidence for this interpretation is compelling.

METAPHOR	*REFERENT*
Thorn	A personal referent
Angel	A personal referent
Buffet	A personal referent
Remove	A personal referent
Masculine Pronoun	This person
Num. 33.55	A group of persons
Thorn	Sick group of people

If it is probable that Paul refers to a group of persons, the remaining task is to identify the person(s) to whom the enigmatic metaphor refers. All of the statements in the foolish discourse are ironic and thus have tiers of meaning. A parodist, Paul employs irony that is 'a double-leveled literary phenomenon in which two tiers of meaning stand in some opposition to each other' (Duke, p. 17). In his parodic healing story Paul makes the thorn a consequence of his heavenly rapture. Understood as an instrument of execution, an interpretation quite possible in Corinth, a 'thorn' would have meant the termination of Paul's apostolate.

P.E. Hughes (p. 447) misses the irony and his tier of meaning becomes a Corinthian interpretation! He sees a body helplessly impaled, 'transfixed, painfully held down and humiliated'. The hypothesis offered here is that the 'thorn for the flesh' is a sick Corinthian church. Witherington (p. 447 n. 93) calls this hypothesis (cf. McCant, pp. 550-72) 'a novel thesis' and suggests there are a 'host of reasons' to reject the thesis, including the observation that it 'is not clear that the Corinthian church had simply or totally rejected Paul. There are notable troublemakers but not rejection by the majority.' If there so many reasons to reject the thesis, Witherington should produce the evidence. Paul writes 2 Corinthians to the whole church, but makes distinctions between the majority and the minority throughout. His 'thorn' is not the majority but the minority. Witherington's conclusion of a 'visionary with poor eyesight' depends on the tired theory of Lightfoot and is a poor substitute for the hypothesis he rejects. Paul's tier of meaning allows the 'thorn' to be an irritating splinter and allows the situation to remain open.

Why the Corinthians? Parody functions to expose or criticize, and throughout 2 Corinthians Paul invokes invective against the Corinthians. When Paul concludes the parodic healing story, he exclaims, 'I have become a fool; you have forced me to it' (12.11). The pain of the 'thorn' is consonant with Paul's allusion to a 'painful letter' in 2.4-5. Since the Corinthian leaders have disciplined the ringleader, the problem was certainly in the Corinthian church. The Corinthians felt the pain of that letter but Paul has no regrets because it led to repentance (7.8). However, Paul alleges that he wrote the letter 'not for the sake of the offender, nor for the sake of the one offended, but that my earnestness on your behalf might be made known to you in the sight of God' (7.12). Paul wants to 'build up' the church (10.8; 12.19; 13.10).

Consistent with conventions for self-praise, and the irony inherent in a parodic defense, Paul denies he is writing a defense (12.19). The ambiguity that has surrounded the 'thorn' for centuries may be a clue that Paul means it for the Corinthians. There is no good reason to suppose the Corinthians missed the meaning of the ironic metaphor. Paul writes to the Corinthian church to deal with problem people there, not to outside opponents who rival his apostleship.

Aristotle advises: 'Now what you should do in your introduction is to state the subject, so that the issue may be perfectly clear; whereas in the epilogue you should give a summary of your proofs'. In his 'Fool's Discourse', Paul pleads for forbearance in 'a little bit of foolishness'. He writes of his 'godly jealousy' for the Corinthians and his desire to present the church to Christ as a pure virgin; he is their 'father'. His fear is that the serpent will deceive them as it did Eve (11.1-3). In his conclusion (12.11-18) Paul blames the Corinthians for forcing him to boast and failing to commend him (12.11). He alludes to signs of the apostle, the free gospel and identifies himself as their 'parent' who does not 'want what is yours, but you' (12.14). Immediately he denies having 'defended' himself. Thus, Paul reminds them that he began 'in foolishness' and ends 'in foolishness'. The entire speech, and the entire letter, have been a parodic defense. Probably unwittingly, Paul has structured his speech on Aristotelian principles.

Betz ('Christus-Aretalogie', pp. 288-305) has shown that form-critically, 2 Cor. 12.7-10 is a healing story in aretalogical style, citing significant parallels in Hellenistic healing stories, especially the Delphic oracles.

These parallels reveal a five-point division in the healing story: (1) Description of illness (v. 7); (2) Paul turns to the Lord (v. 8a); (3) Paul prays to the Lord (v. 8b); (4) oracle and a 'cure' (v. 9a); (5) recognition of healing and praise to God. In addition, Betz has shown that the healing story is parodic. The healing story has no healing, in the normal sense of the word. Paul's 'healing' is the assurance of God's sufficient grace. A healing story without a healing is parodic. In the end, Paul has no evidence because there is no healing. Again, he is inverting the Corinthian criteria. With or without a healing, Paul is an apostle of Jesus Christ.

Paul caricatures his relationship to Corinth as a 'sickness'. However, he uses terms requiring personal referents so the careful reader knows his prayer is for the healing of a 'sick church'. Parody continues since he has no evidence of 'healing' and boasting is 'useless' (12.1). The perfect tense of the word 'said' (12.9) indicates that God says there will be no healing and 'grace' is all Paul will get. Grace is constant, but there may be no healing at Corinth.

Paradox elucidates Paul's expression of a christological resolution of the 'thorn for the flesh'. 'Power is being perfected in weakness' (12.9). 'When I am weak, then I am strong' (12.10). Philo (*Vit. Mos.* 1.69) provides a striking parallel for Paul's statement. Commenting on what Moses learned at the burning bush, he says, 'Your weakness is your power'. Out of his weakness Paul discovers that 'the power of Christ will spread its tent upon me' (12.9). Perhaps the best commentary on 2 Corinthians comes from an interpetive paraphrase of Paul's declaration: 'By the grace of God I am an apostle of Jesus Christ' (1 Cor. 15.10). The 'thorn' reveals a source of grace sufficient for all Paul's needs.

Paul's reference to the triple appeal in prayer is probably a stereotypical expression for urgency in prayer. As Jesus prayed three times in Gethsemane and found no reprieve, so Paul prays three times but finds no healing. Euripides (*Hippolytus* 46) has Aphrodite say it is 'not in vain to pray to the deity three times in succession'. Horace (*Odes* 3.22.3; *Satires* 2.1.7) reflects a knowledge of the magic of triple performance. Paul regards the 'oracle' from God as final. His use of a perfect and an aorist in 12.8, 9, is a conscious attempt to tell the Corinthians that now rather than pray, he will 'boast in my thorn'. The word translated 'sufficient' is a present tense continuous verb: 'My grace continues to be enough' (12.9).

Weakness does not cause 'the power of Christ' to dwell on Paul, but in his weakness he finds the sufficient power and grace of God. The result is a paradoxical boast; v. 9b establishes what Paul says in 11.30

and 12.5, that he boasts only in weakness. Paul's parodic story becomes one of triumphant endurance in the face of incredibly difficult crises. The endangered benefactor emerges as a miraculously victorious paraplegic. God has granted to Paul the 'high privilege...of suffering for Christ' (Phil. 1.29). Nothing can separate him from the love of God (Rom. 8.31-39). He has learned in all circumstances to be 'Christ-sufficient' (Phil. 4.11-13).

Verse 10 shows that Paul's paradoxical boast is not against others, but in joyful acceptance of suffering. 'I take pleasure in weaknesses, insults, hardships, persecutions and calamities for the sake of Christ.' Paul offers a second catalog of hardships in the 'Fool's Speech'. The phrase 'for the sake of Christ' stands at the end of the sentence but belongs to the verb 'to please' rather than with the catalog. The context requires a causal interpretation; that is, Paul does not accept hardships as a benefit to Christ, but because Christ's power becomes evident in weakness. As in vv. 5 and 9b, Paul mentions 'weakness', but now it is the first item in a list of hardships with which he has had to cope (cf. 2 Cor. 11.29a; 1 Cor. 4.10b). The items following 'weaknesses' are appositional to and illustrative of weaknesses.

This catalog of hardship concludes with a triumphant, if paradoxical, affirmation, 'When I am weak, then I am strong'. The 'when...then' form accentuates the paradox. With the indefinite particle, 'whenever', Paul includes not only the thorn, but places his entire ministry under the rubric of 'weakness'. Paul's third tier of meaning for the thorn is Christological. The catchwords 'weakness' and 'power', in 12.9 and 13.4 indicate his christological interpretation. Paul defines his whole ministry christologically. He so identifies with Christ that 'the sufferings of Christ are mine' (2 Cor. 1.18). Paul's theology is Christology.

At Corinth, his message was the foolishness of 'the word of the cross' (1 Cor. 1.18) and 'Christ crucified' (1.23; 2.2), both in contexts of weakness. He carries 'in the body the dying of Jesus' and this earthen vessel is 'delivered over to the death of Jesus' (2 Cor. 4.10-11). The apostle wants to be 'conformed to the death of Jesus' (Phil. 3.10) and he is 'crucified with Christ' (Gal. 2.20; cf. Rom. 6.6). In his schema of apostle, there is suffering, which explains 'boasting in weakness'. Paradox empowers the christological resolution: 'Power is being perfected in weakness' (12.9) and 'When I am weak, then I am strong' (12.10).

Remarkable parallels in the passion narrative and the parodic healing story confirm Paul's christological understanding of the 'thorn' and his ministry. Consider the following parallels:

A Comparison of Jesus and Paul

Jesus faces a *stauros* (cross), an instrument of death (Mk. 14.32-35, par.)	Paul has a *skolops* (thorn), a possible instrument of death (2 Cor. 12.7)
Three times Jesus prays, 'Let this cup pass from me' (Mk.14.35)	Three times Paul prays, 'Remove this thorn from me' (2 Cor. 12.8).
Jesus prays, 'Not my will but your will' (Lk. 22.42).	Paul receives an oracle: 'For you, my grace is sufficient' (2 Cor. 12.9)
Jesus dies on the cross (Mk. 13.24)	Paul's thorn will remain (2 Cor. 12.9).
Jesus' 'own people' reject him (Jn 1.11)	Paul's 'own church' rejects him (2 Cor. 10.14)
God raised Jesus from the dead (Mk. 16.1)	Paul will live with Christ (2 Cor. 13.4).
Jesus is the 'Rejected Messiah'	Paul is the 'Rejected Apostle'
Jesus is the Suffering Servant Messiah	Paul is the Suffering Servant Apostle

So many parallels suggest that Paul is consciously using the story of Jesus as a paradigm for his apostleship. By the power (i.e. grace) of God that has made itself at home with Paul and 'tents' upon him, Paul is 'an apostle of Jesus Christ' (1.1). Ironically, even though he is a 'nobody', (12.11), he is not at all inferior to the 'super apostles' and God reveals divine power in Paul's ministry. Corinth has received all 'the signs of a true apostle' (12.12). Paul's 'defense' is parodic. No one at Corinth has jurisdiction over Paul's apostleship. His purpose is not self-defense but 'building up' the church to which he was 'father'.

d. Correction for the Offended Reader (12.11-18)

Observing cultural conventions, Paul offers an epidiorthosis (subsequent justication, 'rhetorical ointment') because what he has written has the potential for offense. His epidiorthosis (12.11-18) matches his prodiorthosis (11.1-21a) and is equally parodic. Some scholars (BDF, §495.3) think of only v. 11 as an epidiorthosis. Others (e.g. Furnish, p. 554) treats vv. 11-13 as epidiorthosis. Thematic unity in 12.11-18 argues much more in favor of these eight verses being a unit. The epidiorthosis allows Paul to change his tone. However, because it is parodic, what he says in this 'correction for offended readers' does little to assuage the offensiveness of what he has already written.

Paul has become a 'fool', but he transfers the blame to the Corinthians (v. 11). Invective 'shames' the Corinthians for failure to commend him. Their commendation could not make him an apostle (3.1) but they are Paul's commendation letter from Christ (3.2) and they have failed. His expectation is not a contradiction. His apostleship originated with God (Gal. 1.1) and only God has jurisdiction over him (1 Cor. 4.3-5) but the

Corinthians are his seal of apostleship (1 Cor. 9.2) and their existence as a Christian community attests his apostleship (1 Cor. 3.6, 10; 4.15). With a devastating blast of wit, Paul adds, 'For in nothing do I come short of your superlative apostles, even though I am nothing' (12.11c; cf. 10.7; 11.5). The irony is humorous and the joke is patent. In his 'nothingness', recounted in detail since 11.23, he is superior to the super apostles.

In obvious parody, Paul asserts that the Corinthians have seen the 'signs of an apostle'. The expression 'signs and wonders and powers' is not common in the New Testament (cf. Acts 2.22; Heb. 2.4). Paul seldom speaks of miracles he has performed, but see 2 Cor. 6.6-7; Gal. 3.5; Rom. 15.19). The Paul of Acts is quite a healer (13.6-12; 14.8-18; 15.12; 16.16-18; 19.11-12; 28.3-6, 7-10). However, Acts provides no miracles during Paul's tenure at Corinth. Witherington (p. 455 n. 3) thinks of Paul's reference to miracles here as a 'supplementary argument'. Furnish (p. 555) suggests that miracles attested 'any valid religious truth' in ancient times.

Neither Paul's view of ministry nor the present context support Witherington and Furnish. Here Paul mentions miracles as an inversion of apostolic criteria. Apparently they want an apostle who is heroic (*corona muralis*), ecstatic (rapture), and performs miracles (miracle story). Paul characterizes his ministry as one of sincerity and holiness (1.12; 2.17; 3.4-6; 4.2; 5.11; 6.3-13; 7.2; 10.13-18; 11.6, 23-29). The 'sign of a true apostle' is suffering triumphantly (cf. 4.8-9; 6.4-10; 11.23-29; 12.11). The Corinthians have seen the 'signs of an apostle' when God demonstrated 'extraordinary power' (4.7) through a slave who can only boast in weakness. His suffering authenticates his apostleship. To proclaim himself a miracle worker would be promoting himself, a practice he disdains (4.5). Paul subordinates miracles to the proclamation of the gospel (Rom. 15.18-19; Gal. 3.5, possibly 1 Cor. 2.4).

By the use of parody, Paul accedes to the necessity of boasting but inverts their criteria for apostleship in the process. By using parodic examples in 11.30–12.10, two of which are aretalogies, he makes it clear that miracles do not confirm apostleship. Paul brings no evidence from his experiences, but he is still an apostle. He knows that a quacksalver, even the 'Man of Lawlessness' (2 Thess. 2.3, 9) can produce miracles. Two aretalogies and failure to scale the wall, all of which exhibit no evidence, make it highly improbable that at 12.12 Paul points to miracles he has performed as proof of his apostleship. For the apostle, the 'signs of an apostle' signify weakness and direct attention to one 'crucified in weakness' (13.4) whom he emulates.

Sarcasm is acidic when Paul asks in what way the Corinthians have been treated as inferior to his other churches. Acridity increases as he wryly adds, 'except that I myself did not burden you? Forgive me this wrong!' (12.13). If he is salving the wounds he has inflicted, why does he revisit an unresolved issue (cf. 11.7)? Mocking sarcasm parodies their inferiority complex as Paul observes, 'my only mistake, evidently was my refusal to take advantage of you'. A parodic apology provides more invective: 'Forgive me this injustice' (12.14b).

Verse 14 is splendid, double-edged irony as he responds to his question in v. 13. Paul subordinates his mention of a 'third visit' here, unlike 13.1, to the theme of 'burden', which persists through v. 18. He is preparing for a third visit but his fiscal policy has not changed. Now, speaking as a 'parent', he says 'I want you, not what you have'. Parents set aside resources for their children, not children for their parents. Paul's compassionate appeal is double-edged: he does not want their possessions, but he wants the Corinthians. He is not trying to make a profit (2.17), but he is asking for their loyalty. What he asks is far more demanding than if he simply asked for money (cf. Phil. 4.17); he is asking for their hearts.

A parental metaphor (12.14c) allows a gentler, more compassionate apostle to emerge. Paul, as parent, is responsible to his Corinthian children. With this metaphor Paul expresses affectionate, pastoral interest and this pastor is a parent. Paul's poverty (6.10) and the metaphorical statement shows that he does not mean to provide a material inheritance. Rather, he lifts the discussion to a higher level, showing that just as what he asks is a greater gift than money, so he also offers them an 'inheritance' that is more precious than money. What Paul most wants to communicate takes the form of a simile: 'I am your father' (Atkins, pp. 176-79).

Pursuing the parental figure, Paul not only does not want what the Corinthians have but is prepared to say, 'I will most gladly spend all I have and even give myself in order to help you' (Louw *et al.*, §57). Verse 15a amplifies the simile of father to a concrete case. Although he speaks as a father, the invective still evokes the question: 'If I love you more extravagantly, am I to be loved less?' This question functions to expose the egregious ingratitude of the community that does not reciprocate with more love for its spiritual father. The question Paul poses, camouflaged in a simulated naïveté, is: if he loves them prodigiously, why have they followed others and rejected the legitimacy of his apostleship? Paul's motive is not as much to reaffirm his love for the Corinthians as to accuse the Corinthians of failing to respond to his love. Acerbic sarcasm does not call into question Paul's pastoral concern. It does not diminish his claim: 'I promised you in marriage to one spouse, to present you as a pure virgin to Christ' (11.2). He wants to give to the Corinthians, not receive something from them.

In an apparently imaginative dialog with Corinth Paul says, 'Now, we agree that I did not burden you. Notwithstanding, being a crafty person, I took advantage of you by deceit' (12.16). Danker ('II Cor.', p. 202) paraphrases Paul's words colloquially: 'Very well, "You did not free-load", you will say to me. But in the same breath, "Ah, but you were clever and took advantage of us in our naïveté"'. Verse 16 amplifies vv. 14-15 with diatribe form that enables Paul to continue the invective. If the Corinthians concede that Paul has not been a burden (v. 16a), they must disagree with his assessment of his motives (v. 16b; cf. 11.11). Their assessment seems to be that Paul's pretense of independence is because he embezzled from the Jerusalem collection (v. 16b; cf. 8.20-24). Paul has been at great pains to preserve his probity (8.20) and wants 'to do what is right not only in the Lord's sight but also in the sight of others' (8.21). It seems beyond doubt that 12.16-18 has a connection with 8.20-24 and that Paul wrote chs. 8–9 before chs. 10–13 (Barrett, *Second Corinthians*, p. 324). There seems to be no finger of accusation against Titus and his cohorts.

Although missing in the Greek, NRSV include the words 'you say' at 12.16b. Filson (p. 414) wants 'they say' because he thinks the words should be on the lips of Corinthians interlopers. The NASB and KJV take the safe road, 'Nevertheless, crafty fellow that I am, I took you in by deceit'. We do not know that anyone, insiders or outsiders, made such a charge. Since it amplifies the obvious satire, Paul may well have formulated the 'charge' in keeping with the diatribe style in vv. 16-18. To advance his argument, he provides a self-portrayal of a con artist: 'Being a person capable of anything, I took you to the cleaners'.

In Greek, the word here translated as 'took' is a metaphor for fishing or hunting: 'I caught you' (BAGD, *s.v.* §1c). The term for 'deceit' is a metaphor for the bait with which to catch a fish (A.T. Robertson, *Word Pictures*, p. 268). He 'baited' them with the offer of becoming benefactors to Jerusalem and 'caught' them by embezzling the funds. With the reference to Titus in v. 18, he surely alludes to the Jerusalem offering. That anyone made such 'charges' against Paul is by no means certain but Paul is using an anti-sophist *topos* to make his argument.

Continuing the *topos* of fraud, Paul poses four rhetorical questions. The first two questions begin with a negative particle that indicates Paul expects a negative answer. 'With respect to any one whom I sent, did I defraud you through anyone for gain?' (v. 17). The compound verb, 'to defraud' means to take more than one's due and connotes greed or exploitation. Exploitation has been an ongoing issue in 2 Corinthians (7.2;

8.20-21; 9.5; 12.17). Verse 18 repeats the question in v. 17 more specifically: 'With respect to any one thing, did Titus defraud you for gain?' (v. 18b). With the 'anyone' (v. 17) and 'anything' (v. 18), Paul challenges the Corinthians to be specific with their evidence of fraud. The ironic tone here makes certain Paul's allusion to himself as an embezzler is also ironic. Paul assumes the only appropriate response to the two questions is 'No'. He is confident that no one in Corinth can produce a single shred of evidence against him.

There is circularity in Paul's argument (Bultmann, *2 Corinthians*, pp. 235-36). He seeks to prove his impeachability by appeal to Titus and to prove Titus' irreproachability by virtue of common cause with Paul. With the third question preceded by a different negative particle, Paul expects an affirmative response. 'Did we not conduct ourselves in the same spirit?' The 'same spirit' in the third question parallels the 'same steps' in the fourth question. The fourth question, 'Did we not take the same steps?' reiterates the third question. If the Corinthians give the expected 'Yes' to these questions, they cannot have suspicions about the apostle's integrity. In Corinth, as well as other large cities, charlatans passing off themselves as philosophers was a familiar sight (Betz, *Der Apostle*, pp. 116-17; Hock, p. 49). Fully aware of this situation, Paul does not want anyone to think of him as an impostor (cf. 2.17; 4.2).

3. Paul's Final Word to Corinth (12.19–13.13)

Socrates rejects self-defense in court. The orator, Lysias, composed a speech for him to deliver at his trial. Socrates declined, saying it was a good speech but did not fit him. He offered no apologia, in the technical rhetorical sense, but only as a philosopher might do. Socrates told the court that he made his defense, not on his account, as some might suppose, but on their account, in order that they might not put to death their chief benefactor of the city, whom God had given to them and whose like they would not easily find again. Paul begins his conclusion by denying that he has been defending himself and informs the Corinthians: 'Everything I do, beloved, is for the sake of building you up' (12.19). Paul rejects a rhetorical apologia because Paul thinks rhetoric is inadequate to proclaim the gospel (1 Corinthians 1–2). Paul's 'defense' is parodic and resembles a philosopher's *apologia* rather than that of a rhetorician.

Verse 19 is hardly 'rhetorical protective ointment' (contra Danker, 'II Cor.', p. 204). Paul's statement certainly would not mollify the Corinthians. As a declarative statement, v. 19a is more like diatribe style with Paul assuming he knows what the Corinthians think. Verse 19b functions as a *correctio,* and between v. 19a and v. 19b, Paul implies, 'You are wrong'. Verse 19b repeats verbatim what Paul said at 2.17, 'I am speaking in the sight of God in Christ'. The court to which Paul is accountable is God (cf. 1 Cor. 4.3-5). There is no defense because Paul cannot and will not recognize the Corinthian community as a judicial body; only God can judge him. Paul will not venture even to judge himself (1 Cor. 4.4).

Paul can deny offering a defense because his stance is parodic and he had no intentions of 'defending' himself. His 'Fool's Discourse' is ironical and he has offered three distinct parodies (at 11.30-12.10). Here he subverts expectations by announcing he has made no defense of himself. All that Paul has done has been 'in the sight of God' in order to edify the Corinthian church (v. 19c). He speaks only 'in Christ' (2.17; 5.17; 12.2) and only God is his judge (1.18, 23; 4.2; 5.11; 7.12; 11.11, 31). He is not accountable to the Corinthians. The parody is for his 'beloved' and intends to 'build up' the church. The parodic form shows that Paul rejects rhetorical apologia just as he rejects boasting as 'according to the flesh' (11.17) and 'useless' (12.1).

Consonant with the anti-sophistic tradition, Paul rejects rhetorical apologia; that would give too much credibility to the Corinthian complaints. He does not write from self-interest but out of concern for his congregation. Sometimes the harsh sarcasm in chs. 10–13 causes the modern reader to overlook the tender affection Paul has for Corinth (2.4; 6.11; 7.2-4; 11.1-3, 11; 12.14-18). With tender, pastoral tones, he addresses them as 'Beloved', denoting a close relationship, especially that of a parent and child (BAGD, *s.v.*). He hopes they will receive benefits from his ministry (1.7, 15, 24; 3.2-3; 4.5; 7.3, 8.16). The apostle is careful to say he exercises apostolic authority to edify the community (10.8; 12.19c; 13.10).

Affirmations in v. 19bc introduce vv. 20-21. Resuming the first person singular, Paul expresses two fears: (1) I may find you not as I wish; (2) you may find me not as you wish (v. 20ab). Paul expresses similar anxiety at 11.3. He expresses fear in a chiastic structure.

A I may find you
    B Not as I wish
    B' Not as you wish
A' You may find me

He hopes when he comes to Corinth for his 'third visit' (12.14; 13.1a) that discipline will not be necessary (13.2). 'Fear' is a major theme in vv. 20-21. Paul fears he will find various forms of sin at Corinth (v. 20); if that happens, Paul will not find Corinth as he wishes. If the Corinthians need discipline, they will not find the apostle as they wish.

Scholars think the sins in v. 20 suggest a rival mission (Barrett, *Second Corinthians*, p. 329) or that Paul has arranged the eight items in pairs (Plummer, p. 369). Furnish wisely cautions against over-analysis of the catalog of vices (p. 567). All the vices are traditional and appear in other lists in the New Testament, as well as in Hellenistic catalogs. All eight vices suggest partisan politics. 'Discord and jealousy' focus on partisanship and the six following describe problems generated by such divisiveness. Two particles in the sentence indicate that Paul is not suggesting the majority are guilty, but that some of them may have reverted to pagan vices.

Verse 21a is elliptical and depends on the 'I fear' of v. 20. Paul fears a second humiliation at Corinth. Paul's allusion to humiliation may be an echo of 11.7 and 10.1. Combined with 'to mourn', as well as the parallelism with v. 20, the humiliation lies in not finding Corinth 'as I wish', but immersed in party strife and immorality. The humiliation will come if the apostle must use his authority, to 'tear down' Corinth. While rejection by the congregation would be painful, Paul's greater concern is the possibility of strife and immorality that might require severe discipline. God, not the Corinthian, determines his apostolic status.

Paradoxically, Paul fears humiliation from God (v. 21a) because of sin in Corinth. One expects to hear that God will humiliate the Corinthians. Paul cannot exalt himself because the Corinthians are Paul's letter of commendation from Christ (3.3), but their persistence in sin makes the letter humiliating. At Corinth Paul constantly faces the humiliation that his ministry has failed to produce a Christ-like church. That only the work of God can produce holiness might be liberating, but it is not for Paul due to his paternal love for his children.

The proper and effective use of his authority may leave Paul discredited (Jones, p. 55). The verb 'to sin' is a perfect tense and suggests persistence in sinning. The aorist participle for 'repent' with the aorist 'practice' implies persons who continued to sin and did not repent. Paul seems to be saying that their conversion was not genuine or that they have regressed to previous sinful behavior. He fears God's humiliation. Their sins will cause grief for his pastoral heart. He identifies with his 'children'; their shame is his shame; when someone causes them to stumble, he burns (11.29).

The apostle repeats his intention for a 'third visit' (13.1; cf. 10.2; 12.14, 20-21), making it emphatic. Having stated his intention at 12.14, he must believe that repetition will support the warning he is preparing to give. With an allusion to LXX Deut. 19.15, Paul announces his plan to hold court on his third visit. They must substantiate any 'charge' by the witness of two or three witnesses. In light of 13.2, Paul is likely thinking of the use of the Deuteronomic rule in Palestinian Judaism to support the requirement to convict a person. In a general way Paul is telling Corinth that he has given sufficient judicial warning. 'The ones who have continued in their former sinning' refers to persons who were living sinfully prior to and at the time of Paul's second visit. As if to cover all bases, Paul adds, 'and all the rest'. By designating 'ones continuing in sin' Paul signals that condemnation is not for the entire church, but 'all the rest' affirms that anyone persisting in sin will deal with his wrath.

Already Paul has expressed fear that the serpent might deceive them (11.3) It appears to Paul now that the serpent has indeed beguiled some Corinthians. The 'that' is like quotation marks and repeats his departing words on his second visit: 'If I come again, I will not be lenient'. If there was uncertainty about a third visit when Paul first gave the warning, there is no doubt now. He definitely plans a third visit and he will act with apostolic authority; he will not spare them. The verb 'to spare' is a military term and means 'to have mercy on' someone (LSJ, *s.v.*). Paul will 'not have mercy on Corinth' when he arrives.

From what did Paul spare Corinth (1.23) that he now says he will not spare them (13.2)? The context of 1.23 suggests he was sparing them the pain of his scathing denunciations. At 13.2 he promises no longer to be lenient. Assuming the military metaphor is still in view, Paul is pledging he will no longer refrain from destroying the Corinthians in battle. If they persist in sin, he will use his authority to 'tear down' and not to 'build up' (13.10). A nonspecific threat of 'destruction' creates an aura of suspense that leaves one wondering what Paul has in mind. If necessary, he will deal harshly with recalcitrant and unrepentant sinners at Corinth.

Even the threat of punishment is parodic. At Corinth, Paul's authority is precarious. On the second visit, Paul had the support of the majority (2.6). Now, he is hardly in a position to exercise authority of any kind in Corinth. Instead, he faces the possibility that even the majority will reject him permanently. Paul has boasted of 'weakness' and now he has an excellent opportunity to test his principle 'Power is made perfect in weakness' (12.9). An earlier letter (2.9) had been to test their obedience. Now the Corinthians are putting Paul to a test of his apostolic credentials. Verse 3 continues the sentence in v. 2; the Corinthians want 'proof' that Paul is an apostle. 'Since' in v. 3a informs why Paul will not show mercy when he arrives. In effect Paul says, 'Since you are demanding proof, I will demonstrate the authority to tear you down'.

When the unrelenting apostle of destruction appears, the Corinthians should know they have provoked the war. 'To desire' (NRSV) in v. 3 is too weak; they are 'demanding' proof (BAGD, *s.v.*) as the NIV renders the verb. Paul's spirituality is not the issue here as Bultmann (*2 Corinthians*, p. 242) assumes. The Corinthians are disputing the legitimacy of his apostolic office. The issue of who is 'approved' and who is 'not approved' is the basic question in 13.1-4. Paul responds that he will demonstrate 'proof', but the Corinthians will not like the show. His 'proof' will be the use of his authority to 'tear down' unrepentant church members. In Paul they will confront the Christ who is 'not weak in dealing with you, but is powerful among you' (13.3). Paul uses an affirmation with which the Corinthians will agree, he is baiting the hook for the affirmation of the source of his 'power' to function in weakness as an apostle of Christ.

Grammatically, Paul tells the Corinthians that the Christ who speaks 'in me' is not 'weak toward you', but is powerful 'among you'. The sarcastic invective in v. 5, 'Or do you not recognize about yourselves, that Jesus Christ is in you', reveals the ironic character of 13.3b. An ironic statement, it reveals the tiered meaning of Paul's words. If we take Paul at face value, the Corinthians interpreted 'Christ in you' as 'signs and wonders and powers' (12.12). Contrarily, Paul understands 'Christ in you' to mean 'Christ among you as your judge'. He is saying the 'power' in the Corinthians is different than they have imagined.

Paul is probably alluding here, as he does again at 13.9, to their triumphalist boast that they are 'strong' (1 Cor. 4.10) and will reign with Christ (1 Cor. 4.8). However, Paul thinks believers do not rule with Christ's power; that is the subject of irony in 1 Cor. 4.8-13. Rather, the power of Christ rules them (2 Cor. 5.14). He writes of Christ being powerful 'toward' and 'among you', but not 'in you'. On his arrival, Paul will be an agent of Christ's power as he dauntlessly chastises errant, unrepentant persons in the community.

Power and weakness are dominant motifs in 13.1-10. Paul contrasts 'to be weak' (13.3, 4) and weakness with 'to be powerful' (13.3, 4, 8), 'power' (13.4) and 'powerful' (13.7). This section also places great emphasis on 'passing the test' (13.3; 7) and 'not passing the test' (13.5, 6, 7). Of the seventeen occurrences of 'to pass the test' and its cognates in 1 and 2 Corinthians, six appear at 2 Cor. 13.3-7. The force of Paul's argument lies in the sequence of these terms.

Since you demand proof (v. 3)
Examine yourselves (v. 5)
Whether you pass the test (5b)
I passed the test (v. 6)
Not that I appear to have passed the test (v. 7a)
I may appear to have failed the test (v. 7b)

The christological affirmation in 13.4 supports the claim of Christ's powerful presence with the congregation and is pivotal for developing the 'strength and weakness' theme at 13.1-10. The sequence of these terms reveals the potency of Paul's strategy.

> Christ is not weak toward you, but is powerful among you (v. 3b).
> Christ was crucified in weakness, but lives by the power of God (v. 4a).
> I am weak, but I will live with Christ by the power of God (v. 4b).
> I am not powerful against the truth (v. 8a).
> I rejoice when I am weak and you are strong (v. 9).

The 'power' of Christ is effective in Paul, who is 'weak' and lives in 'weakness', because 'weakness' and 'power' unite in Christ. Christ went to the cross as a 'weakling', but lives by the 'power' of God. Paul is 'weak', but he will live by the 'power' of God. The crucified Christ is 'weak', but the living Christ is 'powerful'.

Christ's death and resurrection are one event for Paul. Christ's death is not merely a past event followed by the resurrection. A Pauline view sees the cross as a continually present event. The Risen One remains the Crucified One and the Crucified One remains the Risen One. Anyone who shares the power of Jesus must also share his weakness (cf. 4.10; Phil. 3.10). Christ has been 'among' the Corinthians (13.3) where Paul appeared in weakness; that is Paul's 'approval rating'. If necessary, he can be 'powerful' (13.4) but he prefers to appear 'weak' while the Corinthians appear 'strong'. His 'weakness' and 'power' make him like Christ and thereby 'certify' him.

In this passage the apostle is polemicizing against a 'theology of glory' that presents Jesus only as a powerful figure. His kenotic theology (Phil. 2.5-11) requires 'weakness' (Phil. 2.7, 8) as well as 'power' (Phil. 2.9). The Christ-Paul analogy lies at the heart of 13.4 (Güttgemanns, pp. 152-54). Paul asks that the Corinthians consider that 'weakness', not overlording superiority (1.24; 11.19-21), is Christ's mode of operation and, and likewise, that of an ambassador of Christ (5.20). Like Christ, Paul came to them in weakness, and Christ was among them, which is characteristic of the gospel (4.7-15). Corinthian Christians fail to realize that in the meaningful necessities (12.10) of the apostle there is mirrored the shape of the cross of Jesus. Even if he must deal harshly with unrepentant Christians, he will act from power in weakness and he will suffer humiliation (12.21).

Unless they accept his weakness, Paul has no credential to show he has 'passed the test'. His parodies (11.30–12.10) show that he has no evidence but weakness and humiliation. The evidence for the legitimacy of his apostleship is his weakness. He has 'passed the test' because in the weakness of a cracked pot, God has displayed extraordinary power (4.7). Existentially Paul lives in the dialectic of weakness and power; they are complements, not contradictions. Among the Corinthians Paul has imitated the cruciform pattern of Christ's ministry (Kraftchick, pp. 625-28). Power is being perfected in weakness.

The difficulty for the interpreter of 2 Corinthians is that, if they ever existed, we do not have the prosecutor's charges. If the Corinthians made charges, we do not know what they were. What Paul tells us probably reflects the general situation at Corinth, but it is impossible to formulate the Corinthian 'charges'. All we have is Paul's parodic defense and surely he is capable of some distortion, misrepresentation and bias. Just as there is no dialog between Socrates and Athens, there is none between Paul and the Corinthians. What we know is that Paul's defense is parodic. In the closing statements he chooses an emotional appeal, and this appeal is congruous with the aims of the entire discourse: restored relationship with his converts. Kitzberger (p. 134) suggests that Paul's admonition to self-examination (13.5) is the purpose of 2 Corinthians.

Paul turns the tables on anyone demanding proof of his apostleship with the challenge: 'Examine yourselves to see whether you are living in the faith' (13.5a). 'Test yourselves' signals that they, not he, are on trial. The test for them is whether they are 'living in the faith'. Paul calls the authenticity of their relationship to God into question. 'Do you not realize that Jesus Christ is among you?—unless, indeed, you failed the test' (v. 5c). With obvious appeal to self-pity, Paul pleads, 'I hope you will find out that I have not failed the test' (v. 6). The apostle prays they will 'do nothing wrong' (v. 7), but quickly notes that the purpose of his prayer is not that he may 'appear approved'. Pastoral pathos brings the apostle to say that he wants them to do what is right even if it makes it appear that he has failed.

Pathos continues with the claim that Paul 'cannot act against the truth', but only 'for the truth' (v. 8). He rejoices when he is 'weak' and the Corinthians are 'strong'; he prays that they may 'become perfect' (v. 9). The purpose of his letter, while he is 'absent', is that when he is 'present' he will not be forced to act 'severely' (v. 10). The 'absent...present' theme echoes 10.1, 10. Paul's burning passion is that the Corinthians will 'pass the test' and that his 'third visit' will allow him to be a builder and not a demolitionist.

As he has been throughout 2 Corinthians, Paul continues to be the prosecutor, not the defendant. Antithetical terminology provides continuity between vv. 1-4 and 5-10. He issues an imperative: 'Test yourselves' at v. 5. To assure clarity he places 'yourselves' in an emphatic position, literally: Yourselves you test! (Moule, *Idiom*, p. 120). Instead of scrutinizing Paul's test results, they should test themselves. The proof that Paul seeks is not a legitimizing demonstration of pneumatic power, but the genuineness of their Christian profession. The Corinthians have clearly shaken Paul's confidence in their confession of faith. Against R.P. Martin (p. 479) who thinks Paul dismisses the idea that the Corinthians will fail, the grammar introduces the possibility that the Corinthians have become reprobates (v. 5b). Paul has now placed three tests before the Corinthians: (1) Test of obedience at 2.9; (2) test of love, loyalty at 8.8; (3) test of genuineness of faith at 13.5. Paul's purpose in 2 Corinthians is to call them to self-examination!

'Testing' here means 'to discover what kind of person one is' (BAGD, *s.v.*; Louw *et al.*, §27.45, 46). Having challenged them to 'discover who you are', Paul poses a rhetorical question 'Or, do you not know yourselves that Jesus Christ is in you?' (v. 5c). The 'in you' here corresponds to the 'in you' in v. 3 and both instances should translate 'among you'. The 'you' and 'yourselves' are plurals, indicating that Paul's question is at the corporate level. The statement is ironic. At the level of 'in you', the Corinthians would assuredly answer affirmatively, but Paul is asking 'Or do you not know what it means that Christ is among you?'

Of utmost concern to Paul is whether they understand Christ 'among you' as a critical power and that they always stand under the judgment of Christ who comes 'in power'. Now he assumes if they will use the correct criteria for their self-examination, they will correct their criteria for judging their apostle and understand the 'proof' of his apostleship. With a bit of needling, Paul adds to his question, 'Unless, of course, you have not passed the test'. Wordplay manipulates 'passed the test' and 'failed the test'. To 'fail the test' reveals one as a counterfeit, and 'disqualifies' the person. To 'pass the test' reveals that one is authentic and qualified. Paul's motive is not to get a verdict for or against the Corinthians. The crucial question is whether they are conscious of 'Christ among you' as one who judges and convicts. Paul seems to be asking if they recognize 'Christ among you' in the person of their apostle.

In a somewhat surprising move, Paul expresses 'hope' that they will learn he has passed his test (13.6). Symmetry anticipates a corresponding 'and that you did not pass' or 'that you did pass'. He writes neither statement. Corinthian Christians are Paul's letter of commendation to the world (3.2) and the seal of his apostleship (1 Cor. 9.2). The question, not the answer to the question, is crucial here. Paul hopes self-examination will ascertain that Paul 'passed the test'. If they conclude that

Paul, their founding father, does not pass the test, the Corinthians cannot pass. In that case, the community ceases to be apostolic and the community is counterfeit. If Christ is 'among' them (vv. 3, 5), their faith is authentic and Paul's apostolate is genuine. It is Paul who establishes their 'approved' status; they must recognize Paul as 'approved' unless they wish to 'fail the test' and be disqualified.

'Passing the test' is a recurrent theme in vv. 5-7. In each instance, Paul uses the term differently. At 13.5 it refers to discovering one's personal identity. At 13.6 Paul tries to tease them into 'testing' him while at 13.7 the terms 'approved' and 'disapproved' refer ironically to Corinthian criteria. Not only does Paul assure that he is praying for Corinth, he also discloses the content of the prayer. The structure of v. 7 reveals exquisite balance in Paul's thought.

A That you do nothing wrong
B Not that I may appear approved
B' But that you may do what is right
A' As though I am unapproved

Parallelism in this structure functions as amplification and makes it emphatic. Amplification is a device that allows a speaker to dwell on a thought, repeat, but vary the way it is said to give it greater emphasis (G.A. Kennedy, *NT Interpretation*, p. 21).

Here, as elsewhere (e.g. Phil. 1.9-11; Phlm. 6), the 'prayer disclosure' becomes an exhortation to readers. Paul exhorts as he prays that the Corinthians are to do nothing evil and do only what is good (Wiles, p. 247). This hortatory prayer may be responding to concerns of 12.20-21, that they cease behaving like pagans. It is a restatement of Paul's hope that the Corinthians will examine themselves. With the prayer disclosure, there is a disclosure of the apostle's motive. Paul is not anxiously awaiting, from self-interest, an acknowledgment that he is 'approved'. 'Doing what is right' and avoiding 'what is wrong' will prove that the Corinthians are 'approved'. Ironically, the disclosure of their 'approval' would simultaneously reveal Paul's 'disapproval'.

Paradoxically and ironically, if the Corinthians 'do what is right', Paul will be 'unapproved' because he will not have proof that he can be 'strong'. With no need to be 'severe' at Corinth, he would revive the spook of one who is bold in his letters but timid in face-to-face encounters (10.1, 10). His motive is 'that you may do good while I may appear as disapproved' (v. 7). From the Corinthian perspective, he will not be strong unless he come(s) as a general and makes war with them. Paul wants their full acceptance because their obedience is the only valid proof of the authenticity of their faith and his ministry among them.

Whether the Corinthians accept his apostolate is not a matter of indifference to Paul, as Furnish (p. 578) alleges, but his motive is that they 'pass the test'. Paul is willing to appear superficially 'approved' even though from their perspective he will seem 'unapproved'. The legitimacy of his apostleship does not depend on the Corinthian decision, but Paul thinks their salvation depends on it. Verse 7 echoes 12.19 and anticipates 13.10, all of which affirm that everything Paul does is for the edification of his Corinthian children. Beyond his ironic and parodic strategies, Paul reveals the heart of a pastor in v. 7. He prefers to be 'approved' rather than 'unapproved' at Corinth and he prefers acceptance over rejection. However, he is willing to seem 'unapproved' if that will bring allegiance to the gospel.

Parody becomes paradoxical as Paul concludes. There is not much chance that the Corinthians will do good and accept Paul. 'Doing good' and rejecting Paul are mutually exclusive, but the strategy diverts attention from the apostle to the Corinthians. He wants the Corinthians to continue their self-examination. Verses 5-7 function to challenge his readers to reconsider their criteria of legitimate apostleship but he does not need their 'approval' to authenticate his apostleship. Regardless of the Corinthian response, Paul can do nothing 'against the truth'. He is capable only of acting 'on behalf of the truth'. In the dialectic of weakness-in-strength (12.10) and acceptance-in-rejection (13.7), Paul conducts his life in the interest of truth. It is not possible for him to do otherwise.

As the 'for' shows, v. 8 explicates v. 7. As in 4.2, 6.7 and perhaps 11.10, 'truth', is the gospel in contrast to 'another gospel' (11.4). Paul proclaims, not himself, but 'Jesus Christ is Lord' (4.5). Since the gospel is his only criterion of action, his person is not an issue; he can do nothing that it is not on behalf of the gospel. His dialectic is that he is simultaneously 'approved' and 'unapproved', both 'powerful' and 'weak'. For Paul, this dialectic is the authentic existence of gospel reality. Whether he arrives at Corinth 'building up' or 'tearing down', it will be on behalf of the gospel and the best interests of the Corinthians.

The dialectic of weakness (10.10; 11.21, 30; 12.5-10; 13.3, 4) and power (10.4; 12.9, 10; 13.3, 4) becomes important again. Through weakness God discloses divine power (4.7; 10.3, 4; 12.9, 10; 13.3, 4, 9). Verses 7-9 are closely connected and the 'for' clause in v. 9 continues the thought of v. 8, although reference to praying for the Corinthians resumes the thought of v. 7. Apostolic behavior on behalf of the gospel means 'we rejoice when we are weak and you are strong' (v. 9). As in 12.9, 10; 13.4, 7, here the strength-in-weakness dialectic is paradoxical.

The 'weakness' of Paul (v. 9) corresponds to 'unapproved' (v. 7) and 'strength' (v. 9) parallels 'approved' (v. 7). Paul is 'unapproved' and 'weak', but he is also 'approved' and 'strong'. Paul does not simply endure weakness; he embraces it and glories in it as the 'signs of a true apostle'.

With 'I pray', Paul resumes and expands on the prayer disclosure in v. 7. While Paul's Greek word for 'to pray' in v. 9 may mean 'to wish' (as in Rom. 9.3), in v. 9 it has the same force as in v. 7 and means 'to pray'. Now, Paul prays not only that they may 'do what is right' (v. 7), but now he prays for their 'perfection' (v. 9). As in v. 7 the prayer disclosure functions not only as a prayer for the Corinthians, but also as an exhortation to the Corinthians. The RSV rendering 'improvement' is anemic and Lietzmann's rendering 'betterment' (p. 162), is hardly any improvement. Originally the Greek term, here rendered 'perfection', was a medical term referring to the setting of dislocated bones (LSJ, *s.v.*; Louw *et al.*, §75.5). Although the term denotes religious and moral perfection, it is not perfectionism (Filson, p. 421; P.E. Hughes, p. 484). Paul prays for their 'restoration', that a dislocated relationship might be reset and healed (BAGD, *s.v.*). This prayer captures the essence of the entire letter: reconciliation of the children with their father.

The contrast of 'being absent' and 'being present' in v. 10 recalls 10.1, 10, 11 and 13.2. Paul explains that he is writing 'these things' while absent so that when he is 'present', he will not need to use apostolic clout. He hopes still that he will not need to act 'harshly' with Corinth. However, in spite of hope (v. 6) and prayer (vv. 7, 9), the Corinthians' behavior is still an issue. Knowing that his letter might provoke a negative response at Corinth, Paul returns to his warnings at 10.1-11 and 12.19–13.4. From Paul's standpoint, the warning serves the best interest of a community in conflict. The apostle never prostitutes authority into authoritarianism. He does not renounce his apostolic authority but allows the principle enunciated in 10.8 to govern his conduct: apostolic authority is for building up and not for tearing down (13.10b).

The phrase,'for building up and not tearing down' forms an inclusio and indicates the argument in chs. 10–13 has come full circle. He is not a power-hungry bureaucrat who misuses and abuses authority. He is their benefactor and benefactors prefer construction over demolition. Paradoxically, Paul cannot lose and he cannot win. If he goes to Corinth 'unapproved', he will know he is 'approved'. If he arrives in 'weakness', Paul will be 'strong'. Thus, ironically if he must 'tear down', he will at the same time be 'building up'. Indeed, Paul seems to believe that 'tearing down' must precede 'building up' at Corinth. What Paul says in 12.19–13.10 is scarcely 'rhetorical ointment', as an epidiorthosis should be. Paul is still heaping invective on Corinth and uses paradox, sarcasm, and irony to make the invective more pungent. If 2 Corinthians is a 'defense', it is surely a parodic defense; it is not a serious, rhetorical apologia.

In his epistolary conclusion, Paul offers a series of five admonitions (v. 11a), a promise (v. 11b), greetings (v. 12) and a benediction (v. 13). In general, this epistolary conclusion follows the usual pattern in Pauline letters: greetings, doxologies and benedictions. With five imperatives in v. 11, the concluding statements of his argument intrude into the epistolary conclusion. The usual personal remarks and greetings are missing in this conclusion. Paul's strategy, especially with five rapid-fire staccato injunctions, is to continue the pressure and make the Corinthians defensive in the hope that they will realize that they must set their house in order before Paul arrives.

An adverb, 'finally', alerts the reader that Paul is making a transition and preparing to close the letter. With 'brothers and sisters', an address that is warm in tone, and pastoral in nature, Paul acknowledges that the Corinthians are Christians. 'Brothers and sisters', a common address in early Christianity, encompasses the entire congregation. It may also remind hearers that Paul, the preacher, is speaking. In 1 Corinthians Paul uses the address twenty times, but in 2 Corinthians only three times (1.8; 8.1; 13.11), but 'beloved' (12.19) is roughly synonymous.

Following the affectionate address, Paul releases a torrent of five pulsating, drumming imperatives: 'rejoice, restore yourselves, admonish yourselves, agree with one another, live in peace' (v. 11). The abrupt, disconnected style gets attention and gives the imperatives the appearance of interjections. In 'the briefest of all paraneses' (Talbert, p. 129), Paul issues orders with all the authority of an apostle. First he commands 'Rejoice', and certainly not 'good-bye' (NIV). The 'rejoice' here corresponds to the one in v. 9. Here Paul has in mind a rejoicing that is characteristic of the life of faith.

'Restore yourselves' is problematic because one must decide if the verb is passive or middle. Scholars have not reached a consensus on this issue. Since Paul prays for 'restoration' in v. 9, the cognate verb here is likely passive. However, since it is imperative, a paraphrase such as 'aim at restoration' (R.P. Martin, p. 498) captures the author's intent. The same problem exists with the third imperative. As a passive it may mean 'Pay attention to my admonitions' (cf. Heb. 13.2). As a middle, it could be 'Exhort one another'. Based on the imperatives and admonitory character of the context, it most likely it has to do with 'exhortation' rather than 'comfort'.

'Think the same thing' is a call to unity, especially unity in the divisive issue of Paul and his gospel, and may indicate that the old disharmony (1.10-12; 3.1-4; 12.20) was still a source of trouble. This imperative occurs at Rom. 12.16; 15.5; Phil. 2.2; 4.2 and most likely has its origin in political discourse. In view of Paul's fear at 12.20-21, the exhortation is apt. Undoubtedly, Paul has in mind for Corinth, as for Philippi (Phil. 2.5-11), that they adopt a kenotic (i.e. self-emptying) theology. He does not want them to deny their individuality and maintain a diplomatic truce of superficial uniformity. Rather he wants them to realize their identity and purpose for existing as a Christian community.

'Living in peace' is a consequence of living in unity and to live in peace is to experience God (v. 11b). Paul's final appeal is a string of imperatives suggesting continual action (Moule, *Idiom*, pp. 20-21), although v. 12 may provide an exception to the rule. Perhaps Paul is reminding the Corinthians that the qualities to which he refers in his thrumming list of imperatives are both a gift and a task (cf. Eph. 4.3). To these commands, Paul appropriately attaches a promise: 'And the God of peace will be with you' (v. 11b).

The phrase 'the God of love' appears nowhere else in the New Testament, but Paul does refer to 'the God of peace' (Rom. 15.33; 16.20; Phil. 4.9; 1 Thess. 5.23). The order of the two genitives, 'of love and of peace' formed as a unit may reflect the influence of the two preceding imperatives. The 'God of love' also anticipates 'the love of God' in the benediction. Paul expands 'the God of peace' to 'the God of love and peace'. This expression amplifies that aspect of God that is most supportive of the preceding admonitions. As the God of love and peace is with them, the Corinthians can be of one mind and be at peace. The promise is conditional.

Characteristically, there are greetings, 'Greet one another with a holy kiss' (v. 12a). The aorist tense of 'greet' may appear striking, coming after five present imperatives in v. 11, but Paul always uses the aorist when he asks his readers to greet someone (cf. Rom. 16.3-16; 1 Cor. 16.20; Phil. 4.21; 1 Thess. 5.16; Col. 4.15). Since Paul regularly gives this instruction, it is not likely that here he continues the theme of peace and harmony in v. 11. The 'holy kiss' is no more than a kiss of greeting within a religious association (Thraede, p. 508). From Justin (*Apology* 1.65) we learn that following the prayer and before the eucharist, the people 'salute one another with a kiss'. By the end of the fourth century, Christians considered the practice imprudent, but in Paul's churches the kiss seems to have been a fully communal and inclusive act. With the 'kiss' command, Paul seek to get the Corinthians to affirm their existence as

Christ's body. The kiss is 'holy' because the saints (the holy ones) exchange this Christian symbol.

Paul now transmits greetings to the Corinthians 'from all the saints' (v. 12b). Note that some translations make greetings v. 13 and the benediction v. 14. Paul customarily has the people who are with him send greetings to his readers (Rom. 16.3-23; 1 Cor. 16.19-20; Phil. 4.21; Col. 4.10-15; Phlm. 23). We do not know who 'all the saints' are in v. 12b. The phrase is more inclusive than greetings from individuals (Rom. 16.21-23; Phlm. 23-24) or co-workers (Phil. 4.21b), but not as inclusive as 'all the churches of Christ' (Rom. 16.16). Possibly, it may be all the Macedonian Christians, or more probably, all Christians in the city from which he is writing, Beroea or Thessalonica. Paul allows no one to be a solitary saint. One can only belong to the company of 'saints', the holy ones. The 'Church of God in Corinth' is a particularization of the universal Body of Christ.

The benediction at v. 13 is the most theologically elegant in Pauline letters. It takes the form of three parallel statements joined by the simple copulative 'and'.

The grace		of the Lord Jesus Christ
	and	
The love		of God
	and	
The fellowship		of the Holy Spirit
	be with all of you	

Customarily, Paul closes his letters with 'The grace of our Lord Jesus Christ be with you' (e.g. Rom. 16.20). Here, he includes Christ, God and the Holy Spirit, in that order. Spicq (p. 126) thinks it is the 'most explicitly trinitarian formula in the Pauline corpus…it establishes clearly both the equality of the three Persons and their separateness'. Witherington (p. 476) suggests that 'Paul implies that since the Godhead works together, surely he and his converts can do likewise'. It is incredible that Witherington should interpret Paul as using the Trinity as a paradigm for his working relationship with the Corinthian Christians. Spicq and Witherington go well beyond the text to reach these conclusions. Before one glibly concludes that Paul uses trinitarian language, one should consider that the order—Christ, God and Spirit—hardly conforms to the trinitarian formula. Paul says nothing about the equality or separateness of persons and suggests nothing about how the Godhead works. Paul's formulation is some distance from 'in the name of the Father, and of the Son, and of the Holy Spirit'.

Most scholars agree that the first two genitive clauses are subjective. If 'of the Holy Spirit' is a subjective genitive, Paul refers to the fellowship created by the Holy Spirit in the church. If it is an objective genitive, it refers to the participation in, or fellowship with the Holy Spirit. Certainty is not possible, but it seems logical to treat it as subjective genitive because (1) the statements are formally parallel and the first two are subjective; (2) Paul's concern here, as elsewhere is reconciliation at Corinth; and (3) Paul shows no interest in hypostases of the Godhead. Rather, he emphasizes grace, love and fellowship. Grace originates with Christ, love begins with God and fellowship emanates from the Holy Spirit.

There is a striking and obvious difference in Paul's conclusion and that of Demosthenes (*De Corona* 324). Demosthenes asks the jury to inflict the severest penalties on his treasonous opponents. On the other hand, Paul does not view his audience as enemies but as 'sisters and brothers' gone astray. In his conclusion he converges on the fathomless magnanimity of God. He still hopes to use the authority the Lord gave him for 'building up' and not for 'tearing down'. Rather than punishment for the Corinthians, Paul blesses them with the grace of Christ, the love of God and the fellowship that the Holy Spirit creates. Unlike the conclusion of the Socratic apology, Paul asks nothing for himself.

When the Corinthians heard Paul's concluding remarks, they must have been livid with anger. He is totally noncompliant regarding their apostolic criteria. There are no signs of buckling under pressure from the church. His 'defense' speech sounds much more like a prosecutor stating charges than a defendant seeking acquittal. Indeed, unless one assumes that the defense is parodic, one must conclude that Paul was seeking conviction rather than acquittal. As a parodic defense, Paul sought neither. Only God could judge him and the Corinthians had no jurisdiction. Strategies used in the parodic defense transform the defendant into a prosecutor. As prosecutor Paul charges that the Corinthians use erroneous criteria for apostleship. Rather than seeking a conviction, Paul endeavors to reorient their perception of apostleship and the gospel. He believes their salvation depends on a more adequate understanding of the gospel and apostleship.

If 2 Corinthians is a 'defense speech', even his epistolary conclusion is parodic. Who ever heard a defendant conclude a 'defense' by delivering orders like a judge? Usually the judge gives the orders, not the defendant. Paul barks, not one, but five imperatives at the Corinthians. This defendant makes no plea for mercy. He makes no emotional appeal for the maximum sentence for the muckrakers. Paul gives no indication of being a man on trial for his apostolic life. Paul speaks with full apostolic authority, not with the lugubrious whine of an insecure defendant.

Defendants seldom address the 'jury' as 'sisters and brothers'. Paul's tone is pastoral and conciliatory, despite the orders he believes he must give. A defendant does not deliver greetings from other persons to the 'jury'. Paul produces a liturgical formula to instruct members of the 'jury' to greet one another with a 'holy kiss'. Such an instruction implies Christian status for the Corinthians and acknowledges them as a worshipping community, but it also signifies that Paul still has authority to preside over this community of faith.

It is conceivable that a defendant might utter curses and condemnation at accusers, but Paul pronounces a benediction on his plaintiffs/jurors. Moreover, his benediction pronounces grace, love and fellowship. Parodically, Paul does not conclude his 'defense' as a defenseless, whimpering defendant at the mercy of the court. His final words are words of blessing and he speaks like a pastor ending a worship service, not like an insecure defendant in a life and death struggle for his apostolic credentials. He can afford to be parodic because the Corinthians have no jurisdiction over his apostleship. He concludes as he began, 'an apostle of Christ Jesus by the will of God' (1.1), over whom only God has jurisdiction.

Bibliography

Amador, J.D. Hester, 'Re-discovering and Re-inventing Rhetoric', *Scrip.* 50 (1994), pp. 1-35.

—'The Unity of 2 Corinthians: A Test Case for a Re-discovered and Re-Invented Rhetoric', unpublished paper (1998).

Allo, E.B., *Saint Paul: Seconde épître aux Corinthiens* (EB; Paris: Gabalda, 2nd edn, 1956 [1936]).

—*Saint Paul: Premiére épître aux Corinthiens* (Paris: LeCoffre, 1956).

Atkins, R.A., *Egalitarian Community: Ethnography and Exegesis* (Tuscaloosa: University of Alabama, 1991).

Barrett, C.K., *A Commentary on the Second Epistle to the Corinthians* (New York: Harper & Row, 1973).

—*Essays on Paul* (London: SPCK, 1982).

Bates, W.H., The Integrity of 2 Corinthians', *NTS* 12 (1965-66), pp. 50-69.

Batey, R.A., *New Testament Nuptial Imagery* (Leiden: E.J. Brill, 1971).

Baur, F.C., *Paul the Apostle of Jesus Christ: His Life and Work, his Epistles and his Doctrine* (trans. A. Menzies from the 2nd edn by Edward Zeller; 2 vols.; London: Williams & Norgate, 1873-75).

Beardslee, William A., *Human Achievement and Divine Vocation in the Message of Paul* (Naperville, IL: Allenson, 1961).

—'What Is 1 Corinthians About?' (unpublished paper, 1994).

Beare, F.W., *St Paul and his Letters* (New York: Abingdon Press, 1962).

Bernard, J.H., 'The Second Epistle to the Corinthians', in W. Robertson Nicoll (ed.), *EGNT* (New York: Hodder & Stoughton, 1903), pp. 1-119.

Betz, H.D., 'Eine Christus-Aretalogie bei Paulus (2 Kor. 12.7-10)', *ZTK* 66 (1969), pp. 288-305.

—*Der Apostel Paulus und die sokratische Tradition: Eine exegetische Untersuchung zu seiner 'Apologie' 2 Korinther 10-13* (BHT; Tübingen: J.C.B. Mohr [Paul Siebeck], 1972).

—'2 Cor. 6:14-7:1: An Anti-Pauline Fragment?', *JBL* 82 (1973), pp. 88-108.

—'Paul's Apology II Corinthians 10-13 and the Socratic Tradition', *Protocol of the 2nd Colloquy*, Berkeley, 1975).

—*Plutarch's Ethical Writings and Early Christian Literature* (SCHNT, 4; Leiden: E.J. Brill, 1978).

—*Galatians: A Commentary on Paul's Letter to the Churches in Galatia* (Hermeneia; Philadelphia: Fortress Press, 1979).

—*2 Corinthians 8 and 9* (Hermeneia; Philadelphia: Fortress Press, 1985).

Bjerkelund, B.J., *Parakalō: Form, Funktion und der Sinn der Parakalō-Sätze in der paulinischen Briefen* (Oslo: Universitesforlaget, 1967).

Boobyer, G.H., *'Thanksgiving' and the Glory of God in Paul* (Leipzig: Noske, 1929).

Bruce, F.F., *Paul and his Converts* (New York: Abingdon Press, 1962).

—*1 and 2 Corinthians* (NCB; Grand Rapids: Eerdmans London: Marshall, Morgan & Scott, 1971).

Bujard, W., *Stilanalystische Untersuchungen zum Kolosserbrief* (SUNT, 11; Göttingen: Vandenhoeck & Ruprecht, 1973).

Bultmann, R., 'Hilaros', *TDNT*, p. 299.

—*Exegetische Problem des Korintherbrief* (Upsala: Wretsmans, 1947).

—*Theology of the New Testament*, I (trans. K. Grobel; 2 vols.; New York: Charles Scribner's Sons, 1951).

—*The Second Letter to the Corinthians* (trans. Roy A. Harrisville; Minneapolis; Augsburg, 1985).

Burton, E.D., *Syntax of the Moods and Tenses in New Testament Greek* (repr.; Edinburgh: T. & T. Clark, 1973).

Calvin, J., *The Second Epistle of Paul the Apostle to the Corinthians and the Epistles to Timothy, Titus and Philemon* (trans. T.A. Smail; CC; Grand Rapids: Eerdmans, 1964 [1547]).

Carpenter, R., 'The Ubiquitous Antithesis: A Functional Source of Style in Political Discourse', *Style* 10 (1976), pp. 426-41.

Chavasse, C. , *The Bride of Christ* (London: RBC, 1930).

Chow, J.K., *Patronage and Power: A Study of Social Networks in Corinth* (JSNTSup, 75; Sheffield: Sheffield Academic Press, 1992).

Conzelmann, H., 'Korinth und die Mädchen der Aphrodite: Zur Religionsgeschichte der Stadt Korinth', *NAWG* 8 (1967), pp. 247-61.

Dahl, N.A., *Studies in Paul* (Minneapolis: Augsburg, 1972).

—'Benediction and Congratulation,' unpublished paper.

Danker, F., 'II Corinthians', in Roy A. Harrisville *et al.* (eds.), *ACNT* (Minneapolis: Augsburg, 1989).

—*Benefactor: Epigraphic Study of a Graeco Roman and New Testament Semantic Field* (St. Louis: Clayton Publishing House, 1982).

—'Paul's Debt to Demosthenes' *De Corona*', in Duane F. Watson (ed.), *Persuasive Artistry* (JSNTSup, 50; Sheffield: Sheffield Academic Press, 1991).

Deissmann, A., *Paul: A Study in Social and Religious History* (trans. William E. Wilson; Harper Torchbooks; New York: Harper & Row, 1957).

Denney, J., *The Second Epistle to the Corinthians* (EB; London: Hodder & Stoughton, 1894).

Delling, G., 'skolops', *TDNT*, VII: 409.

Dillon, J., 'Critique of Betz', in H.D. Betz (ed.), *Paul's Apology II Corinthians 10-13 and the Socratic Tradition Protocol of the Second Colloquy* (1975).

D'Israeli, I., *Curiosities of Literature* (3 vols.; London, 1791–1817).

Duke, P.D., *Irony in the Fourth Gospel* (Atlanta: John Knox Press, 1985).

Dunn, J., '2 Cor. 3:17—"The Lord is Spirit" ', *JTS* 21 (1970), pp. 309-20.

Dutile, G., 'An Annotated Bibliography for 2 Corinthians', *SJT* 32/1 (1989), pp. 41-43.

Egan, R.B., 'Lexical Evidence on Two Pauline Passages', *NovT* 19 (1977), pp. 34-62.

Engels, D., *Roman Corinth: An Alternative Model for the Classical City* (Chicago: University of Chicago Press, 1990).

Fee, G.D., 'II Corinthians VI.14–VII.1 and Food Offered to Idols', *NTS* (1977), pp. 23.

Filson, F.V., 'The Second Epistle to the Corinthians' (IB; New York: Abingdon Press, 1953), pp. 140-61.

Fitzgerald, J.T., *Cracks in an Earthen Vessel* (Atlanta: Scholars Press, 1988).

—'Paul, the Ancient Epistolary Theorists, and 2 Corinthians 10–13: The Purpose and

Literary of a Pauline Letter', in D. Balch *et al.* (eds.), *Greeks, Romans and Christians* (Philadelphia: Fortress Press, 1990), pp. 190-200.

Fitzmeyer, J.A., 'Qumran and the Interpolated Paragrahp in 2 Cor. 6:14–7:1', *CBQ* 23 (1961), pp. 205-17.

Forbes, C., 'Comparison, Self Praise and Irony: Paul's Boasting and the Conventons of Hellenistic Rhetoric', *NTS* 23 (1981), pp. 1-30.

Fridrichsen, A., 'Zum Thema "Paulus und die Stoa", Eine stoische Stilparallele zu 2 Kor. 4.8', *ConNT* 9 (1944), pp. 27-31.

Furnish, V.P., *II Corinthians* (AB, 32; Garden City, NY: Doubleday, 1985).

Georgi, D., *The Opponents of Paul in Second Corinthians* (Philadelphia: Fortress Press, 1986).

—*Remembering the Poor: The History of Paul's Collection for Jerusalem* (Nashville: Abingdon Press, 1992).

Goudge, H.L., *The Second Epistle to the Corinthians* (WC; London: Methuen & Co, 1927.

Güttgemanns, E., *Der leidende Apostel und sein Herr: Studien zur paulinischen Christologie* (FRLANT, 90; Göttingen: Vandenhoeck & Ruprecht, 1966).

Hafemann, S.J., *Suffering and Ministry in the Spirit: Paul's Defense of His Ministry in II Corinthians 2.14–3:3* (Grand Rapids: Eerdmans, 1990).

Hainz, J., *Ekklesia: Strukturen paulinischer Gemeinde-Theologie und Gemeinde-Ordnung* (Regensburg: Verlag Friedrich Pustet, 1972).

Halmel, A., *Der zweite Korintherbrief des Apostels Paulus* (GLU; Halle: Niemeyer, 1904).

Harris, M.J., '2 Corinthians', in F.E. Gabelein (ed.), *EBC* (Grand Rapids: Zondervan, 1976).

Hausrath, A., *Der Vier-Capitelbrief des Paulus an die Korinther* (Heidelberg: Bassermann, 1870).

Heinrici, C.F.G., *Das zweite Sendschreiben des Apostels Paulus an die Korinther* (Berlin: Hertz, 1887).

Héring, J., *The Second Epistle of Paul to the Corinthians* (trans. A.W. Heathcote and P.J. Allcock; London: Epworth, 1967).

Hock, R.F., *The Social Context of Paul's Ministry: Tentmaking and Apostleship* (Philadelphia: Fortress Press, 1980).

Hodgson, R. von, 'Paul the Apostle and First Century Tribulation Lists', *ZNW* 74 (1983), pp. 59-80.

Hughes, P.E., *Paul's Second Epistle to the Corinthians* (NICNT, 10; Grand Rapids, MI: Eerdmans; 2nd edn, 1980).

Hughes, F.W., 'The Rhetoric of Reconciliation: 2 Corinthians 1.1–2.13 and 7.5–8.24', in Duane F. Watson (ed.), *Persuasive Artistry: Studies in New Testament Rhetoric in Honor of George A. Kennedy* (JSNTSup, 50; Sheffield: Sheffield Academic Press, 1991).

Hurd, J.C., *The Origin of 1 Corinthians* (Macon, GA: Mercer University Press, 1983).

Hydahl, N., 'Die Frage nach der literarischen Einheit des zweiten Korintherbriefes', *ZNW* 64 (1973), pp. 289-306.

Jeremias, J., 'Flesh and Blood Cannot Inherit the Kingdom of God', *NTS* 21 (1956).

Jewett, R., *The Chronology of Paul's Life* (Philadelphia: Fortress Press, 1979).

Johnson, S.E., *Paul the Apostle and his Cities* (Wilmington, DE: Michael Glazier, 1987).

Jones, I.H., *The Contemporary Cross* (London: Epworth, 1973).

Judge, E.A., 'The Conflict of Educational Aims in New Testament Thought', *JCE* 9 (1966), pp. 32-45.

—'Paul's Boasting in Relation to Contemporary Professional Practice', *AusBR* 16 (1968), pp. 37-50.

—'St Paul and Socrates', *Int* 13 (1973), pp. 106-16.

—'St Paul as Radical Critic of Society', *Int* 16 (1974), pp. 191-203.

Jülicher, A., *Einleitung* (1931).

Käsemann, E., 'Die Legitimität des Apostels: Eine Unterschung zu II Korinther 10–13', *ZNW* 41 (1942), pp. 33-71.

—*Perspectives on Paul* (Philadelphia: Fortress Press, 1971).

—*Romans* (Grand Rapids, MI: Eerdmans, 1980).

Keck, L.E., *Paul and his Letters* (PC; Philadelphia: Fortress Press, 1979)).

Kennedy, J.H., *The Second and Third Epistles of Paul to the Corinthians* (London: Methuen, 1984).

Kennedy, G.A, *New Testament Interpretation through Rhetorical Criticism* (Chapel Hill : University of North Carolina Press, 1984).

—*Classical Rhetoric and its Christian and Secular Traditon from Ancient to Modern Times* (Chapel Hill: University of North Carolina Press, 1987).

Kent, J.H., 'The Inscriptions 1926–50', *Cor.* 8.3 (1966).

Kierkegaard, S., *Edifying Discourses* II (trans. David F. Swenson and Lilian Marvin Swenson; 2 vols.; Minneapolis: Augsburg, 1962).

—*The Concept of Irony* (New York: Harper & Row, 1965).

Kittel, G., 'angelos', *TDNT*, I: 74-87.

Kitzberger, I., *Bau der Gemeinde* (Würzburg: Echter, 1986).

Knox, W.L., *St Paul and the Church of the Gentiles* (Cambridge: Cambridge University Press, 1939).

Kraftchick, S., 'Death in Us, Life in You: The Apostolic Medium', in E.H. Lovering (ed.), *SBL Seminar Papers* (Atlanta: Scholars Press, 1991), pp. 618-37.

Kuhn, K.G., 'Les rouleaux de guerre de Qumrân', *RB* 61 (1954).

Kümmel, W.G., *An die Korinther* (2 vols.; HNT, 9; Tübingen: J.C.B. Mohr, 1949).

—*Introduction to the New Testament* (trans. H.C. Kee; Nashville: Abingdon/SCM Press, 1975).

Kustas, G.L., *Diatribe in Ancient Rhetorical Theory* (Berkeley: Center for Hermeneutical Studies, 1976).

Lake, K., *The Earlier Epistles of Paul* (London: Rivington's, 1914).

Lausberg, H., *Handbuch der literarischen Rhetorik: Eine Grundlegung der Literaturwissenschaft* (Munich: Max Huber Verlag, 1973).

Leivestad, R., 'The Meekness and Gentleness of Christ', *NTS* 12 (1966), pp. 156-64.

Lenski, R.C.H., *The Interpretation of St Paul's First and Second Epistles to the Corinthians* (Minneapolis: Augsburg, 1937).

—*The Second Epistle of Paul to the Corinthians* (London: Tyndale Press, 1961).

Lietzmann, H., *An die Korinther* (2 vols.; with supplement by W.D. Kümmel; Tübingen: J.C.B. Mohr [Paul Siebeck], 1949 [1909]).

Lightfoot, J.B., *Saint Paul's Epistle to the Galatians* (London: Macmillan, 8th edn, 1884).

Lincoln, A.T., 'Paul the Visionary: The Setting and Significance of the Rapture to Paradise in II Corinthians XII.1-10', *NTS 25* (1979), pp. 204-20.

—*Paradise Now and Not Yet* (Cambridge: University Press, 1981).

Louw, J.P.E. Nida, R.B. Smith and K. A. Munson, *Greek-English Lexicon of the New Testament* (New York: UBS, 1988).

Lütgert, W., *Freiheitspredigt und Schwarmgeister in Korinth* (BFCT; Gütersloh: Bertelsmann, 1908).

Lyons, G., *Pauline Autobiography: Toward a New Understanding* (SBLDS; Atlanta: Scholars Press, 1985).

MacMullen, R., *Enemies of the Roman Order: Treason, Unrest and Alienation in the Empire* (Cambridge: Harvard University Press, 1966).

Malherbe, A.J., *Paul and the Popular Philosophers* (Minneapolis: Fortress Press, 1989).

Dana, H.E. and Julius R. Mantey, *A Manual Grammar of the Greek New Testament* (New York: Macmillan, 1955).

Marshall, P., *Enmity and Other Social Conventions in Paul's Relations with the Corinthians* (1980).

—'A Metaphor of Social Shame: THRIAMBEUEIN in 2 Cor. 2.14', *NovT* 25 (1983), pp. 302-17.

Martin, R.P., *2 Corinthians* (WBC, 40; Waco, TX: Word Books, 1985).

Martin, H.B., *Slavery as Salvation: The Metaphor of Slavery in Pauline Christianity* (New Haven: Yale University Press, 1990).

Mason, H.J., 'Lucius at Corinth', *Ph* 25 (1971), pp. 160-65.

McCant, J.W., 'Paul's Thorn of Rejected Apostleship', *NTS* 34 (1988), pp. 550-72.

Menzies, A., *The Second Epistle of the Apostle Paul to the Corinthians* (London: Macmillan, 1912).

Merklein, H., 'Die Einheitlichkeit des ersten Korintherbriefes', *ZNW* 75 (1984).

Meyer, H.A.W., *Critical and Exegetical Handbook to the Epistles to the Corinthians* (New York: Funk & Wagnalls, 1890).

Moffat, J., *An Introduction to the Literature of the New Testament* (3rd rev. edn; Edinburgh: T. & T. Clark, 1918).

Moule, C.F.D., *An Idiom Book of New Testament Greek* (Cambridge: Cambridge University Press, 1953).

—*The Meaning of Hope* (FB, 5; Philadelphia: Fortress Press, 1963).

Mullins, T.Y., 'Paul's Thorn in the Flesh', *JBL* 76 (1957), pp. 299-303.

Munck, J., *Paul and the Salvation of Mankind* (trans. F. Clarke; Richmond, VA: John Knox Press, 1959).

Murphy-O'Connor, J., *St Paul's Corinth: Texts and Archaeology* (Wilmington, DE: Michael Glazier, 1983).

—'Relating 2 Corinthians 6.14–7.1 to Its Context', *NTS* 33 (1987), pp. 272-75.

—'Corinth', *ABD*, pp. 1134-39.

Mussner, F., *Der Galaterbrief* (HTKNT; Freiburg: Herder, 1974).

Mussurillo, H., *Méthode d' Olympe: Le banquet* (SC, 95; Paris, 1963).

Nickle, K.F., *The Collection: A Study in Paul's Strategy* (London: SCM Press, 1955).

Papahatzis, N., *Ancient Corinth: The Museums of Corinth, Isthmia and Sicyon* (Athens: Ekdotike Athenon, 1977).

Plank, K.A., *Paul and the Irony of Affliction* (Atlanta: Scholars Press, 1987).

Plassart, A., 'Revue Etude Grecques mentionnant le proconsul Gallion', *REG* 80 (19), pp. 372-78.

Plummer, A., *A Critical and Exegetical Commentary on the Second Epistle of St Paul to the Corinthians* (New York: Charles Scribner's Sons, 1915).

Price, J.L., 'Aspects of Paul's Theology and their Bearing on Literary Problems of Second Corinthians', in B.D. Daniels and J.J. Suggs (eds.), *Festschrift S.W. Clark: Studies in the History and Text of the New Testament* (Grand Rapids: Eerdmans 1967), pp. 95-106.

Ramsaran, R.A., More than an Opinion: Paul's Rhetorical Maxim in First Corinthians 7.25-26', *CBQ* 57 (1995), pp. 531-41.

Rensberger, D., '2 Corinthians 6.14–7.1—A Fresh Examination', *SBT* 8 (1978), pp. 25-49.

Ridgway, B.S., 'Sculpture from Corinth', *Hesp* 50 (1981), pp. 422-48.

Riguax, B., *The Letters of St Paul: Modern Studies* (trans. Stephen Yonick; Chicago: Franciscan Herald, 1968).

Roberts, R.J. and R.M. Kreuz, 'On Satire and Parody: The Importance of Being Ironic', *MSA* 8.2 (1995), pp. 97-109.

Robertson, A.T., *A Grammar of the Greek New Testament in the Light of Historical Research* (Nashville: Broadman Press, 1923).

—*Word Pictures in the New Testament*, IV (6 vols.; New York: Harper & Brothers, 1930–33).

Robinson, J.A.T., *The Body: A Study in Pauline Theology* (SBT, 5; London: SCM Press, 1952).

Rose, H.J., *A Handbook of Greek Literature: From Homer to the Age of Lucian* (4th edn, revised and corrected, 1964 [London 1933]).

Rose, M.A., *Parody: Ancient, Modern and Postmodern* (LCT, 5; New York: Cambridge University Press, 1995).

Rushford, G.M.N., 'Triumphus', in W. Wayte and G.E. Marindin W. Smith (eds.), *DGRA* (London: J. Murray, 1891), p. 894.

Saffrey, S.D., 'Aphrodite a Corinthe: Reflexions sur une idée reçue', *RB 2* (1985), pp. 359-74.

Sampley, J.P., 'Paul, his Opponents in 2 Corinthians 10–13, and the Rhetorical Handbooks', in J. Neusner *et al.* (eds.), *The Social World of Formative Christianity and Judaism: Essays in Tribute to Howard Clark Kee* (Philadelphia: Fortress Press, 1988), pp. 162-77

Sandmel, S., 'Parallelomania', *JBL* 81 (1962), pp. 1-13.

Schmidt, K.L., 'kolaphidzo', *TDNT*, III: 818.

Schmithals, W., *Die Gnosis in Korinth* (Göttingen: Vandenhoeck & Ruprecht, 1965).

—*Gnosticism in Corinth* (trans. J.E. Steely; Nashville: Abingdon Press, 1971).

—'Die Korintherbriefe als Briefsammlung', *ZNW* 64 (1973), pp. 263-88.

Sedgewick, D.S., *Of Irony, Especially in Drama* (Toronto: University of Toronto Press, 1935).

Semler, J.S., *Abhandlung von freier Untersuchung des Canon* (Halle: Hemmerde, 1771).

—*Paraphrasis II epistolae ad Corinthios* (Halle, 1776).

Sherwin-White, A.N., *Roman Society and Roman Law in the New Testament* (Oxford: Clarendon Press, 1963).

Smith, M., 'Prolegomena to a Discussion of Aretalogies, Divine Men, the Gospels of Jesus', *JBL* 90 (1971), pp. 174-99.

Smyth, H.W., *Greek Grammar* (Cambridge: Harvard University Press, 11th edn, 1980).

Snodgrass, M.E., *Encyclopedia of Satire* (Santa Barbara, CA: ABC-CLIO, 1996).

Soulen, R.N., *Handbook of Biblical Criticism* (Atlanta: John Knox Press, 1976).

Spencer, A.B., 'The Wise Fool (and the Foolish Wise)', *NovT* 23 (1981), pp. 349-60.

Spicq, C., *Agape in the New Testament* (2 vols.; trans. M.A. McNamara and H.H. Richter; St Louis and London: Herder, 1965).

Spittler, R.P. 'The Limits of Ecstasy: An Exegesis of 2 Corinthians 12.1-10', in G. Hawthorne (ed.), *CIBPI* (Grand Rapids: Eerdmans, 1975).

Stahlin, G., 'ekkopto', *TDNT*, III: 857-60.

Stone, C., *Parody* (London: Martin Secker, 1914).

Stone, I.F., *The Trial of Socrates* (AB; New York: Doubleday, 1898).

Stowers, S.K., *The Diatribe and Paul's Letters to the Corinthians* (SBLDS; Chico, CA: Scholars Press, 1981).

—'Letter Writing in Greco-Roman Antiquity', in Wayne A. Meeks (ed.), *LEC* (Philadelphia: Westminster, 1986).

Strachan, R.H., *The Second Epistle of Paul to the Corinthians* (MNTC, 15; New York: Harper, 1935).

Strelan, J.G., 'Burden-Bearing and the Law of Christ: A Re-Examination of Gal. 6:2', *JBL* 94 (1975), pp. 266-76.

Sundberg, A.C., 'Canon Muratori: A Fourth-Century List', *HTR* 66 (1975), pp. 1-41.

Talbert, C.H., *Reading Corinthians: A Literary and Theological Commentary on 1 and 2 Corinthians* (New York: Crossroads, 1992).

Tasker, R.V.G., *The Second Epistle to the Corinthians* (TNTC, 8; Grand Rapids: Eerdmans, 1958).

Thayer, J.H., *Greek-English Lexicon of the New Testament* (Chicago: American Book Company, 1889).

Thiessen, G., *The Social Setting of Pauline Christianity: Essays on Corinth* (trans. and ed. J.H. Schütz; Philadelphia: Fortress Press, 1982).

Thraede, K., *Grundzüge griechisch-römischer Brieftopik* (RAC, 8; Munich: Beck, 1970).

Thrall, A.H., and W.F. Addison Hibbard, *A Handbook to Literature* (New York: Odyssey Press, 1960).

Thrall, M.E., *Greek Particles in the New Testament* (Grand Rapids: Eerdmans, 1962).

—'The Pauline Use of Sunēidesis', *NTS* 14 (1967), pp. 118-25.

—'The Problem of II Cor. VI.1–VII.,1 in Some Recent Discussion', *NTS* 24 (1977), pp. 132-40.

Travis, S.H., 'Paul's Boasting in 2 Corinthians 10–2', *SE* 6 (1973), pp. 527-32.

Turner, N., *Grammatical Insights into the New Testament* (Edinburgh: T. & T. Clark, 1965).

Vlastos, G., *The Philosophy of Socrates: A Collection of Critical Essays* (repr. Notre Dame: University of Notre Dame Press, 1980 [1971]).

Weiss, J., *Earliest Christianity*, II (trans. F.C. Grant *et al.*; 2 vols.; New York: Harper & Row, 1965).

Wendland, H.D., *Die Briefe an die Korinther* (Göttingen: Vandenhoeck & Ruprecht, 1954).

Wiles, G.P., *Paul's Intercessory Prayers* (SNTSMS, 24; Cambridge: Cambridge University Press, 1974).

Williams, C.K., 'Corinth 1977: Forum Southwest', *Hesp* 47 (1972), pp. 1-39.

Windisch, H., *Der zweite Korintherbrief* (MeyerK; Göttingen: Vandenhoeck & Ruprecht, repr. 9th edn [1924]).

—*Paulus und Christus* (UNT, 24; Leipzig: Hinrichs, 1934).

Winston, D., *The Wisdom of Solomon* (AB; Garden City: Doubleday, 1979).

Winter, B.W., 'Are Philo and Paul among the Sophists? A Hellenistic Jewish and Christian Response to a First Century Movement' (unpublished dissertation, MacQuarrie University, 1988).

Wiseman, J.R., *The Land of the Ancient Corinthians* (SMA, 50; Astroms, 1978).

Witherington, B., *Conflict and Community in Corinth: A Socio-Rhetorical Commentary on 1 and 2 Corinthians* (Grand Rapids: Eerdmans, 1992).

Wüllner, W., *Paul and Rhetoric: Unpublished Papers and Classnotes* (Berkeley: Graduate Theological Union Library, 1992).

—'Rhetorical Criticism', in George Aichele *et al.* (eds.), *The Postmodern Bible* (New Haven: Yale University Press, 1995), pp. 149-86.

Zmijewski, J., *Der Stil der paulinischen 'Narrenrede': Eine analyse der Sprachgestaltung in 2 Kor 11.1-12.10 als Beitrag zur Methodik von Stiluntersuchungen neutestamentlicher Texte* (BBB, 52; Bonn: Hanstein, 1978).

Index of References

Old Testament

Classical

Index of Authors